# Growing People, Growing Companies

Mark Hollingworth
*5i Strategic Affairs*

ISBN 0-9730752-0-1

Copyright © 2003 by Mark Hollingworth
*5i Strategic Affairs*
Montreal, QC, Canada

Cover Design: Lora Tamburri
Publishing Assistant: Dina Cindric
Interior Design and Format: Michael Pereira
Copy Edit and Index (1st edition): Jodi A. Lewchuk | safoworks.com
Designed and typeset using QuarkXpress on an Apple Macintosh.

Every reasonable effort has been made to obtain permission for non-original material in this edition. If errors or omissions have occurred, they will be corrected in future editions provided written notification has been received by the publisher.

For more information about
*5i Strategic Affairs* and/or VIP Leadership workshops,
contact Mark Hollingworth.

Web: www.5istrategicaffairs.com

E-mail: mark.hollingworth@5istrategicaffairs.com

This book is dedicated to all the very special people who see me as a VIP and to you, the reader, for taking the risk to grow to your full potential.

A special thanks to all of the following for playing a crucial role in supporting the creation of this book: George and Jane; Sugarloaf and Ile Cadieux; Denis and le *Vieux St. Laurent*; Tom and Killer; Renee De Gagne and Michel Knuebuehler; Pierre, Andre, and Lise; and most importantly, Dina, Jodi, and Michael for their creativity, quality work, support, and patience.

# Table of Contents

**It's Broke, So Let's Fix It**

When he retired twenty years ago, my father had been working for the same aerospace company as an engineer for over forty years. He had enjoyed a well-planned career, job stability, fringe benefits, and was looking forward to a generous pension. His formal education ended at the age of sixteen and his mission was to be the family provider, with the hope that his children would have better and more than he had. Over the years his job certainly presented challenges and responsibilities; however, he worked in an environment characterized by constancy, order, and the feeling that the world of tomorrow would be pretty much the same as today's. His employer was loyal to him, but in reality the company viewed the steady supply of raw materials, the inventories, the plant and the production equipment, and the access to cheap financing as its real source of competitive advantage. Organizational growth meant increasing the amount of physical assets owned and the organization made a profit by managing those assets efficiently. My father was an unavoidable expense.

I'm now in my early forties, already on my fourth career, and I recognize that the stable environment, aspirations, and career objectives that my father enjoyed—the very reality he took for granted—are meaningless to me.

Today, knowledge is growing exponentially. The half-life of an engineering degree is estimated to be three-and-a-half years. Competition comes from companies and countries that did not exist even five years ago. New technologies can be outdated in six months or less. I can now send a message to the other side of the world in a fraction of a second, and the recipient can return it just as quickly. Managing change, information, and time is vital—work preoccupations that my father would have found meaningless. I'm certain that tomorrow will *not* be the same as today, and those physical assets my father's employer sought to acquire are no longer a source of competitive advantage; indeed, they are liabilities—possessions to be avoided whenever possible.

The world of work, its base assumptions, and its way of operating have all changed except for one crucial thing: the management roles and systems, organizational processes and paradigms we currently are expected to work within are largely unchanged from the era of my father's career, which finished twenty years ago. Yet now there is only one source of competitive advantage in knowledge-based businesses: the knowledge and skills possessed by employees. In the past, organizations were centred on and built around their most important assets. Shouldn't the same principle apply now? Shouldn't today's organizations be built around employees?

> *Now there is only one source of competitive advantage in knowledge-based businesses: employees.*

Imagine visiting a city for the first time. You have just rented a car at the airport to get to an important meeting at your hotel—and you're using my father's city map, which he bought when he was last in town. That map is twenty years old. There may be a few monuments, museums, and streets that still correspond to it, but there are new housing developments, large office towers, a one-way traffic system, an inner city ring road, and new highways that cut old streets in two. You're late for the meeting at your hotel and you're trying to get there using this twenty-year-old map. It's ridiculous to keep using it and you throw it away.

But if everyone can so easily discard a twenty-year-old map after recognizing that it's no longer applicable, why hasn't the system that was in place during my father's career been discarded too? Why do so many companies working in what is a radically altered environment still use "the map" when it is obviously obsolete and harmful to both the organization's performance and the people working within it?

If an organization still expands through the growth and production capability of its assets—which are now its employees—it's surely the time to design a new knowledge-based blueprint that acknowledges different roles, current and essential skills, and new behaviours, allowing us to effectively negotiate the new territory. In this way, organizational growth and success can be built on the professional and personal development of its employees.

# V I P

## Part 1: The Foundation

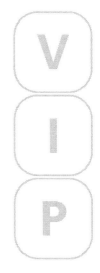

## Chapter 1

A few years ago, I attended a seminar on the changing needs of students on a university campus. The panel at the front of the room consisted of students from a variety of different academic programs while the audience was predominantly members of the university's administrative staff who possessed years of experience. The discussions had progressed quite well until the students mentioned how they believed many of their requests for information on programs, course timetables, marks, etc. could now easily be dealt with through the Internet rather than face-to-face interactions with staff members.

In general, the suggestion was welcomed by the university employees who saw a potentially huge reduction in the repetitive and time-consuming questions that successive students often pose at reception desks or over the phone. They recognized that their time would be freed to pursue more interesting activities that would add value to the students' education. However, they also realized that providing services on-line would entail more change and learning to use new software. One administrator suddenly voiced a nagging but seldom voiced frustration that all present could somehow relate to: "It's fine, all this talk of technology, new services, and new software programs, but when are they going to get it right and come out with the *final* version of the software?"

Some in the room laughed openly while others smirked inwardly; yet the comment touched a chord with everyone. The people attending the seminar wanted to be good at their jobs, make use of more technology, and learn new skills, but they recognized that it surely has to stop somewhere! Students will always want easier access to more information in more user-friendly formats. University staff, already trying to be more flexible in an old and rigid system, lacking resources and time to train themselves, and feeling a little overwhelmed, just want to change one last time and have the final, bugproof version of "the" software installed on their machines. At that point, working life will reach a new and improved status quo; everything will return to "normal."

Whether the environment is a university, a large public multinational, or a privately owned business, most people are currently feeling a sense of frustration from having to play a new, high-speed, and continually evolving game while simultaneously having to abide by old and often constraining rules and paradigms that were not created to function in a constantly fast-changing world.

## *Constant Change*

It is widely recognized that very few people crave constant change. Although change can be exciting and stimulating, allowing both professional and personal development, most people are usually more comfortable making a conscious decision to change one aspect of their life at a time rather than having change forced upon them. Take, for example, the prospect of moving to a new home. Such a move can be an extremely positive experience when you outgrow your current home; when you can afford a bigger, better place in a nicer neighbourhood; or when you decide to live beside a lake. The experience is not the same if you're forced to move when you can no longer afford the rent, when the government has expropriated your land to build a highway, or when you're breaking up a household because of a divorce.

> *The truth is that people do not like to be changed, but they can learn to enjoy changing and seeing themselves evolve and grow.*

Even when the motivation for your move is positive, it's still a more manageable and enjoyable experience when you have a stable income, a stimulating job, a healthy relationship with a partner, and kids that will not have to change their schools or friends. If only one of those factors is at less than optimum—if one partner is working only on a contract basis or when the new home is in a different school district, for example—the decision to move can all too quickly become one that is risky, stressful, and difficult to make. Even those who say they love change can usually only handle so much at a time. The truth is that people do not like to be changed, but they can learn to enjoy changing and seeing themselves evolve and grow—if they're in an environment conducive to such change and growth and see it as being in their best interest.

Today, despite society's best efforts to mystify corporate existence, pretending that organizational culture is "apersonal" and suggesting that people be rational and unemotional individuals at work is preposterous. Companies are but groups of people, each with accompanying human creativity, drives, fears, and frailties. Perhaps in the past it may have been understandable to expect employees to leave their personal lives at home, as they were considered just "minor cogs in the big wheel." Now, with technology, funding, and raw materials available around the globe on a twenty-four-hour basis, the only real competitive edge a company can possess is the knowledge, competencies, and motivation of its employees. Those employees are human beings and must be dealt with as such.

## A New Environment and New Rules

It is obviously easier to introduce a new computer system, manage a change in Human Resources (HR) policy, unveil a new product, or raise additional financing when your people can focus on one project at a time. In reality, however, this seldom happens anymore and it is unlikely to ever happen again in the future.

The now old adage, "The only constant is constant change," is true. Everyone is operating—on both a corporate and personal level—in a constantly evolving and often threatening environment. Notwithstanding the constant small changes in both our professional and private lives, every now and again the rules of the game are dramatically and irretrievably altered by the introduction of a major radical innovation, be it a new product, procedure, service, technology, or process. This kind of change can happen at any time; your company may lead the change or it may be introduced by a current or—even worse—a new competitor in the arena. It is always easier if you introduce the change, if you can reinvent the way things are done in your industry. If you are one of the "followers" and change is forced upon you, you will likely feel more pressure and stress, and will have less knowledge about the new competitive environment, not to mention less time to implement any program for change.

> *Companies are but groups of people ... those employees are human beings and must be dealt with as such.*

Irrespective of who makes the first move, the old game is over and a new possibly completely different one, has begun. Overnight, or at least within a very short time frame, new products or services will have to be made and offered; new business sectors and strategies will have to be identified and introduced; new work processes, different competencies, and novel individual skills will be required—and it is clear that the recipe for doing all of this is not contained in last year's strategic plan. That document was prepared twelve months ago when you were using an outdated map, playing a different game on a different terrain. It is quite likely that the new service or initiative was not even conceivable when the old business plan was prepared. You and your teammates have to quickly adapt to the new reality without missing a beat and while (hopefully) relishing the opportunity to do so. With these kinds of challenges to face, is it any wonder that so many people burn out and so many initiatives fail?

If companies and individuals are to flourish in this new environment, the old ways of doing things, throughout every level of an organization, obviously must be changed. Good people in a bad system, structure, and culture will produce bad results regardless of their efforts. And you, as their leader or co-worker, cannot afford to have employees and colleagues feeling overwhelmed by rapidly evolving client needs, constantly changing software, increasingly stringent time pressures, etc. Likewise, you certainly can't expect them to be effective, grow as individuals, and be assets to your company or team when you ask them to work in structures and cultures and with business strategies and reward systems that were suited to a previous era. These systems were simply not designed to be operational in an environment of constant change.

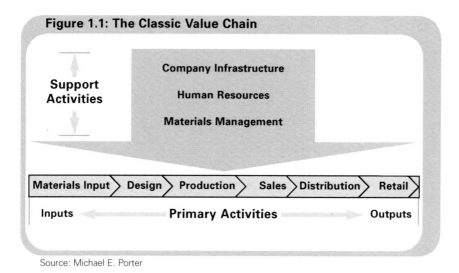

Figure 1.1: The Classic Value Chain

Source: Michael E. Porter

# The New Playing Field: What to Consider

## Today's Organization

When you look at a traditional theoretical value chain (see Figure 1.1), from the raw materials through to the finished product and the end customer, you'll notice clear, well-defined boundaries between different companies in the chain. In reality, these boundaries no longer exist; they have become extremely vague and difficult to locate. Various degrees of vertical integration, strategic alliances, electronic data interchange (EDI), share swaps, partnerships, etc. mean that corporate boundaries are barely visible—one company simply blurs into another.

Within organizations, a focus on core competencies has given rise to the subcontracting or outsourcing of many primary and support activities in the value chain. A company may simultaneously use employees located in Birmingham, Bombay, and Boston to design a product; have another company in London conceive its marketing and advertising; employ a world-class manufacturer in Singapore to produce it; have it assembled and packaged in Marseilles; and hire an e-commerce company in California to handle sales and distribution. Even the HR function may be administered by an outside contractor. Alternatively, all partners may be in the same city—location no longer really matters. Such companies exist today, and they are not all large organizations. Even small companies may subcontract or partner with others in order to receive better-quality, cheaper, or speedier services than they could produce for themselves internally. This is the new reality. The challenge is to build an organization that can flourish in this new environment and a management process that is appropriate in such a context.

## Strategic Planning vs. Strategic Thinking

The classic annual strategic planning process has always, at least superficially, taken into account the effect of the so-called macroenvironment: the macroeconomic, technological, political and legal, demographic, and social factors that impact the business environment and corporate strategy. Often, however, company personnel treated this part of the strategy development process as simply a necessary warm-up before getting to the meat of their discussions. In fact, in the interest of saving time away from the job, many companies even dropped this "unproductive" brainstorming session and focused more time on strategic battles over organizational issues such as departmental budget allocations. Those involved felt they had more control over these kinds of internal, territorial concerns.

Furthermore, many companies, in an admission that they were unable to keep up with the rapid rate of change and new developments in their industry, recognized the futility of preparing a five-year strategic plan each year. Instead, they turned their strategic planning into budgetary planning—they simply crossed their fingers and prayed that their corporate strategy would develop reactively as the company tried evolving with the changing competitive landscape. Obviously this is not a style of proactive leadership that is going to make a company into an industry leader. If a company is going to prosper on the new playing field, strategic management and leadership needs to happen at the individual level and be part of every employee's job.

Today, almost all of the drivers for changing customer demands, organizational change, and sources of competitive advantage originate from events that occur in the macroenvironment, be it deregulation of the telecommunications or trucking industry, new international trade agreements, new government programs to help aerospace and pharmaceutical companies, or new technological developments that impact on all industry sectors and all departments in an organization. Leading companies are now realizing that they have to maintain a constant "environment watch," and look for early indicators of change and new trends in the macroenvironment.

In many cases, a company might not be in a position to exploit many of the trends it identifies. It may not have the financial resources, the expertise, the contacts, or even the drive to exploit all opportunities. But all a company really needs to transform itself is to recognize one opportunity and develop and bring it to fruition. By constantly examining market trends and possibilities, it will one day find that opportunity. In doing so, the company will also have looked at most of the strategic moves that a competitor might be considering and will know each opportunity's strengths and weaknesses. Even if it does not find a radical way of transforming itself during the macroscanning process, it will undoubtedly identify many incremental improvements to ensure that it optimizes its value creation process and minimizes the associated costs. It will be a very competitive company with a low risk rating simply because it has done its homework better than its competitors.

One simple but effective management model that illustrates why change is necessary for success in this new environment is the Diamond-E Framework (see Figure 1.2). It shows why most organizations (and the individuals inside them) are now out of equilibrium. As presented by Joseph N. Fry and J. Peter Killing, this model has been around for many years and demonstrates the dynamic relationship between different parts of an organization, its strategy, and its environment. In an ideal company, management preferences are ideally aligned with organizational structure and resources. In turn, these factors support the corporate strategy, which is optimized to the company's environment. The model suggests that if a change occurs in any one of these elements, all the others need to adapt to the change if the system is to remain in equilibrium. Figure 1.3 shows a typical Diamond-E Framework for an organization during my father's career. It is in equilibrium: the management preferences, structure, resources, and strategy are perfectly aligned and harmonized with the existing environment.

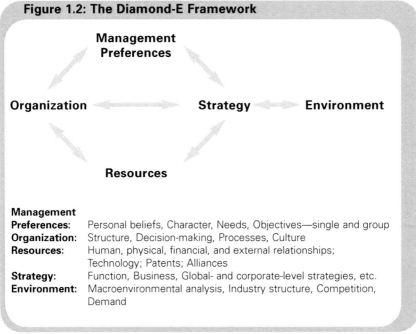

**Figure 1.2: The Diamond-E Framework**

| | | |
|---|---|---|
| **Management Preferences:** | Personal beliefs, Character, Needs, Objectives—single and group | |
| **Organization:** | Structure, Decision-making, Processes, Culture | |
| **Resources:** | Human, physical, financial, and external relationships; Technology; Patents; Alliances | |
| **Strategy:** | Function, Business, Global- and corporate-level strategies, etc. | |
| **Environment:** | Macroenvironmental analysis, Industry structure, Competition, Demand | |

Source: Joseph N. Fry and J. Peter Killing, *Strategic Analysis and Action*

Now, what happens when the company's environment changes? Whether it's a macroenvironmental change, new competitors entering the market, globalization effects, currency devaluations, new business trends, the advent of the Internet or home-based working, the model recommends that business strategy be adapted to the new environment. In turn, this adaptation dictates the creation of new resources and a new structure, or even that management generate new preferences or paradigms (or that the company generate new management!) so that a new equilibrium can be achieved.

The catch is that today's environment is in constant flux. As a result, a company must maintain a constantly evolving dynamic equilibrium, one in which all parts of the model are continually adapting to the new environmental context (see Figure 1.4). The model suggests that you need to be asking yourself the following questions:

- ➲ Is your organization or team built on the premise of constant change?
- ➲ Is your organization built to redesign itself as its environment evolves?
- ➲ Is your strategic planning process designed to take this new reality into account or are you simply performing a budgetary exercise, leaving your business strategy to chance?
- ➲ Is your organization flexible enough to react in (almost) real time?
- ➲ As the system needs to be in dynamic equilibrium, are you planning strategically on a continual basis?
- ➲ Are your employees, as individuals, thinking and behaving with this paradigm in mind?

## Figure 1.3: An "Old" Diamond-E Framework

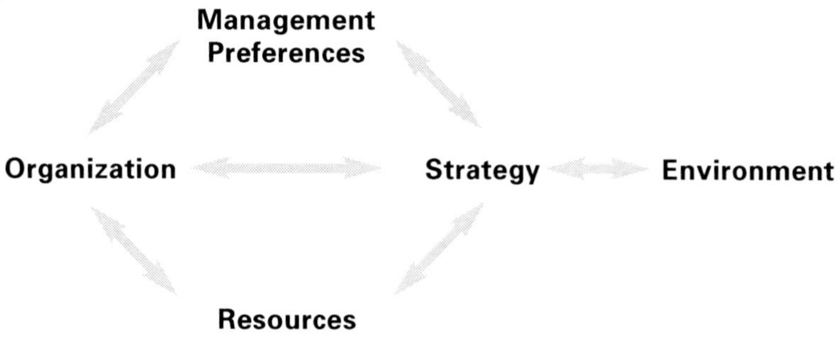

**Management Preferences**

**Organization** ⟷ **Strategy** ⟷ **Environment**

**Resources**

| | |
|---|---|
| **Management Preferences:** | Control and monitoring of employees; "Manufacturer of product" culture; Shareholder satisfaction paramount |
| **Organization:** | Structured for budgeting and planning processes; Rigid hierarchy and communication channels; Decisions made at senior levels; Executive committee deals with strategic issues; Strict procedures to be followed by emplyees; Little employee empowerment; HR has little power |
| **Resources:** | Assets are buildings and equipment—not people |
| **Strategy:** | Target local, traditional client base; Use past as indicator for future; "Continue doing what we've always done" |
| **Environment:** | Stable growth; Little choice for consumers; Little buyer power; Limited information available; New product introductions released at company's discretion; Known competitors; Serve local markets and export excess capacity; Foreign countries as potential markets, not potential competitors; Traditional distribution channels; Stable rules of competition; Low employee mobility; Time-lags unimportant; Patents easy to enforce; Protected domestic markets |

For example, many organizations still view "playing" on the Internet, reading a publication, chatting informally with colleagues from another department, or, heaven forbid, sitting at a desk just "thinking" (i.e., "doing nothing") as justification for reprimand rather than valuable, creative, and necessary work. If companies are to be knowledge-based in an ever-changing environment, then employees need to work their knowledge and their brains in the same way they worked their bodies, raw materials, and machines in the past. And work in this case means sitting still, sometimes alone and sometimes in groups, and thinking, generating, creating, and analyzing—not rushing around "doing" for appearance's sake. How many people today stay at home to be productive and go to the office for meetings or when they have nothing urgent to create? At home you can take a long coffee break, read the newspaper, or take a walk; but the quality of the ideas, the plan, the report (the value-added) that you've generated by the end of the day is normally far superior to anything you would have produced at the office. The reality is that very few people in knowledge-based organizations are paid for what they do physically; they are paid for what they create intellectually—and that just might require them to regularly sit around and do "nothing." Yet how do you react when you see a co-worker doing something that is seemingly outside of their current business segment?

## Figure 1.4: Today's Diamond-E Framework

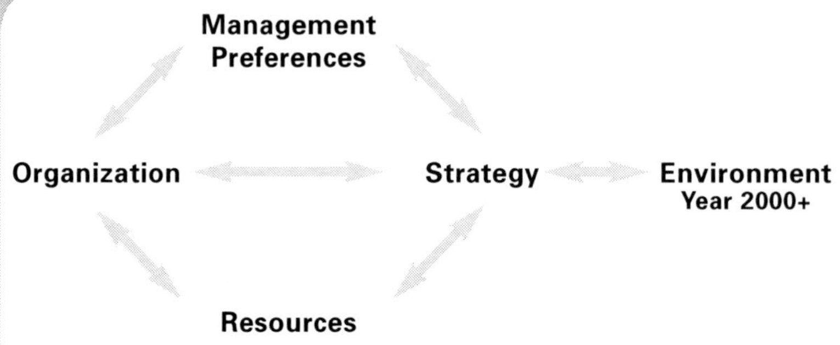

**Management**
**Preferences**

**Organization** ⟷ **Strategy** ⟷ **Environment**
**Year 2000+**

**Resources**

| | |
|---|---|
| **Management Preferences:** | Are focused on personal and professional growth of employees; Flexible recognition systems with sharing of rewards; Development of a sense of mission and community; Liberation of creativity and the building of an empowered, entrepreneurial organization focused on value creation; Satisfaction of all stakeholders |
| **Organization:** | Entrepreneurial with decisions made at the lowest appropriate organizational level (subsidiarity); Continuous strategic thinking process and ongoing evolution of organization; Real-time information systems providing required packaged information facilitating decision making; Formal and informal, electronic, and face-to-face communication facilitated; Flexible guidelines in place to stimulate creativity and problem solving; HR department with executive-level authority |
| **Resources:** | Principal assets are people; Focus on development and retention of intellectual capital; Exploitation of globalization effects; Development of core competencies |
| **Strategy:** | Focus on perceived value creation in the mind of the client; Construction of an interconnected web of activity sets to achieve this unique strategic position; Maximum efficiency; Development of an innovation continuum; Continual horizon scanning for constant reinvention as environment changes; Five-year strategic planning exercise obsolete |
| **Environment:** | Global markets and global competition; Fast-paced technological change; Fierce competition; New business models introduced regularly; Networks, global partnerships, and outsourcing widespread; Information available in "real time"; "Time" a new competitive factor; Quickly evolving rules of competition; Increasingly demanding clients; Employee mobility; Patents difficult to protect; Free trade zones; Virtual companies and offices |

To keep your company at a point of dynamic equilibrium, the Diamond-E suggests that you need to be constantly checking your environment for what's on the horizon, and not just by flipping through your industry trade magazine, but by scanning through and understanding developments in areas far removed from your traditional area of concentration. If even companies like Microsoft fear that a competitor with a new paradigm will create radical, out-of-the-box innovation and competition, surely your organization should have the same fear.

As a starting point for looking at your own strategic management using the Diamond-E Framework, consider the following points:

- Is your Diamond-E in equilibrium now?
- Is there obvious inconsistency or dysfunction hurting your competitiveness, decreasing efficiency and effectiveness, and generating stress for your employees?
- Are you playing catch-up?
- Are you asking the right questions?
- Are you ignoring the fact that the game and the rules have changed and continue to change while you are still playing the old game?

Next, let's look briefly at some of the characteristics of today's environment and ask how well your company (or individuals) "fits" onto this playing field.

# The Current Competitive Environment

## Globalization

Management theorists and many western business people now regard it as fact that financing, technology, and raw materials are available on a global basis. Even if this new reality is entirely true on paper only (try finding venture capital or raising money by going public in Costa Rica or Iran), many company presidents echo the sentiment that there is effectively a level playing field around the globe.

This equitable playing field effectively means that it is only the quality of competent and creative human resources in a country or organization that can make a difference, create intellectual capital, and be the source of competitive advantage. Everything else is equally available to all competitors. Only people are guaranteed to be a unique asset. Consequently, they should be the resource into which you make your biggest investments and the asset that you try to develop, train, and retain. Does your company follow such a philosophy? Do you feel like the most important asset in your organization? Are you seeking to develop, invest in, and grow your people?

Globalization should also mean that, where transaction costs justify it, companies will migrate to areas of the globe where they can best achieve their objectives. Each part of the value chain will be located in the region best suited to maximize value creation or to minimize costs and time. Have you looked into this? Are you taking advantage of location economies where an activity might cost an order of magnitude less?

Global product tastes (and brands) may also be homogenizing, although each local region still maintains its particular preferences. Governments in all nations will, in fact, be hoping that their populations retain and demand regional tastes, as this could require global companies to build local production facilities rather than simply export generic standard products from their home bases. Do you consider local cultural preferences when shaping your product offering or are you still trying to sell a product that you hope people will need and buy? Are you seeking to exploit opportunities around the globe? Have you looked at possible competitive advantages you could achieve by capitalizing on expertise in different areas of the globe? Have you looked at different regions of the globe where you can realize location economies or increase value creation?

## Stakeholder Satisfaction

Traditionally, many companies have concentrated on satisfying only the demands of their shareholders. However, companies that focus on satisfying all stakeholders and building win-win relationships with them have been shown to perform better financially than those that concentrate solely on shareholder satisfaction. Do you know what your employees—local or national governments, suppliers, customers, unions, associations, etc.—want from your organization? Do you know what you really need from them? How strong are your relationships with all your stakeholders? Are you exposing your company to unnecessary risk by not trying to fully satisfy all their needs?

## Horizon Scanning

Today you need to know about every single thing that can affect all levels of your business. However, although there is talk about building a knowledge-based economy or knowledge-based companies, this "knowledge" rarely includes a thorough understanding of the external macroenvironment. The monitoring and use of this information has been traditionally left to the president or CEO, who is expected to scan the future and take care of strategy. The problem with this coping mechanism is that, except in the case of a very small company, it is impossible for one person to be sufficiently qualified to know how each of the macroenvironmental factors (political and legal, demographic, social, macroeconomic, and technical environments) could potentially impact suppliers, manufacturing, packaging, competitors, marketing, or the needs of the end-user. It takes in-depth knowledge of an area along with an ability to create a vision of the future to generate creative alternate scenarios for what could happen. Companies that will be successful in the future will have found a way of ensuring that this environmental watch is maintained at all levels. Failure to do this well means that, sooner or later, a company will fall victim to an unidentified macrothreat or will fail to capitalize on a radical innovation.

## Protected Markets

In the near future, the only protection any world market will have is the distinctive tastes of the local consumer and the shipping costs to certain markets for particular products. A company built to take advantage of existing trade barriers is destined for failure. Only lingering nationalistic prejudices and old wounds will prevent consumers from purchasing the products that best suit their needs, irrespective of country of origin.

## Positioning

Positioning in the marketplace has always been the cornerstone of a successful business. This fact has not changed, even with the remarkable power of technology and the Internet. Satisfying clients' needs by offering a unique product in a new, innovative, and difficult-to-replicate manner still remains the quintessential sustainable competitive advantage. This reality will never change; only the means to achieve it will constantly evolve.

Gary Hamel has preached extensively on the need for companies to reinvent the way things are traditionally done in an industry. Although others may not use the same terminology, many other authors have explored the same ideas. Michael E. Porter examines unique positioning and activity sets; both Hamel and Porter speak disparagingly of the role of benchmarking. Michael Treacy and Fred Wiersema suggest companies must focus on one of three possible value disciplines (customer intimacy, product leadership, or operational excellence) without neglecting either of the other two. I'll discuss these topics in more depth later. The basic message to be gleaned here is that companies must seek to identify a need, satisfy it in a unique way—

preferably one that is very hard for others to copy—and take a radical new approach rather than make an incremental improvement. It is important to develop a new means to satisfy an identified need rather than to benchmark and try to improve on what someone else is already doing. Thinking differently in a radical way is the philosophy of a winner in a knowledge-based economy.

## The Sources of Competitive Advantage

Traditionally, four equally important means for creating competitive advantage have been assumed: superior quality, superior efficiency, customer responsiveness, and innovation. The first two tools of competitive advantage are now merely minimum requirements for a company's existence. Competition is now evolving in such a way that it tends to centre on customer service; the degree of innovation in products and process; and a new source of competitive advantage, the competitive use of time (e.g., time to market for new products; time to respond to changing customer needs; time between receiving an order and delivery of the product or service; time to hire; flex-time; personal time management; etc.). As Stan Davis argues, "Executives who used to worry about the time value of money now manage the money value of time" (13, p. 5). He also presents an interesting point of view that suggests companies are now really competing on three axes: in space (where can I find this product or service?); in matter (what form is it in? small, large, virtual?); and in time (can I use it when I want to?), with an objective of satisfying the client with no physical matter, in any place and at any time. Adoption of this paradigm can only be achieved by listening to and satisfying the client's real needs through constant innovation. And the only people who can accomplish all of this are your employees.

### Companies as Innovation Continuums

Product life cycles have been continually shortening over the last twenty years. To be competitive today, you need to have several subsequent product releases in the pipeline before your latest one hits the (virtual) shelf. No sooner do you launch a new version of a product, technology, or service than you are planning for its obsolescence. Although the release of new software has been the most visible example of this phenomenon, all companies and industries are facing the same challenges, even traditionally slow-moving industries such as transportation, aerospace, etc. Today's successful companies have to be innovation continuums— that is,

> *Today's successful companies have to be innovation continuums.... How well do you manage your idea generation?*

they are continually generating and commercializing new product ideas and making use of new technology to satisfy continually evolving client needs. How well do you manage your creative idea generation? Are your employees encouraged to examine their paradigms and behaviours and to challenge the way things are done? Does the company encourage risk-taking (otherwise known as learning)? If not, how does it expect innovation to occur?

### Patents and Intellectual Property

Ironically, while knowledge (i.e., intellectual property) is now the principal competitive advantage, the historic and widespread means of protecting it, through patents, is now often inadequate and ineffective. Patent protection works to a certain extent for some large and powerful companies and in certain industries (e.g., the pharmaceutical industry) and other sectors where barriers to entry are high and global competitors are known. However, effects of globalization, rapid product obsolescence, and the growing capacity of competitors to innovate and reverse-engineer product means that patents can now be easily circumvented. Most companies have also recognized, at least internally, that their means for pursuing patent-breakers in anywhere but North America or Europe have never been realistic. Excepting radical technological breakthroughs and certain industry sectors linked to biological, medical, or chemical advances, companies are better served by putting the energy (and financial resources) wasted in pursuing patent protection into developing new innovations. Today, in many sectors, a capacity for continual innovation, time-to-market capability, and retention of employees is the main form of intellectual property protection.

## Core Competencies

Having identified the needs of your target clients and the positioning of the product and service that your company produces or intends to produce, you need to decide what type of expertise is vital to your particular value creation activity. What particular aspect of your product or service is vital to your client and will give you a competitive advantage now and in the future? What specific aspect of your product and service does the client see as being the most valuable? Hence, what are you going to have to learn to do exceptionally well? Are you strong in the required core competencies? Are you vulnerable to the departure of your key people? Do you know which core competencies will be needed to produce products for your clients in five to ten years' time? Are you developing them now?

## Efficiency (Not Economy) of Scale

Historically, economies of scale and "riding down the experience curve" were seen as the keys to driving down costs and gaining competitive advantage. But serving increasingly demanding retail and industrial consumers means that having the proper value creation process will be the key to success. This may mean using flexible manufacturing methods, producing in-house or subcontracting, or, as in the case of software, creating a situation where manufacturing ten thousand or one hundred million copies costs almost the same.

## Benchmarking

Benchmarking compares efficiencies. If everyone benchmarked against everyone else and implemented the results, all companies would be doing the same thing the same way. Success comes to those who do things differently in terms of positioning and (difficult-to-imitate) ways of satisfying customer needs. You certainly need to operate at maximum efficiency, but the most important qualification is that you need to be efficient at being effective!

## Delayering Organizations

Financially, organizations can no longer afford to have layers of managers and complex structural and procedural mechanisms in place to monitor and control employee activity. A company must be primarily organized and structured around creating an environment in which each employee can generate the maximum amount of value— that is, knowledge, ideas, and innovation for the company and for its clients.

Everyone needs to be entrepreneurial and disciplined. Everyone needs to feel that they are part of a community and that they are the company's "owners" and share its mission. If a person needs controlling and monitoring, should they be working in your company? If a document crosses your desk and is passed up the reporting chain without your adding any value to it (comments, changes, your own thoughts and ideas) then what was the point in your reading it?

An organization in which the president controls and monitors the vice-presidents, who control and monitor the middle managers, who control and monitor the workers, is doomed to fail—and quickly! Implementing the philosophy of subsidiarity (decisions being made at the lowest possible appropriate level) is the only way for companies to really move forward and stimulate customer service, creativity, innovation, and value creation throughout the company. Employees at all levels need to have the required qualifications, training, resources, authority, and responsibility to do their work. And their superiors' task is to provide subordinates with the optimum tools and environment in which they can do it.

## Technology
In the current climate of e-business and e-strategies, it is clear that technology and the dawn of the Internet have seen companies desperately seeking to gain competitive advantage by being first to market, gaining an e-brand name, and building web share. The Internet has certainly changed, and will continue to change, the way people work, the means by which value can be created, and the way it can be delivered to the clients—and you need to take full advantage of its potential. However, it has not changed the laws of economics or competition: the basics of business management remain the same. Technology must be maximized to generate either product or process innovation and to reduce costs. Employees should not be doing work that can be done by technology. Employers should be using technology to reinforce their market positioning and to lever their value creation activities by identifying new ways of using it to gain competitive advantage.

## The Power of Networks
The management of several types of networks has become a key capability within today's organizations. If organizations have "fuzzy" boundaries, subcontract many activities, continually build and dismantle project reams, and seek to satisfy all stakeholders, then the need for well-built and -managed inter- and intra-business communication networks is clear. Word of mouth (i.e., networking) has always been the best way to obtain new clients, and with highly competitive labour markets the recruitment of new employees now often depends on networks of happy employees. Today, when working in multidisciplinary or global product or product teams, being able to build and manage personal networks is crucial to an individual's success.

On an organizational level, the competitive advantage offered to companies who possess high-quality, reliable technological networks for data transmission and communication also means that "being networked" is a crucial success factor for today's organizations.

## Virtuality
Parallel to globalization and networking is the concept of virtuality. Some companies may indeed be virtual—that is, they have no central physical office and outsource all

major activities except for proprietary work or activities that fall within their core competencies. Other companies will have a virtual feel for their employees because they will be collaborating with colleagues on projects located all over the world. Alternately, employees may be in the same city but not have, need, or want a central office. Charles Handy describes offices that are more like clubs, where employees can get together in a relaxed atmosphere to exchange ideas and information, be creative and brainstorm, etc. Extracting the benefits and dealing with the challenges of working with people in virtual companies is something organizations need to do. Everyone must learn to deal with virtual clients. Are you teaching employees how to build long-distance relationships solely through electronic media? Is the office environment you've created appropriate for your employees' needs? Have you looked at what your employees really need in terms of office infrastructure? Are you helping employees deal with the isolation of working from a home office?

## The Human Resources Function

The HR function in most companies is normally the least important of all the functional departments—if it indeed exists in many small companies. Unfortunately, this low priority is often reflected in the quality of people that the field attracts. Finance, Manufacturing, and Marketing have always maintained a higher profile and many HR heads still do not hold a vice-president title. If they do, they are not allowed a full voice in executive meetings or in strategic planning sessions. This practice must change. Current corporate rhetoric suggests that it has: the next time you read an annual report or attend a public corporate presentation, it is guaranteed that the company president will be spreading the gospel that individual employees are the corporation's most important asset. And they are. But actions speak louder than words and companies' HR strategies and policies continue to betray them. If employees are the most important asset shouldn't HR be the most important department?

# *Like Father, Like Son—Again*

The above characteristics of today's business reality could not have been used to describe the business environment in which my father worked throughout his career. Today's world is completely different. Yet we still have not found a new way to work and function in this so-called knowledge-based economy.

Despite the corporate rhetoric about the importance of personnel, organizations are still structured and managed as though raw materials, equipment, and finances are the basis of competition and as though employees need to be controlled and monitored. However, when you examine the current operating environment, knowledge-based products, and the processes they require, it is clear that a company must be primarily organized around creating an environment in which the employees can generate the maximum amount of value (knowledge, ideas, and innovation) for the company and its clients.

Behind the rise in importance of a company's capability to create value are the owners of that capability—the innovators—who are really your employees applying your (or is it their?) intellectual property or capital intelligence. Why not build a new organization that helps them do just that?

# *What Does It All Mean?*

The challenge presented in this chapter is simple: To be successful today—and moreover, to ensure success in the future—an organization must be designed, managed, and staffed in order to capitalize on the abilities of its most important assets: its employees. Reviewing the previous material, we can isolate ten key criteria that can help an organization be successful in the new environment.

## The Ten Criteria for Success in a Knowledge-based Business

A successful organization must:

1. Constantly scan the macroenvironment for trends that could impact business.
2. Satisfy all stakeholders: win-win must be the operating philosophy.
3. Create and deliver a unique positioning and brand in the minds of customers.
4. Develop a unique way of creating value and a set of core competencies that are difficult for a competitor to reproduce.
5. Ensure that every level and every individual create and add value. No one should be controlling, monitoring, or "managing" others, and no one should need it. Employees should be leaders: good communicators, networkers, and coaches. Above all, they should be trustworthy.
6. Recognize that employees at all levels represent intellectual capital and are the real owners of the organization and its core competencies. Grow and protect your intellectual capital by stretching, developing, attracting, and retaining the owners of this resource.
7. Be employee-owned. Think of the company as a community built around a shared mission and vision and common values. Use technology wherever possible to reduce costs, free up employees for value-added activities, and create competitive advantage.
8. Build up an HR-focused, entrepreneurial, and creative organization and recruit people who can adapt to (and enjoy) constant change and renewal.
9. Build and maintain strong networks.
10. Operate as efficiently as possible.

Although success can never be guaranteed, if you can accomplish these goals you will certainly have built a company, division, or work team that will have maximized its chances for success.

In reviewing the above criteria, the point that stands out is the recognition of employees as the key to a company's success. After all, if knowledge (intellectual capital) is your only remaining true competitive advantage, the only means of turning it into true economic value creation is through people. But this new reality cannot become the operating paradigm within an organization still structured in a manner that sees manufacturing, marketing, or finance as the driving force the behind company.

The objective today is to build a new organization and new roles for all your employees so that both the company and the individuals therein can grow and flourish. More than ever, the growth and development of any company is simply a function of the growth and development of its employees. You need to satisfy the Ten Criteria for Success and your organization must become an ideal environment to nurture such leadership and employee growth. The remaining chapters in this book outline one vision of how such a company can be built, staffed, and operated. They describe the roles and skills each person needs to adopt and develop in order to succeed in today's work environment. It's a new model, a road map that reveals where we want to go. And the key to this map is simple: If you want to grow a successful company, you must grow your employees!

## Key Points in Chapter 1

- ➲ Playing the new game using the old rules is a recipe for failure.
- ➲ Your employees are your only real assets and your source of competitive advantage.
- ➲ Strategic planning is only the first step: everyone at every level of your organization also needs to be thinking strategically.
- ➲ Diamond-E Frameworks in most organizations are out of equilibrium.
- ➲ Adopting the Ten Criteria for Success is crucial.

## Questions to Consider

- ➲ Draw a Diamond-E diagram for your company or team. Is it in equilibrium? If not, why? What do you need to do to re-establish equilibrium?
- ➲ Examine your own paradigm with regards to your management or leadership style. Are you playing by the old rules?
- ➲ Are you ready to change your behaviour? If so, read on!

The previous chapter introduced the simple but informative Diamond-E Framework and demonstrated how a constantly changing environment suggests that some sort of dynamic equilibrium needs to be achieved if your organization's Diamond-E is to be in harmony. Consideration of this Diamond-E model gives rise to the following questions:

- Do the majority of today's organizations achieve that harmony?
- Given the constantly changing environment, are strategies adapted accordingly?
- Are the appropriate resources, structure and culture, or management preferences in place to create a winning organization that can adapt to this new environment?
- Do organizations encourage the growth and development of their employees in the same way as they encourage the accumulation of other assets?
- Do organizations encourage and develop leadership?

I believe the answer is a resounding "No." This chapter will explore the reasons behind the current corporate stagnation, reveal the philosophy of VIP Leadership model, and demonstrate how it can help an organization of any size realize the Ten Criteria for Success.

## *The Old Way: The 4Cs*

Christopher Bartlett describes the old paradigm held by many companies in terms of the 4Cs: Compliance, Control, Contract, and Constraint (7, pp. 11–23). For individuals and companies to succeed using the 4Cs, they were best served by complying with the highly constraining procedures, rules, and organizational structure that prevailed at the time. The 4Cs flourished in the era of the "Organization Man," when all members of an organization functioned as human carbon copies in an automatic, highly predictable way. The management preferences were the 4Cs, the structure was organized to implement the 4Cs, and the workers were deemed secondary to finance issues and equipment. Creativity and innovation were not encouraged; mass production and pre-scribed behaviour reigned. But the Diamond-E was in equilibrium: the structure, resources, and preferences all supported the strategy, which was ideal for the rela-tively unchanging environment.

Today, recognizing that the environment has changed and will continue to evolve rap-idly, I like to believe that there are many managers who see that their organizations are at odds with the new environment and would like to adopt new ways of running their companies and managing their people. However, the reality is that many organizations are still structured according to the static 4C model and still favour and encourage indi-viduals to live according to the 4Cs. It is not unusual for managers trying to implement new processes and systems to find their way blocked by the organization's existing structure and culture. The notion of employees as "carbon copies" has been updated or modernized by changing the term to "clones," yet the reality remains depressingly the same.

A major indicator of the continued dominance of the 4Cs paradigm is that the principal business measuring tool, accounting, has still to come to terms with recognizing the value of intellectual property—never mind the value of having a team of extraordinarily talented employees. Ask any software company how a financial institution values the team of employees it has carefully recruited! If people are a company's main asset, shouldn't training costs, for example, be an investment rather than an expense? By tak-ing a training course, employees should be increasing their value to an organization; the balance sheet, however, will not reflect this at all. How many organizations place the growth and development of their employees above the concerns of the finance func-tion and the depreciation of "real" assets?

For many years, the term "empowerment" has been widely used. Unfortunately, how-ever, the term translates into an employee simply being given more responsibility while still lacking the authority, the environment, or the resources to achieve the objective. Being empowered in a rigid organizational structure is like being given the key to the prison door while remaining attached to the wall in leg irons. Whatever the level of an employee's motivation, after a while of constant tugging and no progress, the chains simply hurt so much that they stop trying to move and simply resort to behaviour that doesn't cause pain. In corporate terms this means reverting to the 4Cs, which repre-sent accepted behaviours that feel safe and are never criticized. After all, intelligent peo-ple rarely commit professional suicide; if they do anything, they will simply move to a competitor who better fits their profile and treats them better.

It is important to emphasize that not all people want to be empowered, take risks, have responsibility, learn—and perhaps fail. For many people, after years of being told what to do and what not to do, making their own decisions, implementing them, and being responsible for them is frightening. Consequently, many will gladly revert to a model where someone else assumes the responsibility for outcomes. Unfortunately, the organizations in the knowledge economy that can support employing these people are few and far between.

## *Major Problems in Today's Organizations*

### No Shared Vision, Mission, or Values

It takes a lot of time to build and communicate a shared vision of the future. When results and performance have to be justified on a quarterly basis, the pursuit of this goal always seems like time misspent and poorly rewarded. Mission statements may look nice on the plaque in the lobby and in the pages of the annual report, but the real sense of mission is often confined to the dust lying in the bottom of the desk drawer. Shared values that can explain why an organization exists and what behaviour is acceptable are pre-empted by the overpowering drive to make profits. If you do hire highly mobile knowledge workers by satisfying only their financial demands, you had better be prepared to lose them to better-paying competitors.

### No Clear Strategic Position

Michael E. Porter has stated that he believes the search for and adoption of a unique strategic value proposition and value creation has been lost in the search for efficiency and the popularity of benchmarking. Too many companies straddle, lack focus, follow the perceived leader, and concentrate on being as efficient as possible rather than on being unique, creative, and innovative in satisfying customer needs.

### Employees Are Not Considered Assets

Although many company presidents will expound at length on how their employees are their biggest asset, this rhetoric has usually not been factored into an organization's culture or way of operating.

### Poor Organizational Alignment

As Diamond-E Frameworks illustrate so clearly, there is a distinct misalignment between the environment; strategy; and structure, resources, and management style that many companies adopt.

### Low Levels of Trust

The low levels of trust existing within organizations and in the competitive environment undermine collaboration, the creation of synergy, and even honest competition.

## *The Need for Constant Renewal*

David Hurst talks about the need to view organizations as ecosystems. A forest, for example, needs an occasional fire to promote renewal and continued health. Hurst states, "Ecosystems, such as forests, are dynamically stable entities whose survival depends upon the effective interaction of many organisms and processes. Ecosystems maintain their stability by going through a continual process of creation, growth, destruction and renewal" (24, p. 33). Without man's interference, a forest's Diamond-E is always in equilibrium!

Look at what happened to forests, particularly ones in national parks, where for many years firefighters adopted the practice of extinguishing all fires, man-made or natural, as soon as they began. The forests became unhealthy, out of balance, and the complex renewal system—of which fire is an integral part—ground to a halt. The mature trees, by their ability to capture the majority of sun and water, began to dominate and young trees and plants on the forest floor faded. The forest floor became dry; dead leaves accumulated, the recycling process slowed, and animal life was affected. The limbs of the large trees that fell to the ground lay there awaiting the required spark to ignite—and when it did, the resulting fires were catastrophic.

> *Organizations need to burn—and you need to hire people who have the confidence to work within this natural process.*

The corporate parallel isn't all that difficult to see. Generalizing slightly, the "old" long-term employees working within the structures, processes, and cultures they helped to create dominate and leave no room for the "young" employees to grow. The natural work processes and systems become inflexible and function poorly; consequently, the young wither or leave. The situation often continues until a crisis is reached: the stock price drops, the shareholders rebel, the clients leave, the bank pulls out. Only then does the necessary "burn" take place, allowing new forms to emerge from the ashes. Organizations need to burn—and you need to hire people who have the confidence to work within this natural process.

Key executives at both Kao and GE have highlighted the importance of corporate renewal: Kao's Maruta is on record as saying, "Past wisdom must not be a constraint but something to be challenged. Yesterday's formula is often today's dogma. My challenge is to have the organization continually question the past so we can renew ourselves every day." GE's Jack Welch echoes that sentiment by stating that "An organization ought to stretch itself to the point where it almost becomes unglued."

### The Need for a New Map

Although many people working within organizations exhibiting the above symptoms recognize that the situation needs to change, they also recognize that it is ineffective and ultimately futile to try to bring such change about. As a result, they end up suffering the status quo. Or they may try to alter perhaps one element of the malaise that they feel they can personally affect. But drawing in one new highway on a twenty-year-old map does not make that map much more useful; a new one is still required.

Is there a paradigm of organizational behaviour and renewal that facilitates meeting the Ten Criteria for Success, keeping the Diamond-E in dynamic equilibrium, and serves as a model of personal leadership at each of the organization's levels? In fact, yes.

## The New Way: VIP Leadership

It is clear that organizing a company around the 4Cs and the "old way" only hinders success in the new knowledge-based business environment. But employing the VIP Personal Leadership model, a model based on the roles of the Visionary, Implementor, and People Manager, can help a company achieve all of the desirable goals outlined above. But before we can explore the model and its three roles in depth, we need to examine the ideas in which they are rooted.

## A New-Look Organization

Christopher Bartlett has described his view of a new type of organization. Again, as organizations are only groups of people, any change can only be built upon individual effort and personal change. He suggests that there are four ingredients for change and renewal:

- ⊃ **Personal Discipline**, where autonomy and self-regulation is emphasized over hierarchy.
- ⊃ **Support**, where the control function of management is changed to providing coaching and encouragement to all employees.
- ⊃ **Trust**, where a level of confidence in employees is built, solidifying a middle-ground position somewhere between an employment contract and a family-like, social-type bond.
- ⊃ **Stretch**, where the organization's goals cause the company and the individuals inside of it to grow and move forward. (6, pp. 23–36)

With these four ingredients in place, organizations can be liberated from the 4Cs' mentality and restrictions, allowing their employees to be innovative and productive while giving them opportunity to develop. Your organization needs to reflect this type of structure if it is to successfully compete in the knowledge economy and retain its most important employees.

The Bartlett model provides broad guidelines for instituting organizational change. Each and every individual must alter their approach so that the company can begin to meet the Ten Criteria for Success at every level of its structure. Flip back to Figures 1.3 and 1.4 (pages 11 and 12) for a moment and consider the change in philosophy that needs to occur if an organization wants to be successful in today's environment.

Looking at these diagrams, it is clear that it is not enough for only an organization's senior executive to alter its behaviour—the entire organization needs to change. Providing that you as an individual have the power to alter elements of the Diamond-E Framework in your own division or on your own work team, you can begin to institute change on a smaller scale. You can encourage personal discipline among your people, work to build a climate of trust, and focus on stretching your team's performance while supporting your team members' efforts. The most difficult parameter of the Diamond-E to change when you're not sitting at the top of an organization is the structure (you may be able to change the decision-making processes within your own unit, but the reward and recognition systems are often established at a corporate level). However, you can certainly change your personal management preferences and, often, how you allocate resources. You can make a start. Change often has a snowball effect and just a small difference in your behaviour may prompt many others to question their own. A rigid remuneration and reward system makes your challenge more difficult, but it does not make it impossible. That's why I call this model "VIP Personal Leadership": it is your choice to make!

## The New Owners of Organizations

Based on the Ten Criteria for Success presented in Chapter 1, let's try to describe the new organization of human beings that needs to be built. Historically, descriptions of companies usually began with a summary of the facilities, the production line, the number of employees, and were accompanied by a copy of the corporate organigram. However, a knowledge-based company is built with people, usually intelligent people, operating in some sort of network arrangement. There may not be a building or a production line and the organigram may be a group of matrices that resemble a collection of spider webs. The description of your organization should be a description of its people—the individuals and the value they generate and the competencies and abilities they possess, as opposed to a description of their posts or positions.

These people are the owners of your main asset. Each one of them, individually or as part of a team, owns intellectual capital (knowledge and skills) that contributes to creating value efficiently for your clients. Your challenge today is to design a unique set of activities within (or without) your organization that generates value for clients and stakeholders and maximizes the intellectual capital the company possesses, preferably at a minimal cost. The activity set should allow you to position yourself uniquely with respect to competitors and clients and satisfy all of your clients' latent or nonverbalized needs. In turn, by pursuing your chosen strategies, your bank of intellectual capital should continue to grow and be reinforced, and you should become even more competitive in your chosen markets.

## *Workers in the Knowledge Economy*

In his book *The Age of Unreason*, Charles Handy gives a good overview of the categories of people that a knowledge economy hires. In essence, a knowledge-based company employs three types of employees: core members (or core professionals), professionals, and contract workers.

- ○ **Core members** (or core professionals). These people possess the principal knowledge your company needs to create value; they are the owners of your core competencies, the heart of your business. In fact, they should feel like the company is theirs—and it is. The company's shareholders are key financial stakeholders whose needs must be satisfied, but they cannot "own" the company. Ownership has always meant possession of the company's assets, and it still does. However, in a knowledge-based company, there may not be any equipment or any type of physical assets at all. A competency or key asset may be marketing or retail sales capability, expertise in logistics or in developing or using a specific technology. It follows that a company's core members are those who bring knowledge and capability to the table; these people are the *real* owners. Despite the fondest wishes of the financial stakeholders, the real owners can walk away at any moment—they are mobile assets.
- ○ **Professionals**. This group includes people such as accountants, financiers, even administrative assistants. These people need to be of excellent calibre, as they offer essential professional services to the company, often in a role that supports the primary activities of the value chain. Like core members, their needs must be fully satisfied, as they can easily change positions and move among companies. The people in this group can easily feel left out of the organization, but they are often the glue that holds the core professionals in place.
- ○ **Contract workers**. In this group I include companies subcontracted to perform certain value chain operations and contractual workers hired on a full-time, part-time, or seasonal basis. Contract workers, in all their shapes and sizes, must also feel a sense of belonging to the organization. Even if they are not the owners of your core competencies, they are important stakeholders in the company and their needs should be fully satisfied. For example, you should recruit

part-time workers who are seeking part-time work and who pursue activities that allow them to fully satisfy their other personal needs. Hiring people for part-time positions when they are really seeking full-time ones only leads to frustration for all parties.

The people in each of the three categories should have a personal mission statement that is complementary or synergistic with the company's. Everyone must be moving in the same direction, towards the same goals, with a shared vision and common values. Figure 2.1 depicts this new organigram, while Figure 2.2 clearly demonstrates how difficult it is to move forward when each employee tries to go their own way.

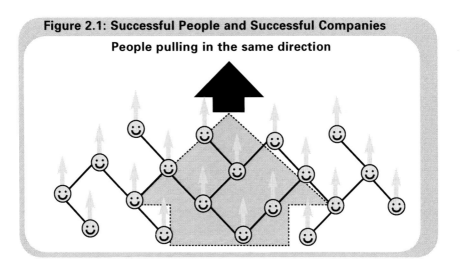

**Figure 2.1: Successful People and Successful Companies**
**People pulling in the same direction**

Most importantly, you must be able to trust all employees implicitly. Communication must be open and win-win relationships must be established with each person. After all, in today's knowledge-based business—or any business—employees may work at home, in another part of the country, or in another area of the globe for a company with whom you have a strategic alliance. You cannot afford to have doubts about any of them. Each person must be 100 percent trustworthy because each is an important link in the value chain. As the saying goes, a chain is only as strong as its weakest link.

In this new type of company, each person will know what their role is and what is expected of them. A shared vision and common values will act as guidelines for behaviour and decision making, and each employee will be fully empowered to be entrepreneurial, to make independent decisions, and to use their own means to achieve specific goals. Each person will scan for new macroenvironmental trends, opportunities, or new technologies that might impact on their particular value creation task. Each will manage their own networks in order to communicate when necessary and receive and transmit the information they and their networked colleagues need. Each will be in a position to be creative, to collaborate with others, and to move both the company and themselves in the direction of the common goal.

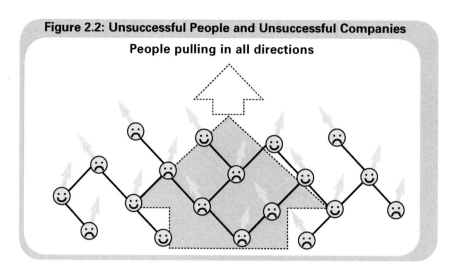

**Figure 2.2: Unsuccessful People and Unsuccessful Companies**
**People pulling in all directions**

Such an organization may seem extremely idealistic. The skeptics will say that it is impossible to create and manage. However, its success requires only one thing: for each employee to accept the responsibility of personal leadership, which includes being trustworthy, entrepreneurial, and accountable, and letting natural creativity, motivation, and enthusiasm drive them towards satisfying the Ten Criteria for Success and fulfilling the company's mandate. Having a clear mandate normally provides sufficient motivation for people to accept the proposal.

What is really happening within the organization is a movement away from management and towards leadership. It is impossible to manage intelligent people; they resist it and want instead to be led. And most want to be leaders themselves. Not necessarily a General Patton or a Margaret Thatcher type of leader, but someone who shows initiative in deciding what should be done and then going out and doing it.

People should be led—only information and processes should be managed. In managing an employee, you are taking away their sense of responsibility, their motivation, and probably their creativity and capacity for innovation. If a person on your team needs to be managed (and unfortunately many people have grown used to it), they are not interested in thinking or acting for themselves. Instead, they are merely a physical extension of you, their manager. If they want to do exactly as you tell them while letting you take responsibility for their actions, it probably means you should be looking for a new employee. Such an individual creates little economic value and synergy and, although their behaviour may be understandable after twenty years of being micromanaged by their previous boss, can a company in today's hypercompetitive market place afford to employ this kind of individual? You are better served by helping such an individual find a position with another company; they will be more satisfied with traditional management and your organization's dynamic balance won't be upset by their presence.

## *Organizations Built on Leadership*

Some people have difficulty envisioning themselves as leaders, usually because they do not have a solid grasp of what leadership actually is. While people such as Gandhi, John F. Kennedy, and Mao Tse Tung were great leaders, not everyone has the desire, capability, or drive to be such an inspirational figure. But everyone *does* have the ability to develop what I term "personal leadership skills."

Robert Cooper defines leadership as "the act of making a difference" and "the ability to achieve priority results through people" (10, p. 3). My definition of personal leadership is quite similar, aptly expressed as, "The ability to move yourself and others towards who you want to be." This definition describes a goal much easier to achieve than becoming another Gandhi! It implies knowing where you personally want to go (i.e., having a Vision) and being able to motivate others who wish to move in a similar direction. It suggests a certain know-how regarding the route you must take (i.e., Implementation) and an ability to mobilize and communicate with others (i.e., being People-focused). In pursuing this mission, the priority results will come naturally as you navigate the voyage of becoming who you want to be.

> *People should be led—only information and processes should be managed.*

But how do you develop leadership qualities? Let's start by looking at what people generally want from their leaders. The table below is derived from Warren Bennis's extensive work on leadership. The left column indicates what Bennis terms the four essential aspects of leadership.

**Table 2.1: Do You Possess the Four Essential Aspects of Leadership?**

| Leadership Aspect(s) | Question(s) to Ask Yourself |
| --- | --- |
| Purpose/Direction/Guidelines | Do you know where you're going and how to get there? |
| Trust/Commitment/Caring | Are you trustworthy? Are you working with positions or people? |
| A Sense of "We-Can-Do-It" Optimism | Do you have healthy self-esteem? Do you enjoy challenges and learning? |
| Action/Results | Do you apply yourself and work hard? |

The first aspect, providing purpose, denotes a shared purpose, something that your colleagues also believe in and want to achieve. If your purpose in life is to get rich, then you will probably only be able to lead people who also believe that getting rich should be the focus of existence. If you want to save the world, then you will probably only attract people who also want to achieve that goal. The problem with such a grand purpose is that it's often outside of what Stephen R. Covey terms the "circle of influence": you might want to do it, but you can't do much about it—it's just not an achievable goal. Purpose needs to be visionary *and* achievable. If it is not, people will quickly lose faith in you. That brings us to the second attribute: people need to trust you completely. They must feel that you're committed to the shared goal and to them. If they feel that you are likely to jump ship when things get tough, they are not likely to give all their energy and commitment either.

Developing faith, trust, and commitment fosters an environment in which the third leadership attribute, a sense of we-can-do-it optimism, can flourish. When people feel that you care about them as individuals, and not just as software designers or accountants, it is more likely that your organization will develop a sense of community, a social aspect that is crucial as we become more dispersed in terms of our physical work locations.

Finally, people want to work with others who have the capability to get the job done. Having a worthwhile mission, being trustworthy, and fostering optimism is worthless if you do not have the skills to deliver the required results. This does not mean that you personally have to accomplish everything on your own. Maybe you just need the wisdom to hire the right people with the appropriate skills. But you do have to be action- and results-oriented. Talking about results is one thing; achieving them is another.

Leadership is a matter of mirroring these four attributes. Individuals are attracted to leaders with whom they can identify and who have a similar vision and common values and desires. When the four aspects of leadership are in place, introverts can lead extroverts; techies can lead artists; urbanites can lead outdoors people. Can an introvert share the same purpose as an extrovert? Can a techie trust and care about an artist? Can both business types and bohemians achieve results? The answer to all of these questions is undoubtedly "Yes."

## Management vs. Leadership

So what are the major differences between managing and leading? Tables 2.2 and 2.3 contrast the two. We have already determined that only information and processes should be managed, as people need to be led. It is not necessary to run down the table and compare the two lists; however, it is interesting to look at the list of activities and attitudes that characterize both "managing" and "leading" and ask, given the environment portrayed in Chapter 1, which of these lists best portrays the characteristics of people you need to build a successful organization. Do you need people focused on control and short-term issues, who accept the status quo and see making an error as failure? Or do you need people who coach and facilitate, who continually reinvent themselves, challenge the status quo, and see making an error as an opportunity to learn? The latter description best outlines the type of people you need to be seeking to employ.

Clearly there will always be information and processes that need managing. However, it is easier for leaders to put on their management "hats" to deal with those issues than it is for managers to temporarily or suddenly become leaders, particularly because the leadership traits of trust and caring take a long time to develop.

### Table 2.2: The Attitudes and Characteristics of Management and Leadership

| Management | Leadership |
|---|---|
| Administrate | Innovate |
| Imitate | Originate |
| Control | Reinvent |
| See the short term | See the long term |
| Ask *How?* and *Why?* | Ask *What?* and *Why?* |
| Do things right | Do the right thing |
| Accept status quo | Challenge status quo |
| Focus on systems and structures | Focus on people |
| Dictate | Coach and facilitate |
| View an error as a failure | View an error as an opportunity for learning |
| Managers abound | Leaders are few and far between |

### Table 2.3: Managing vs. Leading

| OLD: The Organization Man | NEW: Leaders Inc. |
|---|---|
| **Compliance** | **Self-Discipline** |
| • Inflexible procedures | • Keeping one's word |
| • Authoritarian atmosphere (little tolerance for dissent) | • Delivering results |
| • Little debate or exchange | |
| **Control** | **Support** |
| • Delegation with severe mechanisms of accountability | • Horizontal and vertical coaching, helping, and guiding |
| **Contract** | **Trust** |
| • Economic contract vs. social entity | • Strong personal relationships |
| | • Risk-taking |
| **Constraint** | **Stretch** |
| • Live by corporate strategy | • Live with a view to future possibilities, building core competencies and resources |

Personal leadership is constant, ever present. It cannot be turned on when necessary and it can't be faked. The bad news is that people can smell it or feel it when someone pretends to be trustworthy, uses others, or needs to brag about results they've obtained. The good news is that personal leadership is often just a matter of being human. Humans care about others, they do know what they believe in, and most have a sense of purpose—they just need to sublimate those qualities, particularly at work. Most people want to walk the talk, be trustworthy, coach others, and almost everyone prefers to go to work and actually do something and obtain results. In fact, being productive is much easier than being bored and tired while pretending to get work done on a daily basis.

So why don't companies generate more leaders? The main reason is that leaders tend to challenge the system, the status quo, and, in general, companies do not encourage that type of behaviour. It threatens the order of things, the established culture, and the people in charge. The bosses' desire for control, along with their egos, tends to mean that the potential leader's individuality, innovativeness, creativity, and spirit are soon crushed. These leaders learn to stay in line. Alternately, of course, these individuals are lost to competitors who encourage leadership.

Evaluate the company you are working with now. Does it encourage leadership within the ranks of its employees or are there very obvious cultural or structural barriers to people assuming leadership roles? Look at Tables 2.2 and 2.3; which paradigm is favoured within your company? Why?

Let's look at the sorts of leadership skills and capabilities everyone will need to possess in order for a company to fulfill the Ten Criteria for Success. What do all employees need to be doing? I believe that for organizations and individuals to flourish and be successful, it is now essential to adopt the three roles of VIP Personal Leadership at all levels. It is the only way for knowledge-based organizations to move forward. The 4Cs are out and the 3Ps of VIP Personal Leadership—Purpose, Process, and People—are in and need to be instituted from corporate or divisional levels right down to work teams or "virtual team" units.

# The Three Roles of VIP Personal Leadership

Although for discussion purposes the Visionary, Implementor, and People Manager roles are examined separately throughout this book, it is important to note that the three roles are closely connected and interrelated, and are an integral part of each worker. With very few exceptions, each employee must engage each of the three roles. Employees need to recognize, improve on, and master the skills of each role if the team and/or organization are to be successful.

Here is a brief summary of each role:

- ⊃ **The Visionary** establishes Purpose for the unit and determines mission, values, and the strategic positioning and intent that are required for the organization to fulfill its reason for existence.
- ⊃ **The Implementor** establishes Process for the unit by determining short-term corporate challenges and building the core competencies, networks, and strategic system in order to achieve the purpose defined by the Visionary. The Implementor also establishes the Balanced Scorecard™ approach and creates an environment that favours entrepreneurship.
- ⊃ **The People Manager** works in the environment of entrepreneurship and deals with the professional and personal growth and development of the unit's People and creates a culture of synergy, collaboration, and trust.

As an introduction to the three VIP roles, let's briefly examine the skills and challenges associated with the Visionary, Implementor, and People Manager.

## The Visionary: Defining Purpose

There are two different yet overlapping senses of purpose that the Visionary seeks to develop: business purpose and people purpose. Business purpose is the principal guiding

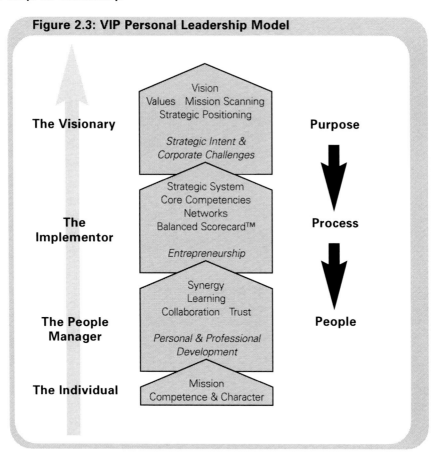

Figure 2.3: VIP Personal Leadership Model

objective that propels the construction of required successful business processes. People purpose fosters the desire to challenge and motivate employees to feel a part of something larger and greater than themselves and to create a legacy.

## Business Purpose

This visionary activity means that individuals continually scan the future to identify possibilities, generate scenarios, and ask the "what if" types of questions that could impact the organization's or team's future direction and performance. These individuals ceaselessly try to see where opportunities and threats for the organization are on the horizon and how evolving demands and the relationships with all stakeholders could affect the unit. Business purpose defines the strategic positioning or value proposition (i.e., the value of an organization's products or services as perceived by its clients) that the company will offer in the marketplace. In turn, the positioning or value determines the intellectual capital or core competencies that the company will need to develop in order to deliver and be successful in that position.

Examples of business purpose could include offering high-quality, fast-response computer system support to small and home businesses; a vast, low-cost selection of on-line books aimed at children aged five to ten; or customized Human Resources (HR) training services to World Bank–funded organizations around the globe.

## People Purpose

There are several activities that Visionaries must undertake to define and effectively develop and communicate people purpose.

The first challenge is to create a vision of the future—what you want to be and do—that is shared by everyone within the organization. Without such a common view, an organization will be forever pulled in different directions as each person tries to achieve their own personal vision (see Figure 2.2, page 30). In this situation, neither the individuals nor the organization will ever attain a shared vision because there simply isn't one.

Examples of people purpose (parallel to the business purposes described above) could include having the best-trained, most highly competent team of computer experts specializing in small systems; overcoming illiteracy by eliminating price barriers to books; or maximizing the efficacy of development projects through transferring top HR practices to overseas countries.

People purpose is also achieved through the translation of a corporate mission statement into a more manageable, tangible, shorter-term message—what Gary Hamel calls "strategic intent." It often takes the form of a slogan or an easily communicated image that challenges employees to achieve results within a three- to five-year time span.

People purpose can also be established with shorter-term (twelve to eighteen months), practical corporate challenges designed to "stretch" the company and its personnel towards the mission. These corporate challenges are not only tangible, but also measurable. Furthermore, using a Balanced Scorecard™–type approach (see Chapter 8 for more details), they can be established as targets for improvement in areas such as financial returns, customer satisfaction, improved processes, and, ultimately, individual learning. Establishing corporate challenges ensures that all action is focused on achieving the strategic intent and supporting the adopted strategic positioning.

## Developing Shared Values

Visionaries also need to develop and communicate shared values. If you want to eliminate the need for restrictive and constraining rules and procedures, each person must understand implicitly what behaviours are acceptable and unacceptable. Employees certainly look for and need guidance regarding behaviour. However, if detailed procedures are used and enforced, employees have little freedom for individual enterprise and creativity. Ideally, employees will be provided with guidelines that provide a basis for decision making while allowing them to be entrepreneurial and innovative in meeting their objectives. To be truly efficient, these behavioural guidelines will reflect the personal belief systems and values shared by all the people within the company. When this kind of culture is established, employees do not need to ask or be told what they can or cannot do. They know implicitly because the guidelines mirror their own vision of how to behave ethically and morally in terms of business practices.

## Developing a Co-Mission

The development of a shared mission statement—a "co-mission"—is also the work of the Visionary. This team mission needs to be developed and shared by all employees, from the president to the office or factory cleaners. The sense of mission should be so strong and meaningful that if potential recruits cannot accept it and learn to believe in its every word, they should not be hired. It should serve as a motivational tool, as a compass showing the unit's direction, and it should communicate the vision and values that all the unit's stakeholders share.

## Developing a Shared Purpose

What will shared vision, values, and a co-mission achieve for you in your drive to be successful in this new environment? According to Christopher Bartlett, it will promote a sense of shared purpose and give meaning to what it is being done as a group. A basic human need is to create a legacy, to leave something behind, and driving towards and achieving a shared purpose provides people with an opportunity to fulfill that need through their work.

## *The Implementor: Defining Process*

Similar to the Visionary, there are several aspects to the Implementor's role, this time focused on creating process. The most important process to create is a unique means of delivering the positioning definition or value proposition to the client. It is preferable, if not essential, that the unit find a unique and difficult-to-imitate means of creating the value proposition that will be offered to the client. Michael E. Porter refers to "activity sets": the arrangement of integrated activities undertaken within a company that allows it to create and deliver the product or service in a unique and very focused way (see "What Is Strategy?"). He argues that every activity should be designed to support, compliment, or enhance the value proposition. Gary Hamel talks about building core competencies and "reinventing the industry"—that is, discarding the existing predominant process presently used in order to produce a similar or improved service or product in a new, preferably unique or lower-cost manner (17). Personally, I like the term "strategic system," which I first saw used by Yvan Allaire (2). This terms suggests the creation of a complete system of strategic activities—marketing, research and development (R&D), production, client service, etc.—totally focused on achieving the desired market position and creating the value proposition for the client (see Figure 2.4). The Implementor's job is to create a strategic system (or value chain) that focuses on creating the maximum value in the shortest time with the least cost, and on creating new or stronger competencies in the key parts of the value chain.

The positioning determined by the Visionary can range from offering a unique product to providing a low-cost service. The first challenge for the Implementor is to design and operate a value creation process that will uniquely deliver this value proposition. They must then design and implement core competencies that will enable the organization to deliver the service today and in the future. The Implementor basically takes the purpose defined by the Visionary and "makes it happen": they make the vision concrete, exploit technology, and create the corporate value chain or processes that will generate the product or service the company will offer.

## Developing Networks

An additional key part of the Implementor's task relates to creating and maintaining two types of networks. The first is used for gaining internal or external support for your work and is particularly important for project groups or divisions within organizations. Without internal political support from company areas, project managers can soon find themselves isolated and without the necessary funding and resources they need to move their projects forward. Even in an entrepreneurial environment, it will always be easier to get things approved, have resources allocated, and gain priority for an urgent initiative if your project has a solid base of peer understanding and support. For a corporate-level project, the existence of a solid base of support among influential members of the external business community can often mean that zoning changes, government assistance, support for infrastructure improvements, or even strategic alliances can be more easily put into place.

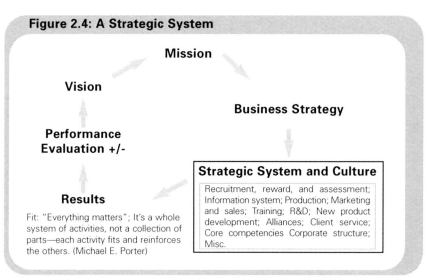

Figure 2.4: A Strategic System

In these days of strategic alliances, partnerships, and inter- and intra-company networks, the second important network for the Implementor to manage is the one required to facilitate exchange through both formal and informal communication and information networks. Providing the right people with the right information in the right format has become an incredible challenge for organizations, even though information is the raw material of knowledge creation, which is vital to the value-added process. Ensuring that information reaches the person who really needs it and who can genuinely benefit from it is the objective of the Implementor. This objective can be attained through electronic intranets, formal meetings, and encouraging informal networking and information exchange around the coffee machine.

## Developing Structure and Culture
The final aspect of the Implementor's job in designing the strategic system is to create an organizational structure and culture that promotes creativity and entrepreneurship. Creating such a culture is essential if the company is truly going to liberate creativity among its employees and encourage innovation, learning, and risk-taking throughout its ranks. If constant change describes the operating environment at all levels of the organization, then constant innovation is the only means by which you can continue to realign yourself and exploit opportunities that present themselves or can be created.

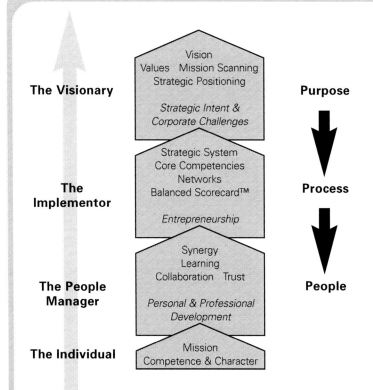

## Figure 2.5: VIP Roles and the Ten Criteria for Success

**The Visionary** — Vision / Values Mission Scanning / Strategic Positioning / *Strategic Intent & Corporate Challenges* — **Purpose**

**The Implementor** — Strategic System / Core Competencies / Networks / Balanced Scorecard™ / *Entrepreneurship* — **Process**

**The People Manager** — Synergy / Learning / Collaboration Trust / *Personal & Professional Development* — **People**

**The Individual** — Mission / Competence & Character

### The Success Criteria

- Constantly scan the macroenvironment for trends that could impact the business. (V)
- Build up an HR-focused, entrepreneurial, and creative organization and recruit people who can adapt to (and enjoy) constant change and renewal. (I, P)
- Ensure that each employee "owns" the company. It must be a community built around a shared mission, vision, and values with a high-tech, high-touch feel to it. Use technology wherever possible to reduce costs, free up employees for more more value-added activities, and create competitive advantage. (V, I, P)
- Recognize that employees at all levels represent intellectual capital and are the real owners of the organization and its core competencies. Grow and protect your "intel lectual capital" while stretching, developing, attracting, and retaining the owners of this resource. (I, P)
- See to it that every level of an organization and every individual is being creative and adding value. No one should be monitoring, controlling, or "managing" others— and no one should need it. Employees should be leaders: good communicators, networkers, coaches, and, above all, trustworthy. (I, P)
- Satisfy all stakeholders; "win-win" must be the operating philosophy. (V, I, P)
- Create and deliver a unique positioning and brand in the minds of customers. (V, I)
- Develop a unique way of creating value and a set of core competencies that are difficult for a competitor to reproduce. (I, P)
- Build and maintain strong networks. (I)
- Do things as efficiently as possible. (I)

## *The People Manager: Growing and Developing People*

Working in an environment of entrepreneurship, the People Manager's challenge is to encourage and nourish the personal and professional growth of each and every employee within a unit. The underlying paradigm the People Manager must understand is that the growth and development of an organization is strictly a function of the growth and development of the individuals therein.

The formula representing this equation is as follows:

Organizational Growth and Development $= \Sigma$ (Individual Growth and Development)$^n$

where $n$ is the power of the synergy created between individuals due to the environment created by the People Manager. And that is the People Manager's challenge: to not only encourage each person's individual development, but to set up an environment based on trust, collaboration, and learning, allowing workers to "synergize" with each other and propel the company forward. The People Manager needs to develop a culture of support, coaching, and open communication if individual and organizational growth is to be maximized.

To achieve this ambitious objective, it is clear that the raw materials must already be present in the organization. In other words, the company must identify and recruit individuals who are trustworthy; who share the company mission and values; and who are, by nature, keen to collaborate, take calculated risks, and learn while maintaining their entrepreneurial spirit. The task of the People Manager, therefore, is not to control or monitor, but to coach, facilitate learning, and offer training programs that fit the needs of both the individual and the company. The People Manager offers remuneration packages and internal recognition systems that motivate desired behaviours and create an environment that promotes synergy, communication, and learning. In essence, the task of the People Manager is not to manage at all, but to lead.

## *The VIP Roles and the Ten Criteria for Success*

Figure 2.5 shows the Ten Criteria for Success alongside the three VIP roles. Take the time to examine how building an organization consisting of VIP employees will allow your unit to satisfy each and every one of the Criteria for Success (the letters in parenthesis signify which of the VIP roles facilitates achieving each criterion).

## *VIP Leaders: The Building Blocks*

Someone may produce results by being a great Visionary or Implementor, but only if they are also a great People Manager. As I will argue throughout this book, although positioning and strategic systems are important, when your competitive advantage is based upon intellectual capital, the difference between a winning company and one that fails is the quality and productivity of its employees. These employees are the building blocks of today's organizations and even heroic efforts come to naught if team members are not of high calibre.

Where do you find high-calibre individuals? While just about everyone has the potential to be an outstanding employee, in reality these people are difficult to find. They are people who want to contribute, grow, and who are willing to work hard to achieve their personal legacy. An organization needs to project these same characteristics and attributes in order to attract the appropriate employees. To use a metaphor, you are a gardener seeking to cultivate a crop of healthy, vibrant plants. At the same time, those plants are sensitive and can be easily damaged. So how do you decide which seedlings will survive? The next chapter describes the kind of building blocks (read: seedlings) that will grow into a strong company—that is, the people who aspire to be VIP leaders.

# Key Points in Chapter 2

○ The "old way"—the 4Cs: Compliance, Control, Contract, and Constraint—only harms today's organizations. The "new way"—the 3Ps: Purpose, Process, and People—encourages personal discipline, support and coaching, trust, and organizational and individual "stretch."

○ Employees are the real owners of today's organizations because they own the key asset: capital intelligence, intellectual property, knowledge—call it what you like.

○ There are three key roles in the kind of VIP Personal Leadership needed in today's organizations: the Visionary, the Implementor, and the People Manager.

○ Visionaries create Purpose by defining where an organization is going and why.

○ Implementors create Process by designing a system for how the organization will go about achieving its goals.

○ People Managers develop the People who "make it happen," and help the organization achieve its purpose.

○ The VIP roles allow an organization to satisfy the Ten Criteria for Success.

# Questions to Consider

○ Who do you want to be? What's your mission?

○ Do the 4Cs still reign supreme in your organization?

○ Do you feel like one of the owners of your organization?

○ Do you share your employer's mission?

○ Are you a core member, a core professional, or a contract worker? Is that the right position for you?

○ At first glance, which of the VIP leadership roles is your strength? Which is your weakness?

○ Do you have the desire to become a VIP leader and develop your VIP Visionary, Implementor, and People Manager skills? If so, keep reading!

## Chapter 3

As highlighted in the first two chapters, an organization's employees are its only real source of sustainable competitive advantage. They are unique assets and technically, they are the organization's true owners. If you remain unconvinced by this proposition, ask yourself which is the worst-case scenario for a knowledge-based company: the exiting of a company's shareholders and/or its financial backers, or the departure of the work team that possesses the company's principal core competencies? Which affects the future revenue-generating capability of the company (and hence its market value) the most?

Often within forty-eight hours of shareholders deciding to sell or financiers deciding to pull out of a small, high-potential, knowledge-based company or project, members of the core team—the owners of the company's core competencies—have started their own company or have been recruited by a competitor. The core team continues on, simply by sporting new colours. In contrast, if the core team members suddenly decide to leave the company and either start their own business or move to a competitor, how valuable are the remaining assets held by the shareholders and financiers? Would anyone want to take the company over? It's not likely.

As demonstrated in the previous chapter, the relationship between the value and growth potential of a company and its employees is very simple:

Organizational Growth and Development $= \sum$ (Individual Growth and Development)$^n$

where $n$ is the synergy created between individuals due to the environment created by the VIP People Manager.

But this formula goes much further than simply suggesting that you should invest heavily in the technical training of a young knowledge worker. Employees must be willing and eager to stretch their development in all aspects of their lives: emotional, spiritual, physical, and intellectual. They need to be balanced people leading balanced lives, and companies need to support such well-rounded and holistic development. The demands placed on people living in a constantly changing environment with a constantly evolving corporate Diamond-E Framework means that they must be strong and healthy in all aspects of their lives if they are to succeed and contribute over the long term. Stephen R. Covey talks about "sharpening the saw" (the seventh of his seven habits of effective people); individuals must take time for the renewal of their physical, mental, emotional, and spiritual lives. People need to explore and hopefully reach their full potential on all these fronts. And discovering your limitations on any one dimension only happens when you overreach—in other words, when you fail! Organizations need to promote adopting such a paradigm and facilitate such an approach to life if they wish to recruit and retain the best employees.

It is also in an organization's best long-term interest to promote such a culture of risk-taking and learning: if employees continually question both their personal and the company's operating models, it will ensure that both remain healthy and productive and that the Diamond-E remains in sync with the changing environment. After all, if the environment changes, the Diamond-E must also change if it is to remain in equilibrium. This means that your people will have to change accordingly—and not just on the intellectual plane. The demands of working globally, virtually, technologically, collectively, and in real time are quite different from those exerted in my father's time when the environment was local, face-to-face, pen and paper–based, and when tasks were performed in isolation. Employees must now be in dynamic equilibrium too—forever moving forward, questioning, learning, testing, and modifying their own behaviour and attitudes. This is the only way for an organization to remain competitive and for an employee to maintain employability.

## Whom Should You Hire?

If you decide that your most important challenge in a knowledge-based company—the one that will determine the very success of your organization—is to build and carefully develop your human resources, the essential starting point is having a very accurate idea about the type of individuals you should be hiring and employing. Here you are not talking about whether they are experts in Java programming, mineral processing, accounting, or marketing (take for granted that they have a high level of technical competence in their field). Rather, you are looking at the type of characteristics that make up the foundation of their being. Many of these foundation characteristics may sound quite similar, one to another. However, each is slightly different and the more of these attitudes you detect in future recruits, the better partners they will be and the better service they will give you over the long term. You want to employ people who possess the following characteristics:

### Unique Intelligence(s)

Excepting the beliefs and practices of formal education systems (which certainly operate in a static equilibrium determined and fixed many decades ago), it's now a widely accepted fact that numerous forms of intelligence exist. Depending on your organization, industry, or strategy, you may need to recruit people with several types or only one type of intelligence. Alternately, you may need to build a "multi-intelligence" team to complete a certain project. One thing, however, is certain: you need to recruit intelligent people throughout all levels of the organization, and you need to choose ones with the right type of intelligence for the task at hand or for the core competence you are trying to build.

In his book *The Age of Unreason*, Charles Handy refers to the existence of at least nine forms of intelligence—and there are probably more! If you are trying to build a multimedia company, for example, you may seek to recruit people with musical, spatial, and analytical intelligence. In contrast, if you're building a construction company, you might hire people with spatial and analytical intelligence to do the design work, individuals with physical and practical intelligence to do the construction work, and someone with intuitive and interpersonal intelligence to do the sales and marketing. Unfortunately, today's reality is such that few people are aware of which sort of intelligence they possess. Hence, they are not really aware of what type of "knowledge work" best suits them (the school systems tend to assess and record only factual, analytical, and sometimes linguistic intelligence). Lastly, and most alarmingly, companies—Human Resources (HR) departments in particular—still tend to be overreliant on factual, analytical, and the increasingly popular interpersonal intelligence, yet have little knowledge, desire, or few tools to assess spatial, practical, physical, or intuitive forms of intelligence, which can be extremely desirable for many positions.

> *Employees must now be in dynamic equilibrium— moving forward, questioning, testing, and modifying their behaviour and attitudes.*

You need to decide which types of intelligence you need to recruit among your core professionals, professionals, and contractuals. Different types may also be required depending on the departmental functions, the level of a position within the hierarchy, and the job goals. However, it is important that both individuals and companies be aware of the differences among types of intelligence and work to find the ideal position for an individual so they can make their best contribution and realize their full potential. Does your company recruit for a position based on the type of intelligence required? Do you know your own strengths in terms of the different types of intelligence you possess?

Given that you need to hire intelligent people, what are the other characteristics that you need to look for when recruiting new members for your team?

## A Defined Life Mission

An obvious prerequisite of recruiting employees whose life objectives and personal mission statement match yours and your organization's is that the potential recruits need to have defined their personal mission statement. This doesn't necessarily mean that they have summed up their mission on one sheet of paper for you to read (although that is preferable). Rather, it means they have taken the time to reflect, to find out who they are and what is important to them, and what they are seeking to do or be in their lives. If they have done this work it means several things: that they recognize working with your organization will help them achieve their life's objectives; that you can work together for an as yet undetermined period of time; and that you will both have moved further towards your respective missions by the time you part ways.

I believe that people who go to work only for their paycheque are missing out on a great opportunity to use their work hours productively to satisfy their own needs and to accomplish their objectives. Once again, Covey sums this up nicely by stating that everyone is looking for the 4Ls:

- ⟳ to Live (satisfy basic needs)
- ⟳ to Love (enjoy social contact)
- ⟳ to Learn (expand knowledge and develop skills)
- ⟳ to create a Legacy (make a contribution and leave something behind)

Although some people strive to inject meaning into their lives outside of paid work time (by volunteering, for example), it still seems a waste to spend many hours a day simply earning money to live—people could be achieving so much more. As an employee, isn't it better for everyone if I satisfy the 4Ls at my paid job? Taking the employer's point of view, do I want to hire an employee who may be saving their most meaningful contribution until the evening when they work or volunteer for another organization? Not really. Instead, I want to offer members of my team the best opportunity to achieve their mission and full potential, to learn and make a contribution to something they believe in. Leading them forward will certainly be much easier if they believe as vehemently as I do in the cause for which we are working.

Individuals who take a position that only satisfies their financial needs risk spending perhaps half of their waking hours trying to build skills and apply them in a subject area or for a cause for which they have no sense of ownership. They are spending half of their waking hours doing something they do not really want to do! Anyone who does their upfront job research well and shows patience and determination will probably find the company or group of individuals who are at taking the time to hire someone with their specific intelligence and mission. Consequently, both parties accomplish—in a collective manner—their respective objectives, which they could never have done individually.

## A Win-Win Philosophy

Stephen R. Covey has written extensively on the "win-win" topic, specifically about the value in adopting such a philosophy. I have a small addition to his material and that is to say, "Yes, it does indeed work" (see Table 3.1 for the six possible win/lose combinations). By simply adopting the most powerful paradigm of thinking—win-win or no thanks (also called "no deal")—in your dealings on a daily basis, you will witness enormous benefits resulting from your own behaviour and the quality of your relationships, and achieve a level of inner peace that is instantly gratifying. We all have probably had moments when we reacted with an "If I'm going to lose I'm going to make sure you do too" (lose-lose) attitude out of spite, or have accepted that someone else would win at our expense (lose-win) when the issue was unimportant to us. As a result, the logic of only accepting win-win arrangements (anything less requires walking away and waiting for the next opportunity) needs little justification.

It's a healthy approach—it can sometimes just be very difficult to do.

Accepting that "no deal" is a possible outcome means that you are also able to handle the tough decisions that can make leadership a lonely pursuit. However, because you know that accepting a lose-win scenario will not only hurt you but also your colleagues, team, or organization over the long term, you will still have an easy conscience knowing that you've been tough for all the right reasons.

**Table 3.1: The Six Paradigms of Human Interaction**

| Paradigm | Result |
|---|---|
| Win-Lose | I win, you lose |
| Lose-Win | I lose, you win |
| Lose-Lose | I lose, you lose |
| Win-Win | I win, you win |
| Win | I win |
| Win-Win or No Thanks (or No Deal) | I win and you win, or we'll try again next time |

Source: Stephen R. Covey, *The 7 Habits of Highly Effective People*

It is now relatively easy for me to identify other peoples' paradigms, be they win, win-lose, etc., and this in itself has helped me arrive at better agreements with such people—or walk away when required. The people I seek to build long-term relationships with are those who also think win-win. When I know I'm dealing with someone who thinks win-win, my trust level and confidence in them soars, my worries diminish, and creating synergy becomes our *modus operandi*.

## A Love of Learning

Although I've already mentioned that everyone wants to learn, it's interesting to delve a little further into the area of people and learning.

Children naturally love to learn; they are designed to do so. From the moment of birth they are constantly fascinated by new things and want to explore, be amazed, try new things, and learn new skills. Unfortunately, somewhere early on life's path they also learn that learning itself carries risks: physical, emotional, or psychological pain; the experience of humiliation upon failing; the shame of being laughed at by friends, teachers, or parents; or being constantly put down. Somewhere children learn that trying new things, being creative, expressing themselves, and trying to improve is often viewed negatively by others, and the best way to avoid standing out is by adopting the same behaviour as everyone else.

Chris Argyris talks about the "defensive routines" that, when adopted, prevent people from learning (3, pp. 77–85). These defensive routines are our postures and ways of speaking, structured to prevent us from exposing our real ideas, thoughts, and understanding to colleagues. They protect us from the potential embarrassment that accompanies being wrong or seeming foolish or ignorant. You will be favoured in many organizations if you can hide behind a façade of being learned rather than risk actually learning. Next time you are due to meet about a controversial issue at work, discuss it first with a friend and see how you present your thoughts. Then, during the meeting, check if you present your views differently; watch for symptoms of stress emerging in your stomach, throat, eye movements, etc. Even when the stakes for you may not be high on a particular issue, you will discover the ways in which you cloak your real views in order to avoid exposing yourself. And you can safely assume that everyone else around the meeting table is doing the same! How can you ever hope to arrive at a win-win agreement if everybody refuses to expose their views? How can you ever hope to really learn if you are not open to such exposure? How can organizations ever grow if people never discuss the real facts or how they feel about them?

Deep down inside, many people still dream of adventure, of daring to take the risks required so that they can do what they really yearn to and be who they really think they can be, which is someone of whom they can be proud. Humans are capable of myriad things; yet most people accept "just enough," the minimum that will get them by. Few seek to find their limits because that would mean ultimately failing in order to truly know those limits. In today's society, it's much safer not to risk anything at all than to try something new and fail.

Peter Senge once defined learning as "the enhancement of capacity to produce results that matter to you" (31, p. 18). In this context, failing at something—perhaps trying a new application of a new technology and finding it doesn't work—can be interpreted as learning. After all, in the wake of such a failure you know more about the new technology, its limitations, or the infrastructure it may need. You may even have stumbled over a new application you never would have appreciated had you not made the initial attempt. For example, if this book remains largely unsold in the book-store's warehouse, it does not devalue the insights, learning, and better methods of communications I will bring to my classroom and workshops—all of which I acquired in the process of writing.

## A Willingness to Fail

It may sound strange, but a willingness to fail is a desirable quality for employees to have. Linked to the desire to learn, people willing to risk failure are also likely to try new things, "push the envelope," and reach beyond their known capabilities in order to try something radically different that will perhaps reinvent their industry. People who understand that failure is an integral part of success know that they may have to fail at something nine times before they succeed on the tenth try. It is often said that the difference between success and failure is simply the fact that those who succeed try again and again. You want these driven people on your team! However, other than forming a trick question in interviews—"Tell me about your biggest fail-ure"—the experience gained and the knowledge learned through failure is seldom recognized when recruiting new personnel. How does your company treat "failure"? Are failed research and development (R&D) projects recognized in addition to suc-cessful ones? Are you rewarded for having had the courage and energy to pursue a "losing" project bid, or do you know that your days are numbered? If you were to vol-unteer to take a course in Spanish but fail to master it, would you be encouraged to take another course or would your training budget be more closely monitored or reduced because you are deemed to have wasted funds?

## *Emotional Intelligence (or People Skills)*

It is almost taken for granted that young graduates from the best universities possess excellent technical skills in their chosen area. However, within two years of graduation, less than a half will still be working in their discipline. Even if they are (assuming they have proved themselves effective in the workplace), their time will be increasingly spent on managing teams and supervising or overseeing other younger graduates rather than doing any technical work themselves. Their major challenges will be leading and coaching others, dealing with communication issues, creating synergy on their teams, motivating individuals, etc. Perhaps this is a positive situation; the half-life of an engineering degree is now about three-and-a-half years. Emotional intelligence (EQ) skills are good for life.

Obviously, this is not only true for new graduates. To be good People Managers, all employees need to have a highly developed EQ in order to manage networks and communicate vision. If you're heading a marketing department, how much time do you spend dealing with people or process issues as opposed to working on new marketing campaigns? If you're working in operations or finance, the same situation probably applies. If you're on the executive committee, you're probably spending much more time on people-related issues than devising corporate strategy.

So what is EQ exactly? According to Daniel Goleman, one of the originators of the term, there are five EQ components:

1. **Self-awareness:** The ability to recognize and understand one's moods, emotions, and drives, as well as their effects on others. This skill is vital when dealing with others, yet there are few courses offered in school about the topic—everyone is somehow just supposed to know about and be aware of this complex area.
2. **Self-regulation:** The ability to control or redirect disruptive impulses and moods; the propensity to suspend judgement and to think before acting. How many people do you know either appear to have no control over their impulses or simply block their reactions and do what they "should" do?
3. **Motivation:** The ability to work passionately for reasons that go beyond money or status; the propensity to pursue goals with energy and persistence.
4. **Empathy:** The ability to understand people's emotional makeup; the skill for treating people according to their emotional reactions. Empathetic listening remains one of the most useful communication tools a person can possess, yet few people have learned this skill.
5. **Social Skills:** The ability to proficiently manage relationships and build networks; the ability to find common ground and build rapport. People without such skills tend to regard those who have mastered them as being "too political"—or worse. However, to be an effective Implementor, managing networks and relationships is a key skill required in today's working environment. (16, pp. 93–102)

These five components are crucial for people adopting VIP Personal Leadership roles and appear throughout the work of Goleman, Covey, and others. Individuals weak in these areas can certainly improve, but they are not skills or abilities that can be gained by taking a one-day course (as is the case for many technical skills).

## Trustworthiness

At the base of all work relationships is a level of trust; trust exists among people in any work group. Stephen R. Covey defines the base of an individual's trustworthiness as being a combination of their competence in a certain field and their overall character (12). For example, though I'd trust an accounting expert with my company's financial books, I wouldn't trust that same person to professionally edit this book— it's not their field of competence. But I wouldn't trust even a great book editor to do the task either if I didn't trust their character sufficiently to know that they wouldn't subcontract the work, deliver on time, or overcharge me.

Warren Bennis describes the 5Cs of building trust: Competency, Constancy, Caring, Candor, and Character. Sounds perfect to me! Trust is certainly not blind: it has to be earned. In fact, there are many types of behaviour that betray a person's real character and either quickly build trust or destroy it. Moreover, trust is easily lost and is tough to regain. However, working in a global, virtual, team-based environment means that trust is even more important today than ever. (Much more on this topic in Chapter 9.)

## Ability to Strive for Balance

> *Self-knowledge helps everyone perform at their best when they have to.*

Although I like to think of myself being 100 percent effective through 100 percent of each and every day, I know that I am neither physically, psychologically, nor intellectually capable of producing the same level of listening, ideas, results, etc. unless I take some downtime, do some training, get some rest and relaxation, and make time for personal renewal. In fact, I find that my best ideas come to me when I'm "goofing off" by skiing or watching a film in the middle of the afternoon! If I continue staring at the keyboard when I'm drained, nothing creative comes out of my brain. By persevering, I simply become more stressed and am doomed to fail. I now recognize that regular downtime and a balanced lifestyle is the only way that I can operate at peak performance when I really need to. I think of myself in terms of a decathlete or a 100-metre runner who only produces their best occasionally—perhaps once every four years at the Olympics—but keeps in top condition so that they can deliver when it counts. Self-knowledge helps everyone perform at their best when they have to.

Balance is also important in terms of ensuring that work does not become the sum total of who we are and what we do. This notion goes beyond Covey's idea of "sharpening the saw" and into Handy's concept of "portfolio lives" (i.e., lives that are balanced between work and outside activities). The reality is that all of my needs probably cannot be satisfied through the work I do for which I am paid. Let's face it—I know I am not a great painter or a wonderful dancer. Furthermore, people are not willing to pay me sufficient hourly fees for "life balance" consultations so that I can earn my living giving them. Yet I love to do these activities. Should I not pursue these interests because I cannot earn money for doing them? Of course not. But I do need to create time in my life for these activities—hopefully time that an understanding employer will realize I need to have if I am to be retained. If I am not given this time, sooner or later I will be seeking other work that will allow me to achieve my own personal sense of balance.

## A Sense of "Stretch"

Success—in society's eyes—is easily defined. In North America, for example, it means earning the biggest salary, working at certain companies, holding memberships at the "best" clubs, having the most attractive spouse, raising respectable children, living in the right neighbourhood, driving the latest car, and wearing an expensive suit. This is the route most people take. They learn to seek what society recognizes as success. It's often a case of "following the flock," the path clearly indicated and judged acceptable by society at large, as well as family and friends.

Creating a unique definition of personal success is different. Moreover, pursuing personal success requires reflection, self-awareness, and courage. The path is difficult to identify, as it is unique to each individual and has never been found or taken before. You are constantly picking your way through virgin forest to create the route with only a vague feeling that you are heading in the right direction. This path can only be created alone and once it's taken, an individual has to take full responsibility for having done so—there is no one else to blame. Pursuing personal success means taking risks and experimenting with yourself. It can be a lonely path and society, family, and friends are known to judge people perceived as being different very harshly: as soon as they become aware that someone does not share their own definition of success, they perceive that person as a threat (or deem them a fool) and readily point our their mistakes. People who choose their own route risk being ostracized and ridiculed; however, that price is normally considered reasonable when the opportunity to accrue self-knowledge, define and achieve one's mission, and discover one's true potential is found. That is true success!

> *Stretch is exciting and liberating: it generates a creative tension that motivates and pulls you towards your target.*

Knowing exactly where you are and then setting reasonable but challenging objectives that move you towards your mission creates a sense of "stretch." Stretch is exciting and liberating: it generates a creative tension that motivates and pulls you towards your target. It's also risky and a part of growing and learning. But if people have an image of who they want to be or what they want their company to be, they can be stretched towards it by setting challenging goals that are supported by the appropriate environment, resources, and rewards. Creating stretch is a major part of every team leader's responsibilities.

People who have determined their personal definition of success (and can therefore be "stretched") are few and far between, but unless they have learned how to mask this quality very well, they are readily identifiable. People living on their own terms are the people that companies should be seeking to recruit.

## *A Commitment to Change and Renewal*

In a state of dynamic equilibrium, organizations constantly have to renew themselves. Their employees need to adopt a similar philosophy. Making ourselves fire resistant—that is, resistant to change and renewal—is dangerous in terms of our employability (although setting small fires in traditional organizations carries the same risk!) and in terms of reaching our potential. How will you ever know just how far you can go in new areas if you are not prepared to give up old positions, responsibilities, aging employers, obsolete software, and outdated processes? You need to throw these things aside every now and again and try out new ones. Continuous, controlled change is better than hanging on to old ways until a competitor (or a younger employee) comes along with a new way and takes your place. If you are to develop all aspects of life to their full potential, you need to reinvent your industry, your organization, and yourself!

## *A Handle on the Complex, Uncontrollable System*

I used to be an unsatiable consumer of news—I couldn't get enough. All the impressive business people on whom I was trying to model myself seemed to know everything. To be like them—and to impress them—I needed to know as much, if not more, than they did. Being continually up-to-date on the latest news was painful, but I was a consultant and was expected to know everything. And the rise of the Internet only made things worse! Why was I doing this? Because I thought if I could just learn more, the big picture would become focused and I would not only know how it all fit together, but would also somehow be in control of it.

Peter Senge points out that handling complexity often happens at the intuitive level and business executives have difficulty accepting that (1) everything is connected and (2) they are never going to understand that connectedness (32). It's like the complex ecosystem of the forest: we know everything in the system is connected, but there are very few people—if any—who know how it all works together so perfectly.

Once people grasp this concept, they are free to let down their guard, empower others, and stop trying to control the activities of bosses, peers, and subordinates.

## *The Bottom Line: Hire Leaders*

When you examine the characteristics outlined above with Bennis's four leadership qualities (see Table 2.1, page 31), it becomes clear that you are looking to hire potential leaders throughout all levels of your organization. You cannot afford to hire "followers" or people who need monitoring and controlling; you need people who are seeking to grow and who want to further develop their leadership skills.

In summary, what sort of characteristics must you include in the job posting for the position you need filled?

**Our company is looking to recruit people who:**
- ⊃ have the appropriate type(s) of intelligence and can do things with it;
- ⊃ know their mission and use a win-win paradigm;
- ⊃ love to learn and are willing to fail;

- are highly competent in their field and are able to make the tough decisions;
- are trustworthy;
- lead a balanced life;
- have defined their own personal definition of success;
- believe in constant change and renewal; and
- can handle the complex, uncontrollable system and can empower others.

Based on my own experience, I'd much rather work with individuals who possess these traits but need to learn a new skill to be on my team than work with individuals who have the technical skills but lack these essential characteristics.

# Why Should I Join Your Organization?

Now that we've looked at the type of person you need to hire, it's time to survey the situation from a future employee's point of view. Why should a talented candidate decide to work with you? What are they looking for?

Imagine that there is an intelligent person (let's say they possess enormous musical and spatial intelligence) who has all the qualities discussed in the previous section and they are seeking satisfying work. What would motivate them to join your company? Will this kind of person be attracted to your organization? Putting aside the financial benefits a salary brings, that person should be looking to join a company where, by leveraging other peoples' efforts or the company's resources, they will improve their chances of achieving their personal mission or goals in life. If they are to do that, you obviously need to create an environment that will maximize the individual's growth and development, as well as your organization's.

## Creating a Work Environment

For your company to be attractive to desirable candidates, there are several key cultural characteristics that they will want to see when visiting your organization. These key characteristics are discussed in the sections that follow.

### Intelligence

The characteristics of intelligence can be listed (realistically, yet somewhat humorously) as follows:

- You can't create it, but you can add to it.
- It has a large appetite.
- It hates being underutilized or undervalued.
- It hates being managed; it likes being led.
- It attracts other intelligence.
- It's very mobile.
- It can be given away but retained at the same time.
- The government can't hand it out.
- It is the source of today's wealth, growth, and value creation.

Are your organization's structures, systems, and controls designed to take into account that your employees represent human intelligence? If not, beware: your intelligent people are either in the process of switching off so that they can bear coming to work for you each day, or they've started to investigate switching companies.

## Shared Vision, Values, and Mission

If you expect your employees to have created their own personal mission statement, then your company or team must also have created one. This statement should communicate an objective, a vision of the future, and the principles the team lives by. Your company should have a management team and process, an organizational structure, and a rewards system that reflect a high level of trust and personal and team stretch, and it should be clear from your organization's culture that the real owners of the company are the people inside it.

## Opportunity Rotation

Some people are born to be architects, linguists, musicians, etc. and have no desire to venture into other disciplines. However, most people are labelled early in their career and never have the opportunity to pursue interests or improve their skills in other areas. If people are to rise up through the organization—or appreciate the work of their colleagues—job rotation should be available and encouraged. As a young engineer I was originally attracted to work with the promise of job rotation every six months during my "management training program." I soon realized that this was not going to happen. How many other people live that same experience?

## Horizontal Careers

On a related topic, flat organizations offer few opportunities to move "up the ladder." Viewed positively, this means there is less chance of everyone rising to a higher level of incompetence! If people cannot rise up, however, they must be provided with lots of opportunities for lateral movement and the company's reward and recognition system must deem such movement valuable and beneficial so everyone is encouraged to try it.

## Freedom to Learn, Freedom to Fail

As discussed extensively in the previous section, failure is often a necessary step in the learning process. Employees who "fail" occasionally are actually cultivating skills and knowledge. Is this process really permissible within your organization? Although poor work should never be rewarded, honest failure when taking on major new challenges and risks must be. Do you reward honest endeavour even if the results of a project or initiative are disappointing? Are failed R&D projects celebrated if the actual work has been done well? Are export marketing initiatives recognized when they have been executed well but entry into a new geographic market fails due to an economic collapse or a governmental barrier?

## Win-Win Employment Contracts

It is unrealistic to expect employees to stay with a company for the duration of their careers. Companies evolve and the skills they need their employees to have also change. Similarly, as employees grow and develop their own needs, challenges and learning opportunities also change. Hence, at some point in the future it may be the right decision for both parties that the employee leave to seek their mission elsewhere. However, until that day arrives, you need to ensure that the partnership satisfies as many needs of both parties as possible.

Coming to agreements that serve both parties well requires communication, real skills, planning, and a genuine effort on the part of your company to enhance a worker's employability during their tenure.

## Strong Human Resource Focus

The HR department of your company is often the first department to make contact with a prospective employee. It serves as a window through which they catch their first glimpse of your organization. In the knowledge-based world, HR's status, capabilities, and the quality of its people often communicate quickly and accurately to potential employees how important an organization's human assets really are. I was recently asked at which stage of development a start-up or small company should create an HR department. The only answer is this: The day it first creates *any* department. The message here is that employees are your biggest asset so you must make sure your organization treats them accordingly.

A vigorous and dynamic HR department that participates in strategic planning and organizational design, offers high-quality training and development programs, and ensures that remuneration and recognition systems reward desired behaviours is vital for all organizations. To win in the knowledge economy, HR needs to play a high-profile leadership role in which it builds an organizational culture focused on encouraging corporate growth through individual growth.

## Personal and Professional Development Training

The key consideration for a new employee in an organization is whether the position is going to help their skill development and employability. If the organization has recruited the right people, developing its human assets should be a case of win-win for both parties. This means developing both an individual's technical and leadership skills.

Hence, at any given time during their stay in an organization, employees should always be positioned to either better serve their employer or move on to another company that can provide new challenges and satisfy personal needs or ambitions that the current company cannot. Upon leaving, however, the individual should have nothing but good publicity to spread about their experience working for you, which should be an asset to your recruitment efforts. In the knowledge-based world, seeing an employee return to an organization later in their career (assuming their previous experience was positive) is far from out of the ordinary. In addition, having ex-employees working elsewhere in the same sector can help individuals and organizations build their information and partner networks.

# VIPs-in-Training

So far I've given you insight into the sort of leadership-based organization you need to build in our knowledge-based society and the types of human "building blocks" you're looking to recruit and develop in order to achieve your objectives.

Most intelligent people I know are highly conscious of the need to keep their skills up-to-date, and there are many resources available to help them develop their technical skills. However, it's your employees' leadership skills that will determine if your organization or team succeeds. Technical skills are a given in the knowledge-based world. It's therefore your employees' ability to develop and apply the skills of the Visionary, Implementor, and People Manager—and your ability to lead them—that will determine if you can build a successful and sustainable knowledge-based organization. And make no mistake: if your employees are developing VIP skills and behaviours, you will need to design an organization or environment that treats them accordingly as Very Important People. If you don't, they'll likely be working for one of your competitors in the near future!

With that in mind, let's go on in the subsequent chapters to look a little more closely at each of the three VIP roles and what each entails. Keep in mind that although we're talking about each role separately, every employee—ourselves included—must be adept at the tasks represented by each role. To be a good Implementor you must be a good Visionary; to be an effective People Manager you must have laid down good groundwork as an Implementor; etc. Think of it as moving seamlessly from one role to another, depending on what a particular situation demands of you.

## Key Points in Chapter 3

⊃ It's crucial to hire a team of intelligent people with the right type(s) of intelligence.

⊃ In addition to excellent technical competencies, recruits need to be trustworthy; have a personal mission, a win-win philosophy, a love of learning, and a willingness to fail; and be seeking a balanced existence that includes constant personal renewal and "stretch."

⊃ Organizations must offer lateral moves, opportunity rotation, win-win employment contracts, and learning environments in order to attract and retain quality employees.

⊃ The HR department has to take a strong leadership role in the management of your organization, thereby demonstrating that people are your greatest asset and the true owners of your company.

⊃ Your employees—your company's building blocks—must be treated as VIPs and be given appropriate roles and training.

## Questions to Consider

⊃ Does your company recruit for a position based on the type of intelligence required?

⊃ Do you know your own strengths in terms of the different types of intelligence you possess?

⊃ Are people in your organization more concerned with "looking good" in meetings rather than exposing their ideas, risking, and learning?

⊃ How is failure defined in your company? How is it treated?

⊃ Does your company offer the sort of attractive work environment and challenge that an ideal candidate would want to work in?

⊃ Do you, as individual, offer prospective employees the type of leadership and empowered environment that would attract them to work for your team? If not, why?

**V** **I** **P**

**Part 2: The Visionary**

## Chapter 4

# Developing Mission and Satisfying Stakeholders

Several years ago, I had an interview with the vice-president of a large nonprofit organization that was interested in recruiting me. Based upon its very positive reputation and image, the organization appeared to have goals and objectives that matched quite closely with my own. As we discussed the objectives of the particular group I would be working with and the flexibility I would have in choosing my own vision and strategy, the manager, an accountant by training and nature, proposed a working arrangement that, again on the surface, appeared enticing: "Providing you're making money, you can basically do what you want without anybody raising any questions."

Being entrepreneurial by nature, the offer seemed attractive to me; yet as our discussion progressed, I realized that the manager's vision and values only extended as far as "making money." I had assumed the manager's vision would be more reflective of the organization's social mission. In fact, the reality was that the social exterior was simply a means to make money—that is, making money was not the means for the company to achieve its mission, but the mission was the means for the company to make money!

It is clear that it would have been foolish of me to accept the position. It would not have been a win-win situation. It would also have been a major mistake for the manager to hire me. He needed someone who shared his values, objectives, and motivations—someone with whom he could communicate and synergize. With me at his side, it would have been a constant battle over which projects we would pursue, where we would put our energies, and how we would measure our results. He needed a "building block" he could relate to, lead, and who would have wanted to follow where he was going.

Now imagine a contrasting scenario where I walk into an interview and a prospective boss paints a picture of the dream they are striving to achieve, the organization they are attempting to build, the contribution they are trying to make, the people they are hoping to develop, and how together, we will make a difference. That prospective boss asks me about my mission and what legacy I'd like to create, and confirms that my contribution will be valued and levered so that the company and I can achieve a common dream.

> *The challenge, then, is to match your company's 4Ls with 4Ls of your employees.*

Acknowledging that the company does not have the funding to pay me the salary I could earn elsewhere, this prospective manager asks me about other forms of recompense: extended vacations, flex-time, working at home, time and assistance to complete other projects (writing this book, for example). Now that sounds attractive! As mentioned in the previous chapter, other than Living (the first of the 4Ls), everyone is looking for a position where, by working within an organization or team, they can have a bigger effect and make a bigger contribution than they could on their own. The kind of manager described in the second interview scenario recognizes that they're dealing with an important "building block," a major asset in the organization, and they're trying to learn as much about me as possible in order to ensure that I share the organization's mission and that it can satisfy my 4Ls. If the company cannot, the manager had better know that immediately and we can both avoid future problems by my seeking employment elsewhere.

If they earn a good salary at their job, some people are content to pursue the other Ls (Loving, Learning, and Legacy) outside of their work through their families, social life, or volunteer activities. However, in order to build a successful knowledge-based company in a highly competitive global market, you need to recruit employees who are seeking all four Ls in their work environment—and then you need to satisfy them all. This is of benefit to both parties: if companies can only grow through the development of their employees, the more you satisfy the 4Ls the faster both your employees and your organizations will grow—and that's without taking into account the costs of recruiting and training that are written off when an employee leaves. The challenge, then, is to match your company's 4Ls with 4Ls of your employees, and a great way of doing that is through mission.

## *Mission, Vision, Credo, Values, and Purpose*

Some may argue that mission, vision, credo, etc. are quite different things. And they very well may be; it all depends on your definition and I've found that each person has their own definition for each. Although I acknowledge that each term can be distinct, I will treat them as part of one all-encompassing "mission" because (1) they all are necessary and interrelated, (2) they all are things a leader and VIP Visionary must constantly and consistently communicate and live by, and (3) they all serve the same objective: they provide the organization with purpose, particularly people purpose. You'll remember from Chapter 2 that people purpose refers to where you are going and why; it gives a sense of the meaning in your life, the values that you live, and the emotional significance of your contribution.

For those who prefer more precise definitions, the various components of my personal definition of mission are as follows, beginning with mission itself:

- ⊃ **Mission.** This is what companies and employees are trying to collectively achieve. It's the what, why, and how, and it binds an organization together. It is more definitive than vision because it includes a description of the organization's strategic positioning (see Chapter 6 for in-depth coverage of strategic positioning).
- ⊃ **Vision.** This provides direction. It is about greatness and what you'd like to achieve and contribute. It comes from the heart and soul rather than from the head, and it can be seen as a powerful headlight illuminating an image of the future, lighting the direction in which you'd like to move.
- ⊃ **Values.** These provide acceptable moral standards of behaviour and represent the right ways to do something as an individual or as an organization. "In the end, managers are loyal not to a particular boss or even to a company but to a set of values they believe in and find satisfying." This quote, attributed to Goran Lindahl, Group Executive VP of ABB, sums up the importance of an organization's values to its employees (4, p. 84).
- ⊃ **Credo.** This most often is a document that accompanies a mission statement. It contains only the business purpose and describes the vision, values, etc. of the organization.
- ⊃ **Purpose.** This is the feeling elicited when an organization and its employees share a mission, vision, and common values.

So part of your objective as a VIP Visionary is to build a company based on the 4Ls and use purpose as a means to motivate; to provide guidance and guidelines; to eliminate the need for procedures and control mechanisms; and pave the way for an entrepreneurial environment that encourages collaboration, learning, and synergy. Sounds like quite the challenge!

However, it's only a challenge to run an organization like this when there is an inconsistency between either the written or verbalized purpose and the actual behaviour, when the purpose is not shared by all the employees, or when it does not include the 4Ls of all its stakeholders.

For example, many founders and presidents of high-tech start-ups are focused solely on developing their organizations to either issue their first IPO or to attract a major company to purchase them. Their objectives are short-term and carry no pretense of creating a real legacy. The goal is simply to push the limits of a leading technology, which will hopefully attract the financial community, allowing the companies to get out of the business with their monetary rewards.

Presidents with such personal ambitions quite rightly set about creating corporate missions and cultures that mirror themselves. Consequently, it can be expected that the employees who will be attracted to work for them are also highly focused on developing technology, getting rich as quickly as possible, and "getting out."

In such organizations, there is little effort to create a sense of meaningful contribution, although time is invested to create a sense of community and a social environment—that's a requirement if employees are to spend as many hours as possible at work. A life/work balance is not a consideration in most high-tech organizations; they simply are not worried about their employees' career longevity or their long-term health. Everyone is focused on being the next "big thing" and each person is aiming for personal financial gain. In a sense, the Diamond-E is in equilibrium in these organizations, as everyone knows the rules.

However, the reality is that people are loyal to the technology and to the dollar—not to any greater mission, vision, values, or purpose. As a result, there is no real corporate loyalty and consequently, competitors can easily woo employees away with better financial packages. Headhunters make themselves rich by encouraging such employees to move from one high-tech start-up to another. High-tech CEOs often talk disparagingly about employees who have been poached by high-paying US or Silicon Valley–based companies. But their employees have only achieved what the CEOs themselves are seeking: to be bought out! If the companies had offered to satisfy more of the employees' 4Ls and different types of employees had been hired (ones who wanted more than a financial return) would the companies have lost their people as easily? Arguably, no.

If you are to create long-term sustainable success in today's knowledge environment, you have to create an organization that is important to its employees, one with which they can identify and feel a part of, and to which they will be willing to commit and invest their maximum energy. If you are to build on the growth of your employees, you must invest in their training and development; the more they feel that they are the real owners of the company (as opposed to the shareholders), the better.

> *If you are to build on the growth of your employees, you must invest in their training and development.*

Peter Senge says that a "social mission is the essence of a successful business: doing something that makes a difference to somebody" (33). Clearly all companies cannot undertake mandates to solve environmental problems, eliminate world hunger, or improve everyone's health or quality of life. Some companies will still simply make pipes, steel, paper, plastic brushes, or shoe polish; sell clothes, furniture, and fast food; and print advertisements. However, depending on your point of view, even the latter group can take on a meaningful mission. After all, steel pipes mean that everyone can have clean water and heated homes; plastic brushes can be useful or useless; shoe polish can be of good or poor quality; and fast food can be a great family experience or bad for your health and your wallet.

The story of the two builders who, each and every day, place one brick on top of another is a poignant one. The first builder, when asked what he is doing, says he is simply constructing a wall; the second, with a genuine sense of being part of something larger than himself says that he is creating a beautiful temple. Both are right, but which is more likely to do the best work? Who will have a sense of achievement at the end of the day? In today's context, which is least likely to be coaxed away by a larger salary to build another wall before the current one is completed?

But Senge takes his point further and goes on to say that, "For organizations to prosper they must contribute something. And the more they contribute on multiple dimensions, the more they are likely to prosper. Those multiple dimensions include communities, customers, and employees."

So the solution appears to be not only making a difference, but also making a difference in as many ways as possible for as many entities as possible. This translates into trying to satisfy not only your employees' 4Ls, but also the 4Ls of every stakeholder in your organization. Your mission or purpose will follow from having identified your stakeholders' needs.

As Senge points out, your stakeholders include your employees, customers, and communities, but the term also includes much more. The following section illustrates the basics of what you need to do to ensure that all your stakeholders are satisfied.

## *Your Success Depends on Others Succeeding*

In these days of hypercompetition, virtuality, globalization, and exponential growth within knowledge-based markets, it may seem passé to be suggesting that the key to success for companies is to recognize and satisfy the needs of each and every one of its stakeholders. However, knowledge-based industries are also characterized by strategic alliances, partnerships, clusters, customer relationships, and supply chain management—all of which require building win-win relationships with stakeholders. In addition, the theory that companies should be more than revenue-making machines for shareholders has been around for a long time. Profit is indeed the oxygen of a company, but profit should not be the company's *raison d'être*. If it were, all companies would end up looking and operating like the "get rich and out quick" technology companies that are focused only on their IPOs.

John Kotter and James Heskett have demonstrated that companies who do take care of their stakeholders—as opposed to only their shareholders—do in fact generate a superior financial performance over the long term. Over the eleven-year period of their study, Kotter and Heskett found that, on average, firms seeking to satisfy three key stakeholders (shareholders, clients, and employees) increased their revenues by four times, expanded their workforces by eight times, increased their share prices by twelve times, and their net profits soared by an average of 756 percent compared to the 1 percent of companies who focused solely on shareholder satisfaction.

Why does this happen? Because these companies are taking care of more of their stakeholders' 4Ls than their competitors are. As discussed in Chapter 1, organizational boundaries within any business sector (particularly if the company is part of so-called industry clusters or integrated value chains) are now often barely distinguishable as individual entities. If this is today's reality, your success is dependent more than ever on the success of all the other organizations in the system; if you do not take care of all your stakeholders (i.e., every part of the network), you are simply not taking care of yourself.

So how can you easily and simply identify, analyze, and strengthen your relationships with all your stakeholders? How can you focus on satisfying their needs? Clearly you must start by examining who your stakeholders are and defining which of their specific needs you need to satisfy.

## *Stakeholder Satisfaction: Using Stakeholder Maps*

Almost everyone can quickly generate a list of their stakeholders, including share-holders, clients, employees, suppliers, banks, government, the community at large, etc. However, to really identify and isolate their specific needs, these traditional groups need to be broken down into smaller subcategories, grouped together by common requirements. For example, although both are clearly clients, are the needs of a multinational located in Europe the same as those of a small customer located just down the street? Do you want the same relationship with both? Probably not.

To generalize a little, the multinational is likely to be focused on low prices and high-quality product; just-in-time (JIT) delivery; and, apart from a once-a-year, face-to-face meeting at the industry's global conference, little in the way of building personal rela-tionships. The local client, although still in need of a high-quality and low-priced prod-uct, may be also concerned with sharing warehouse space, sharing the responsibili-ty of procuring parts, and participating in team lobbying for improved transportation routes in the area. Who knows—perhaps the president of the local client is also the brother of the manager at the local credit union. Ignoring such issues can cost you dearly!

Below is a list of the fifteen stakeholder subcategories for a technology incubator, jointly created by local government and the local university, located in an industrial park. To achieve optimum performance and to minimize its own risk of failure, the incubator needs all of these stakeholders to flourish; it needs to satisfy their needs by creating a win-win agreement with all of them.

### Stakeholders of an Industrial Park Incubator

- Employees
- Consultants
- Clients
- Local Universities
- Alumni
- The Municipality
- Chambre of Commerce
- Provincial Governments
- Federal Governments
- Industrial Park Developers
- Financial Institutions
- Venture Capitalists
- Angel Investors
- Large National Companies
- Large International Companies

Some of these stakeholders are obviously more crucial to the incubator's success than others. To determine the importance of each stakeholder, a few simple but important questions need to be posed:

1. Why is each particular stakeholder subcategory necessary? What is your "win"?
2. On a scale of 1 to 10, how important is each stakeholder to your success?
3. What is the quality of the relationship that currently exists between you and each stakeholder?

4.  Why does each stakeholder want to work with you? What is their "win"? How many of their 4Ls can you satisfy? How much will it cost you to do so?
5.  How important is your company to the success of each stakeholder? Are you important (+1)? Are you unimportant (–1)? Are you neutral (0)?

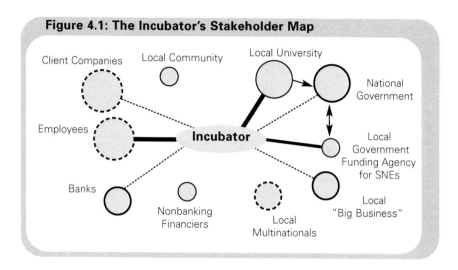

**Figure 4.1: The Incubator's Stakeholder Map**

The answers to these questions should be as complete as possible—a forgotten need can represent a dissatisfied stakeholder. As you may need the opinion of the stakeholders themselves to answer questions 3, 4, and 5, these may be a little more difficult to complete. In asking, however, you gain an opportunity to demonstrate your desire to build good relationships and you may be surprised by your stakeholders' responses and pick up some useful information.

The answer to question 5 is the most difficult to ascertain, but it's very useful. It may give you insight into how you should be working with a particular stakeholder and will give you an accurate indication of how motivated each stakeholder will be to build a strong relationship with you. After all, if you are unimportant to the stakeholder's own success, why should it invest time cultivating a strong relationship with you?

For those of you who are more visual, after collecting this information you can construct a stakeholder map (see Figure 4.1), which figuratively represents your stakeholder relationships and demonstrates the challenges that lie ahead for your organization.

The stakeholder circles are drawn with a circumference in proportion to the level of importance each stakeholder category represents to your organization. The strength of the links between your organization and each group is shown by the thickness of the line linking the groups. A "dashed" outline to a stakeholder circle signifies that your organization is important (positive) to the success of the stakeholder and therefore your efforts to build a strong relationship with that stakeholder should be well received. Simply put, the stakeholder needs you. A thick solid line encircling a stakeholder means that you are unimportant (negative) to the stakeholder and your efforts to improve relations may fall on deaf ears. Next, draw lines that connect your company to each stakeholder circle, using thick lines to represent a strong relationship and thin lines to represent a weak one.

## What is Deduced from Stakeholder Maps?

Consider these points:

- ⟳ Large stakeholder circles with only thin lines connecting them to your organization means that you urgently need to build a relationship; you are in a high-risk and vulnerable situation. What is the problem? What can you do to better satisfy that stakeholder's 4Ls?
- ⟳ Small circles linked to you by thick lines indicate that you have been investing too much time with a minor stakeholder. This often happens when you have built strong personal relationships with individuals in the organization and you enjoy spending time together.
- ⟳ Any stakeholder circles—regardless of size—that are floating free on the diagram also represent a high-risk situation. One dissatisfied stakeholder, irrespective of its importance, represents a major risk for an organization. How are you going to start the process of building a link?
- ⟳ Large circles with a thick line around their circumference represent the biggest challenge. These stakeholders are important to you yet you are unimportant to them. They have little motivation to invest time and energy in improving their relationship with you. Here, in the case of the national government and the incubator, it may be useful to employ other stakeholders to improve the situation. The incubator could quite possibly lever the positive relationship it has with the local university or local government funding agencies to gain the mind space of the national government (via the smaller entities' ties, lines of communication, and power).

Creating a map clearly shows the enormous interdependent network of which your business is a part. Some partners are larger, more important, and have stronger links with you than others. However, your organization is only as strong as the weakest link on the map.

Hence, the last step in your stakeholder analysis is to prepare (and implement) an action plan in order to rectify the weaknesses identified on the relationship map. You need to prepare a plan to build strong relationships based on your understanding of your stakeholders' needs, the importance of each to you, and your relative importance to them. By doing this, not only will you ultimately build stronger relationships, but based on Kotter and Heskett's evidence, you will also improve your profitability.

## *The Mission*

So now that you've identified your stakeholders' 4Ls and have found employees who share your vision and values, how do you finish the job of building a joint mission that satisfies stakeholder needs and instills a sense of purpose? The process of developing mission often includes the development of a mission statement. Unfortunately, many consider the finalization of this statement the end result. However, if the statement is not widely known and adopted by the organization's employees, it will not serve the objective of developing purpose. It is the same with any agreement, be it a marriage contract or a peace treaty between two warring nations: if all the stakeholders do not accept, support, and abide by the spirit or purpose of the agreement it will be worthless, irrespective of what has been written on paper.

Everyone in your organization needs to know the collective statement and abide by the purpose it incites as if by second nature, thereby avoiding the need for rigid controls and detailed procedures. You want everyone to be entrepreneurs guided by the business purpose and people purpose described in Chapter 2. You want everyone to have the same sense of belonging to and ownership of the mission upon which you are embarking as a team. It should be a mission that stretches all of you forward to achieve the shared objective while providing you with guidelines as to what behaviour is acceptable on the road to success.

Think about the many lobby and activist organizations that work in such a mode— Amnesty International, Greenpeace, and Save the Children immediately come to mind. There are also organizations operating on a global scale who have strong cultures and shared mission statements—The Body Shop, GE, ABB, and Marks & Spencer, for example. People who work for or supply these organizations know what the companies stand for and how they should behave. These organizations are models for tomorrow's successful knowledge-based businesses.

If you are to forge a great company or a great team, you need to find people with whom you can co-mission. These human building blocks will be people who have already asked themselves who they are, what they value and believe in, and what they want their legacy to be. Consequently, you can brainstorm and synergize together about ways to achieve a common mission and perhaps create something even greater.

## What Should the Mission Statement Express?

Once complete, the mission statement must communicate a true sense of purpose. It should be timeless and it should have a sense of "greatness" about it that will inspire everyone as it helps them to achieve their legacy. It should encourage a high degree of commitment among the people who prepared it and it should be used as a hiring tool—new employees or team members should be evaluated on their willingness to buy into it.

The values set forth in a mission statement express what the team believes in; the creators should feel proud to live up to the standards set down in the document. Making a 20 percent return on equity for shareholders is hardly likely to inspire an employee to go that extra mile for the client; however, doing something the "right way" because they believe in it may provide such motivation—particularly when the employee knows their teammates will do the same. If a prospective employee cannot agree with the values that the team lives by and aspires to, hiring the individual will weaken the team and possibly cause dissent in the future—little, if any, long-term value will be created through that particular hiring.

## A Mission Within a Mission

Obviously the process of developing a co-mission will differ depending on whether you are starting your own company, taking over an existing operation, or assuming responsibility for a division within a multinational. If you're starting from scratch with other colleagues, you can co-mission a statement that will ensure you are all trying to achieve the same objective and it can be used as a recruiting tool for bringing in new associates.

If you're inheriting an operation (whether you own it or not), co-missioning with existing employees is an excellent change management tool and, providing you really do intend to walk the talk, it will communicate to everyone what it is you're trying to achieve together and what culture you want to introduce. If you're taking over a division of a multinational, co-missioning is very similar to taking over an existing business—except that you have a history to deal with and a major stakeholder (the corporate office) who needs to be fully satisfied and who will set some of the rules that you will need to follow. In fact, the division may already have an existing and operating mission statement. If the organization operates as recommended here, this should not be an issue—you will have been exposed to it during recruitment and you will hopefully have matched your purpose with the organization's before having accepted the post.

> *Making a 20 percent return on equity for shareholders is hardly likely to inspire an employee.*

When you begin to talk about creating a mission statement, there will undoubtedly be detractors who cannot or do not want to see any benefit in the process. In particular, if your new company, department, or team already has a mission statement—one that has never been really used, but is perhaps embossed on a plaque or appears in the annual report—there may be a lot of voiced and unvoiced resistance from employees to the idea of creating "yet another one." This reaction is understandable and it will continue until employees realize you intend to include them in the co-missioning process, give them a chance to have their say, and ensure the final outcome will be something valuable for all involved. Viewing their resistance another way, it's good to know that members of your new team don't like having their time wasted!

Even if it is not in wide circulation, most companies do have a mission statement. I would suggest that you find it. Halfway through the process of creating a new one, you do not want one of the last resisters arriving with a copy and announcing, "We already have one—I told you we were wasting our time!" In fact, the old version can serve as a great starting point for the mission process, even if only an exercise in demonstrating how *not* to prepare and use one (although you should be sensitive to the fact that some of the team members may have been involved in its creation). It may even contain great information that will be of use to you.

If your corporate office does have (and actively lives by) a mission statement and you are running a division or team within the organization, you should ensure the mission you create is coherent with the corporation's. The head office is an important stakeholder that needs to be satisfied and operating within the bounds of its mission is a key part of ensuring its full satisfaction.

## The Co-Missioning Process

Even if creating the mission statement takes time—and it does—it is time well worth investing in order to get everyone's full input and allow them to "buy in." Not only will they feel a part of something, but you might draw some ideas out of them regarding purpose, vision, and values that add worth to your own.

## Developing Mission and Satisfying Stakeholders

A lot of the value derived from creating a mission comes from the process itself; the statement is only the end result. Co-missioning as a process helps to develop understanding; build a sense of community; and communicate a sense of who you are, what you do, and why and how you do it. I would say the most important aspect of creating any mission statement is total participation in its preparation. Some would say it's adequate to include only core members in the process. I disagree, however. I believe even your part-time workers and your cleaning staff should be involved. To succeed today, organizations do not depend just on the owners of their core competencies. Every single person needs to subscribe to the mission, understand its values, and achieve their legacy through the company's growth. The cleaning staff should understand that their work is an important part of the organization's success: have you ever tried working in a dirty, unkempt office?

The following equation illustrates why it is so important that everyone be involved in co-missioning:

Outcomes of the decision = (Quality of the decision) x (Buy-in by the team)

Alone, you may have the best possible answer (10 out of 10), but with a low "buy-in" by the team (2 out of 10), the outcomes that will result once the decision is implemented will be poor: 20 = 10 x 2. After all, the team is not working on its own project—it's yours! A less optimal decision (6) supported with the buy-in (7) of the majority of the team will result in much better actual outcomes: 42 = 6 x 7.

Hence, as many people as possible should participate in the creation of the mission. If you've just become manager of a group of twenty employees, then everyone can easily participate. If its one hundred or more, groups can work on different sections that can then be incorporated into one document by the best writer—preferably someone other than you. Alternatively, work teams can nominate spokespersons to represent them at mission creation sessions. The spokespersons then report back to their groups as required. Reviewing draft versions of statements through the web, e-mail, or even internal mail along with an open invitation for input will serve equally as well. People must feel involved and feel that their input is heard, acknowledged, valued, and incorporated.

> *Once complete, the mission statement must communicate a true sense of purpose.*

The mission creation process is not complicated, but the development of a sustainable mission statement is not something that can be achieved at a single weekend retreat—although much progress can be achieved in that time. The process may take months or even years. It does not entail simply writing or changing a document; it involves changing a mindset and during the change period, the new message has to be consistently sent, digested, and integrated. Otherwise your document will be confined to lining the desk drawer.

The process used to develop the statement is the same whether it is for an individual, spouses, a family, or an organization, division, or work team. The term "unit" is used in the following section to refer to all possible groups.

## A Step-by-Step Co-Missioning Process

1.  **Prepare a complete list of stakeholder groups and subgroups** (sharing common characteristics) for each unit.

    The strategic positioning to be adopted by the unit—that is, the business purpose—may be defined by the corporate office, the owner(s)/founder(s) (if it's a private company), or it may be something that is to be determined during the mission process (the latter is usually only the case when the mission process is being done for a group of professionals). This strategic positioning is included in the statement as being a key deliverable to two stakeholders: the client and the owner of the unit. They will decide whether you sell widgets or widget services and to whom they will be sold. You and a team of senior staff should prepare the list of your bosses, your superiors, and the company's 4Ls: you and this group should know them best.

2.  **Analyze the 4Ls of each stakeholder**; the challenge is to come up with something both concise and meaningful. Where appropriate, this work can be allocated to individuals or teams. For example, sales departments can be asked to prepare an initial draft of client needs; public affairs people can be asked to define government needs; etc.

    Obviously, it may not always be possible to describe a stakeholder's needs in terms of only the 4Ls. But it's important to think about what sort of economic requirements they have; what they are seeking to learn (as an organization and from you); what kind of social environment or relationship they would like to have with you; and what legacy they are trying to achieve and how you can best make a contribution to it. The 4Ls represent a framework to guide you; they are not meant to serve as a list of exclusive rules.

3.  **Circulate these preliminary drafts of stakeholder needs**—one document for each stakeholder group—and invite everyone to provide feedback. This may continue for a number of iterations until people are satisfied and the 4Ls are really complete.

4.  **Ask everybody to provide input** in terms of the values and behaviours that are important to the unit. Questions that can be posed include:
    - What behaviors should exemplify this unit?
    - What behaviour is unacceptable here?
    - What is important here? What are you proud of?
    - How would you like visitors to describe the people who work here?
    - How would you like to be treated here?
    - How do you think others should be treated?

5.  **Give people the chance to comment** on the 4Ls of each stakeholder and the values that describe the unit and then merge the documents into one draft. Circulate the mission statement again for discussion (as mentioned previously, this can include posting it on the web, sending it via e-mail, or passing around hard copies for discussion). Highly visible visits and invitations for input by the unit's high-profile leaders can be beneficial to the process.

6.  **Arrive at consensus** by starting at the "lower-levels" of the hierarchy; allow these levels to pass their version of the mission statement up the unit via their managers, who have the task of merging all the contributions to the different teams' satisfaction. Once that has been accomplished, the versions of the text can continue to rise up through the unit with the proviso being that new versions always return to the lower levels for input and approval through an iterative process.

7.  **Deal with divergences** that appear between two groups' contributions by having them swap statements: send each team the other's version to work on. With

both teams trying to keep the best parts of the statement intact while ensuring the most important portions of their own are incorporated, the next submissions from the two teams will often be surprisingly similar.

8. **Prevent the essence of the mission statement from being lost** in large units—this is a real danger as divisions submit their own versions to head office. Intelligent and creative writing coupled with continual input helps to bypass this problem and the benefit is that each of the teams, business units, etc. will have developed their own customized mission statements and achieved a co-missioning process within their units.

The ideal situation following the missioning process is that each unit, from the "lowest" level of the hierarchy to the corporate unit, will have a version of the mission compatible with everyone else's but also representative of their particular unit's distinctiveness, way of operating, and contribution to the whole.

## Ensuring the Mission Achieves Its Objective

How should the mission be used and made visible? In everything.

If it's been created—pardon the expression—"by the people for the people" and truly represents the organization, it should be a vital tool to be referenced during most activities: from strategic planning to sales meetings, from the way new employees are treated to the cleanliness of the parking lot. It should provide guidelines that allow employees to be and feel liberated from procedures and bureaucracy so that they implicitly know if a decision, activity, or behaviour is appropriate within their unit. They should be free to make decisions based on their fit with the mission and the behavioural norms contained therein.

Employees should also be aware that their bosses will support them, particularly if they've made a decision that represents a risk but is aimed at satisfying a stakeholder. I think everyone has heard of cases where employees of courier companies have gone to extraordinary lengths (never mind expense!) to ensure that a package arrived at its destination on time and to the satisfaction of the client. Result: the employee has been publicly thanked for showing such initiative and pride in their work—and for helping the company achieve its mission. Such examples show all the organization's employees that the mission statement is more than a document—it is the way of working and behaving.

It's obviously important that you still feel that you can lead your unit after the co-missioning process is finished. The unit should still reflect your own ideas, beliefs, and values; you should have actively participated in the process and your input should be just as important as your team's. As the leader, you are offering your people the chance to participate in the missioning process—you are not abdicating your role. You need to be genuine throughout the process and express your views openly. If you do not, and perhaps express values which you think your team wants you to have but in which you don't actually believe, they will sense it immediately and the entire process will be undermined.

It is always possible, although very unlikely, that you will fundamentally disagree with the final mission statement. For example, the process may bring to the surface some issues, truths, or behaviours that are accepted or supported by your corporate office but that you are simply unwilling to accept. However, it's better to make that kind of discovery as early as possible; the message is that you are in the wrong place—not that the process is flawed.

## *From Control and Procedures to Mission*

The best way to ensure that the mission is used is to "measure" it. To paraphrase John Roth, former president of Nortel Networks, if things are measured it quickly shows employees that they are important. Some items are easily measured: customer satisfaction, quality levels, office cleanliness. But some aspects of the mission are more qualitative than quantitative—although that does not mean they cannot be measured by an associated activity.

For example, although the professional development or growth of employees is difficult to measure in itself, it is possible to measure the number of courses or training hours that each employee takes each year; it is also easy to ensure that each employee has a professional development plan that is reviewed on a regular basis with their team leaders. Incentives can also be put in place to ensure that achievement of the objectives set out in the plan is rewarded. Measurement of these parameters will go a long way towards ensuring that the paragraph in the mission statement committing to the development of all employees is achieved. If you want to be an ethical organization, you can quantify that commitment by stating that within three years you will be in *Fortune* magazine's top 100 ethical or best companies. You may have to be a little imaginative, but you will eventually find some quantifiable metrics that show you are indeed achieving qualitative objectives. (More on this in Chapter 8's section on Balanced Scorecards™.)

The use of stories and metaphors—such as the courier company example mentioned earlier—are simple, inexpensive ways to communicate important aspects of the mission to all employees. Metaphors and stories are much stronger and better received than logic and statistics. The language of the message should be geared to different audiences, but it is vital that the "song remain the same."

By making the mission highly visible (in annual reports, Human Resources [HR] recruitment materials, offices, and on the web site), by using metaphors and stories, and, most particularly, by "walking the talk" and designing and using metrics to measure how you are doing, the mission can be motivational. It can show each employee why they should work hard for the unit and how to behave, thereby eliminating the need for expensive and limiting procedures. The mission is also a vital tool used by both the VIP Implementor and VIP People Manager (see Parts 3 and 4). Developing a sense of mission represents a major, indeed essential, step towards becoming a creative and entrepreneurial organization.

## Key Points in Chapter 4

➲ A sense of purpose is what you feel when you share a mission, vision, and common values with your colleagues. It keeps you pointed in the right direction and guides behaviour.

➲ Not fully satisfying all your stakeholders leaves you vulnerable and creates risk.

➲ Use stakeholder analysis to determine why stakeholders need you and why you need them. Create an action plan to help you rectify any weak relationships with key stakeholders.

➲ Create a mission that satisfies the 4Ls of all stakeholders.

➲ Mission statements can be created at all levels of an organization—or for individuals, couples, and families. They are empowering and eliminate the need for numerous procedures and control mechanisms.

## Questions to Consider

➲ Do you know who your unit's stakeholders are? Do you have weak relationships with key stakeholders? How can you strengthen these relationships?

➲ Do you have your own personal mission statement? Do you know what values you live by? Do you know your 4Ls?

➲ Are your 4Ls being satisfied? What can you do to satisfy them?

➲ Do you know your organization's mission? Is it used? Do you share the sense of purpose it generates?

## Chapter 5

George Bernard Shaw once said, "There are those who see things as they are and ask why, and there are those who see things as they could be and ask…why not?" His observation sums up the VIP Visionary's role in horizon or future scanning. To a great extent, horizon scanning is simply a matter of continually asking "Why not?" It involves seeing things differently and pursuing new opportunities and new ways of doing things. "Why not?" There may be some very good reasons; but you need to pose the question to yourself and others before accepting that something cannot be done.

Living in a time of rapid change means that many types of horizon or future scanning need to be undertaken by many different people inside an organization. The future of an organization can no longer be left to the president alone; everyone has to share the responsibility. As part of their role as VIP Visionaries, every employee must scan the horizon in their field to detect the first signs of new trends. New trends, after all, are the chief source of opportunities and threats to organizations—and even to individual employability.

This chapter will examine the different types of horizon scanning that must be carried out at levels of organization, from the president to the administrative staff. If you want to create radical innovations, if you want to reinvent your industry, if you want to find new ways of doing things, and if you want to ask "Why not?" you need to be looking at your environments in new ways—or someone else will.

## Trends in the Macroenvironment

Today, almost all of the drivers for change originate from shifts that occur in the macroenvironment. Leading companies now realize that they have to maintain a constant environment watch and look for early indicators of change and new trends. Companies have recognized that the source of, or motivation behind, most competitive advantage originates in changes that are identifiable through a macroenvironmental scanning process. Hence, if we decide that we want to be driving change rather than being forced to change, a great place to start is by putting on our "futurist caps." We need to spend time monitoring trends—even (or perhaps particularly) those apparently far removed from our domain—and generating future scenarios for our industry and our company's activities to see how they may be impacted by macroenvironmental developments. Doing this once a year is no longer sufficient; you need to be constantly scanning and analyzing trends and occurrences in order to identify possible opportunities and threats.

## All Markets Are Global

So what types of trends should you be seeking to identify? In essence, all global trends have the potential to impact either positively or negatively on your industry, your competition, or your own operation. Any and all global changes are a potential source of opportunity or threat because irrespective of our industry sector or business, everyone is playing in the global marketplace. At first glance, that statement may seem like a slight exaggeration. However, although it is clear that all companies do not actually compete on a global level, they can all be influenced by, impacted upon, or take advantage of factors in the global macroenvironmental arena. So-called multinationals, technology companies, and exporters and importers of all types of products are obviously participating in a global market.

*All global trends have the potential to impact either positively or negatively on your industry.*

But even fragmented industries and local businesses such as hair salons or video stores can take advantage of, or fall victim to, global changes. Although all hair salons in Montreal, Canada may have the latest technology in razors, shower attachments, sun beds, etc. imported from all areas of the world, only one particular salon may have a line of environmentally friendly shampoos and conditioners made by the indigenous populations of the Ecuadorian rainforest. The signing of such an exclusive agreement for the sale of these products in Montreal offers a hair salon a distinct and possibly sustainable competitive advantage in terms of its ability to differentiate itself from competitors. It would also be a priceless item for any publicity campaign aimed at the "socially aware" demographic market that favours the protection of the Amazon jungle and its indigenous peoples. Interestingly enough, even in a small village in Costa Rica where the "salon" may consist of only a chair, a mirror, and a pair of scissors, scanning (and studying) the hairstyle trends in North American and European magazines gives the owner a chance to offer the latest popular cuts not only to locals, but also to the prosperous and plentiful tourist population. It really is a global market!

Similarly, a local video store in London, England, while still facing enormous technological challenges from other media on the horizon, may be able to take advantage of demographic changes and population movements by building an incredibly loyal and profitable clientele by specializing in a selection of films from India, available only in the Hindi language. In the business-to-business (B-2-B) environment, companies that grew up supplying their local manufacturers with raw materials recognized years ago that they were competing for business with other companies located all around the globe. They, in turn, are also in a position to supply around the world if they can build up a competitive distribution network. Any company in the world producing and supplying product in a digital format can seek ideas and clients anywhere it chooses—location is barely an issue.

If the case can be made that all businesses are global businesses, it is also apparent that some of them are going to be better than others at taking advantage of global opportunities and trends. What's more, those companies actively scanning for emerging trends are likely to be the most successful, both in terms of capitalizing on opportunities and being better prepared to face any threats. So let's look quickly at the different macroenvironmental factors and trends that you should be seeking to identify, monitor, and exploit. This is not meant to be an exhaustive examination, but it should provide a good starting point for you to generate your own list of macrotrends that your business or team should be evaluating on a continual basis.

## Macroeconomic Trends

Within the macroeconomic environment, the effects of trends such as the growth rate of the economy, interest rates, currency exchange rates, and inflation rates are widely covered in daily newspapers or magazines and can obviously impact a company's fortunes. Most individuals are at least aware of the macroeconomic conditions that exist within their own country, even if they do not actively include projections of these factors into their business planning. But in recognizing that it is possible to either benefit or be harmed by economic disruptions in other areas of the globe, it is worthwhile to consider what effects changes in these parameters in Europe or South America may have if you are planning to sell to, or purchase products and services from, these continents. Like any other macroenvironmental changes, a change in the economic conditions of any region or country in the world (e.g., the economic problems in Japan, explosive growth in Malaysia, devaluations in Mexico and Argentina) can impact directly on the economic conditions of one's own country.

In addition, changes in the economic health of any nation obviously impacts the competitiveness of its industries and its attractiveness as an import or export market. For example, overseas companies whose products were overpriced and uncompetitive at one exchange rate may suddenly become very attractive given a rapid fall in the value of the country's currency. Perhaps a sudden devaluation could impact your own supply chain, your equipment and service suppliers, your overseas clients, and could suddenly make your idea of opening a sales office in that country seem preposterous. Alternatively, the rapid rates of growth achieved in many so-called developing countries may mean that ground-floor and long-term business opportunities are available for those with the VIP Visionary skills to spot the trends.

## Trends in the Developing World

Economic conditions in different areas of the globe can, at any one time, be an opportunity for one company and a threat to a competitor. Many western economies and their populations see developing countries as a bed of opportunity for large and often subsidized hydroelectric projects and telecommunications networks, a source of cheap labour for low-value repetitive work, and a pool of potential new consumers of products. At the same time, they also feel threatened by the developing world, viewing it as a new competitor with hardworking, well-educated, ambitious, and talented people working in environments unburdened by decaying infrastructure and overbureaucratic social systems, and with much of the world's manufacturing operations already established in its territory. In fact, the perceived threat posed by developing countries is now a major force behind western countries' endless and exhaustive drive for innovation and change. With all these issues and their potential consequences, can we afford not to be monitoring who will be our best export markets and competitors in the near future?

## Demographic Trends

An example of a demographic trend is the "greying" of North America's population, which has lead to a steady growth of opportunities in tourism, healthcare, and nursing, while also adding more weight onto the social services system.

In another example, fewer stay-at-home mothers has created competition for men in the job market, a healthier management style in many companies, and an increase in demand for daycare and many convenience services. It has also meant more disposable income for some, less disposable time for many, and there are suggestions that it has contributed to the doubling of house prices in some areas. Having more women in the workforce has affected marketing and advertising aimed at women; has encouraged new distribution methods for businesses; and has even prompted the launch of completely new lines of clothing, cars, electrical, and food products.

Other factors such as more heterogeneous societies, people working from home, home use of the Internet, urban sprawl into the suburbs, and even the reality of the "haves" and the "have nots" (in a financial, educational, and technological sense) represent changes to the demographic and social environment, which in turn represent real market opportunities or threats for businesses.

Investing in a new business, marketing strategy, or product that targets an existing but declining demographic segment can be disastrous for any business. On the other hand, identifying new needs, designing new products, and delivering them in a unique way to a new demographic market can lead to corporate success.

## Social Trends

As highlighted previously, changes in social trends also impact upon industry and individual businesses. These trend changes may be local or global in nature. Trends such as increased health awareness (e.g., less consumption of red meat) mean more opportunities for seafood, soya, and poultry businesses. Increased environmental awareness has generated "green" investment funds, sales of hemp products, environmental technology, and an increase in the sale of plastic containers to be used as recycling boxes. Companies that were tracking and evaluating these trends in their early stages made the most of the opportunities that the trends created. Those caught unaware suffered or missed opportunities.

## Political/Legal Trends

Changes to political and legal frameworks can also impact heavily on your business. Depending on your degree of awareness and preparation, events such as the breakup of countries or the reunification of others; the creation and continual expansion of the EC, NAFTA, and diverse environmental legislation; and industry regulation or deregulation can either harm or benefit your company. French companies now compete (at least in theory) in the same domestic market as companies in Germany, the UK, and Italy—as do companies in Mexico selling their products in the US. There are no artificial barriers keeping jobs in France, and the French government can no longer simply alter fiscal or monetary policy to help its industry compete with its neighbours. If you are a British company thinking about opening a US facility, then the opportunities and threats associated with opening that plant in Chihuahua, Mexico rather than San Francisco, California need to be analyzed. Only after making an exhaustive analysis of each potential location can you be confident that you're making the right location decision. If you are not even aware that a plant in Mexico is a possibility, then the site evaluation process will never be initiated. For this to happen you need to be macrowatching and macroaware.

## Technological Trends

Of all the macroenvironmental factors that now require constant surveillance, the one that can radically change industries with the least warning is a technological advance. If you're scanning for economic, demographic, legislative, and social trends, they are often fairly visible on the horizon and offer companies the time and opportunity to at least react (if not be proactive) before the impact is felt. On the other hand, analyzing the possible effect of a technological development on an industry may take a certain level of technological know-how.

What's more, the introduction of new technological innovation into an industry sector—particularly an advance that has been tried and proven in another sector—can change the industry structure and basis for competition almost overnight. Hence, advances in, or application of, new technologies are increasingly proving to be the major source of radical and incremental innovation, and thus competitive advantage. With technology, products can be differentiated and become more functional; they can be produced more quickly and with better quality; and they can be delivered to the client in new and different ways or in previously inaccessible geographic locations.

In addition, products, processes, costing, the level of client service, existing distribution methods and, most importantly, the time-base of competition can all be altered almost immediately as new technology is introduced. Such applications can mean the halving of product development times, real-time collaboration on projects between colleagues working locally or internationally, the synchronization of production times with shipping schedules for just-in-time (JIT) delivery, and instantaneous client service and customer responsiveness offered twenty-four hours per day.

In essence, technology can make a mature production or delivery process obsolete within a matter of months. Overnight, it can offer value to your existing (or a new) client, drastically reduce your production costs, increase your selling price, and thus improve your profit margin. Alternately, it can do the same for your competitor! Who benefits depends on who is macrowatching.

## General Business Trends

One other macroenvironmental trend that should be observed closely relates to "general business." This trend is sometimes a derivative of technological or social change, but it can also represent a pervasive cultural change that needs to be taken into account when viewing companies strategically. Recent business issues to consider include: the increasing use of strategic alliances; network management; JIT delivery; virtuality; outsourcing; electronic data interchange (EDI); e-commerce; reductions in number of full-time staff in favour of contractual workers; and stock options. In fact, the list is endless. And, some would argue, worthless. However, it is worth maintaining a surveillance of what is happening just in case your clients or suppliers begin implementing one or another of the items that may affect you. For example, if a major buyer begins to implement EDI, you need give the introduction of that technology (and process) into your company some consideration, as the client may be in a position to force you to adopt such a system.

> *Of all the macro-environmental factors, the one that can radically change industries is a technological advance.*

ISO9000 series qualification is a similar example. Although it can be "massaged" to fit the criteria of a political or technological macroenvironmental watch, the ISO9000 issue is really a business trend and it was almost forced on North America by the European business community. Organizations that were actively monitoring business trends in Europe were well warned about ISO's arrival in the North American business environment. They were able to take early measures to start the ISO qualification process and therefore took an advantage by gaining access to the largest single market in the world while their US competitors trying to enter Europe behaved reactively and floundered in red tape.

## Theory into Practice

Having briefly outlined these trends, let's look at an example—and not an Intel, IBM, Federal Express, Airbus, or Sony, where technological innovation is an integral part of the business model. Let's imagine a small pine furniture business located in Europe. Its main task is to source old pine furniture, strip it of old varnish, make necessary repairs, and then resell it to retail antique furniture outlets. The business is located in an industrial part of town due to its use of chemicals in the stripping process. It already purchases small volumes of old furniture from suppliers in continental Europe and has previously sold to clients in the US. This is not a company that you would traditionally consider a global, knowledge-based business. However, with the pine furniture market being almost of a commodity nature with low entry barriers, high levels of competition, lots of substitutes, diminishing sources, and increasing buyer power, it's a market in which a com-pany located in an industrialized country must generate added value or suffer being put out of business by low-cost overseas competition. It's an example of a business that must turn itself into a knowledge-based business—and quickly—if it is to survive. So what sort of macroenvironmental trends should it be scanning? What could help the business create opportunities or impact it negatively?

### Economic Trends
- ➲ The value of the local currency against key European and US currencies.
- ➲ Consumer purchasing power in developing countries where pine furniture may be unique and therefore could be priced higher.

### Demographic/Social Trends

- ➲ Furniture trends in other countries (e.g., design, wood type, finish) or the possibil-ity of adapting old furniture into new products (e.g., turning old wardrobes into "hideaway" computer workspaces).
- ➲ An increasing number of people living alone in small apartments requiring compact, space-efficient, and multipurpose furniture.
- ➲ A rejection of the modern, plastic appearance of contemporary furniture in some markets.
- ➲ Exploitation of the recycling nature of the business by marketing low-end "remade" products as high-end "recycled" products.

### Political Trends

- ➲ New government programs for helping some small businesses, training employees, etc.
- ➲ Government initiatives to promote recycling of forest products and more efficient use of natural resources.
- ➲ Reductions in tariffs on exported products.
- ➲ The opening of new markets in an expanding EC where pine furniture might have high-end appeal.

### Technological Trends

- ➲ Exploitation of the Internet's potential: scan for sources of pine furniture in other countries; post a web page to advertise the company; sell products on-line; design custom recycled products for Internet customer needs; research competitors; check for new furniture designs; find distributors and sources in other countries.
- ➲ New chemical (and nontoxic) products to strip furniture, allowing for relocation into commercial space and a healthier, cleaner work environment.
- ➲ Replacements for the nails, screws, etc. that lower the perceived value of the product in the customers' eyes.

### Business Trends

- ➲ The people working at home who need furniture in which they can hideaway or house computers, printers, and fax machines in a home environment.
- ➲ Partnership with interior designers who incorporate the "olde worlde" look into their designs, generating high-margin business.
- ➲ Outsourcing the stripping operation to another company in order to move into a better location.

## *The Results*

Although the pine furniture company might not be in a position to fully exploit all of these trends, it could conceivably transform itself if it only developed one of them. Within six months it could be operating out of a new location and offering the latest high-end, environmentally friendly Scandinavian furniture designs for home offices through a network of interior designers. And then again, it might not. A Diamond-E analysis may determine that pursuing even one of the trends is not feasible at the moment. However, by constantly examining the trends and possibilities, the company will some day find at least one opportunity for introducing a radical innovation and reinventing itself. By continually scanning, it will also have examined most of the strategic moves that a competitor might be considering and will have assessed those opportunities' strengths and weaknesses. Even if the company does not find a radical way of transforming itself, it will undoubtedly identify many incremental innovations that will optimize its value creation process and minimize its operating costs. As a result of its horizon scanning, it will be a very competitive knowledge-based company with a low risk rating.

## Trends in the Markets

Having examined the macro level, it's now time to look at the horizon scanning activity focused on your markets, to see how you can best project their development and prepare yourself to be a winner with your clients long into the future. In this situation, the term "market" is used deliberately instead of "industry."

Everyone has been told that they must become "market-driven" (i.e., focused on satisfying clients) yet many companies still associate themselves with being a part of a particular industry rather than one of a selection of companies that seek to satisfy a particular market's needs.

To say that "industry" no longer exists may sound ridiculous, especially since even I have used the word on several occasions in this book. After all, everyone knows that the steel industry is still making steel, that the aerospace industry is still manufacturing airplanes, and that members of the trucking industry continue to rack up the miles along our highways and autobahns. However, it may be very beneficial to view the business world as though industries do not exist, mainly because saying a company is part of an industry is only a good way of describing a company in terms of the products it sells. It is not a useful term when you're trying to be market-focused, as it says nothing about who your clients are.

> *"Industry" is not a useful term when you're trying to be market-focused, as it says nothing about who your clients are.*

When looking at strategic issues for these "industries," it's easy to see how dangerous and limiting it is when a company considers itself solely as a member of its particular industry. Let's look at one of the three examples I mentioned above. If a member of the steel industry only considers issues that affect it and its fellow steel manufacturers, it will rarely take serious notice of companies in other industries. But these other industries may be producing a product that a client could use instead of steel (Chapter 6 explores the idea of potential substitutes and Michael E. Porter's Five Forces model in more detail). By ignoring or only giving these other industries a cursory glance, the steel company may be oblivious to the fact that plastics or ceramics producers may be making significant product developments with more flexible, corrosive-resistant, and cheaper materials, and may be targeting and building relationships with its clients.

## Strategic Groups

The term "strategic groups" also warrants a mention here as it is often said that a company's fiercest competitors lie in its own strategic group. Members of a particular strategic group generally follow the same basic strategy in satisfying the same clients. An obvious example for illustrating this concept is the pharmaceutical industry, which has two strategic groups: (1) the proprietary manufacturers, who are research and development (R&D)–intensive and who focus on developing new proprietary drugs and (2) the generic manufacturers, who have low-cost R&D and focus on copying products that no longer have patent protection. Each group produces the same end product by pursuing completely different strategies.

Examples of other strategic groups include: cable and satellite versus regular TV services (which in many areas all now offer very similar programming); large long distance telephone service providers versus telephone resellers (which offer the same level of service, except one invests heavily in infrastructure and the other does not); and major book stores and on-line virtual bookstores (which usually offer the same books but, some may argue, a different purchasing experience).

However, committing yourself to a narrowly defined strategic group entails the same risk as committing to a particular industry: it tends to place blinders on a company in terms of scouting business opportunities and competition. By focusing on competition within the same strategic group, a company may overlook the most dangerous competition of all: an organization in another industry that has looked at client needs and has found a completely new way to satisfy them—one that may be better, cheaper, and satisfies underlying needs or several different needs in the same product package.

The source of the problem is our paradigms. An industry is often defined as "a group of companies offering products or services that are close substitutes for each other." Unfortunately, the phrase "close substitutes" has limited our thinking. Instead of brainstorming on the term for any potential substitutes, we've taken the word "close" too literally. Similarly, why worry about which industry you are operating in anyway? Industry affiliation my be useful for naming associations, combining lobby efforts, and driving up stock price, but as a tool for planning and running businesses, it is a meaningless and limiting practice.

The only question that is crucially important for defining your industry—that is, your potential markets and clients—is, "For whom can I create value?" If you can be as creative and expansive as possible when answering this question, you are likely to "maximize your return on capabilities" (MRC). While technically this is a financial ratio that doesn't really exist, it is at the same time the only representation of the real measure of your effectiveness and efficiency in exploiting your portfolio of competencies.

## Defining Your Markets

Geoffrey A. Moore gives the most appropriate definition of a market in his book *Crossing the Chasm*. There, he defines a market as:

- A set of actual or potential customers
- For a given set of products or services
- Who have a common set of needs or wants, and
- Who reference each other when making a buying a decision. (28, p. 28)

Notice that the word "industry" does not appear in the definition. Notice also that the definition narrows the concept of a market (or segment thereof) by making it clear that if purchasers cannot reference each other, they are not in the same market. Hence, someone buying this book in Canada is not in the same market as someone buying this book in South America—unless they have a reasonable basis for communicating with each other (e.g., an Amazon.com-type company). An airline in the UK purchasing new short-haul aircraft would be in the same market as a company in Brazil considering the same purchase: industry magazines, global trade shows, even references offered by the aircraft manufacturer would mean that there would be communication between the UK and Brazilian companies.

However, you will have noticed that I included the words "short-haul" in the aircraft description. You may argue that this term encompasses different distances in the UK compared with a large country like Brazil—and you'd be right. This is precisely why it is difficult to use traditional market segment definitions; it's the reason I prefer to break everything down into specific and individual markets rather than market segments. Segmentation makes it too easy to assume that the common traits of the overall market are in fact common. It's better to treat markets individually, a strategy that will avoid misunderstandings and complacency.

In terms of your markets and your competition, you are really better served by examining who else is trying to satisfy your existing and potential clients, irrespective of what "industry" they actually belong to. What clients you are competing for is what really determines your industry and your competitors.

According to Derek Abell, what you are really doing here is putting aside the definition of what you do and focusing instead on three questions: (1) Who you are serving? (2) What need are you seeking to satisfy? and (3) How will you do it? (1) The first question leads you to closely examine your markets and market segments using both new and traditional tools such as the Five Forces analysis (see page 111). You can use the industry life cycle curve (see pages 90–91), but you'll be looking at it with eyes focused on the life cycle of a market or a product.

So assuming you are not in any particular industry, what are you in exactly? Well, you're in the value creation business, targeting anyone who can use your products or services in a cost-effective manner. And your geographic market? As demonstrated in the earlier hair salon and video store examples, you may only be serving local markets but you can still take advantage of global trends. The reality is that you are competing with all other businesses around the world who are trying to offer that same need-satisfying or value-added product or service to your target clients.

What you have to do is scan this market for potential clients that you want to target, develop relationships with, and exploit. You will obviously divide into various submarkets or market segments (although it's probably always better to treat each one as a separate market), but why not start with an open mind and look at the world markets? If you are an individual starting a new business or if you are beginning a new strategic market analysis process, you can simply examine your personal mission, your skills or expertise, and then start examining the who, what, where, and how of value creation.

## Filling the Blank Spaces

If you are part of an existing company, consider what Gary Hamel says about looking for white or blank spaces between current product offerings. Let's say that at the moment, you are offering a certain range of products with specific functionality in a selection of markets to a group of customers. To produce these products or services, you have had to develop a whole range of expertise (what Hamel defines as a portfolio of core competencies). Perhaps you have expertise in making delicious spicy food, photonics, miniaturizing electronic products, or you have direct mailing know-how that is unrivalled. If this is the case, you should be scanning the world for lucrative (and preferably long-term) business opportunities where you can apply an existing or a new combination of your competency portfolio (see Figure 5.1). If you really play your competency strategy well, you should even be able to find opportunities for improving and developing an existing competency, which you can then pass on to your current customers in other products.

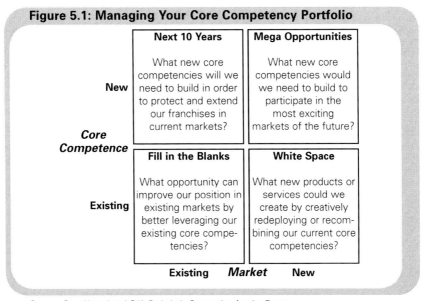

Source: Gary Hamel and C.K. Prahalad, *Competing for the Future*

For example, let's say you have a great deal of expertise in preparing prepackaged Indian food. Your competencies are your ability to recreate the taste of old recipes with new, easy-to-obtain products and your highly automated packaging capability. By scanning the globe with these competencies in mind, you may be able to identify opportunities in different geographic markets seeking easy-to-prepare Thai or West Indian food. Or you may find customers who want to package easy-to-open, robust, but small volumes of industrial or chemical products, health foods, or dehydrated products for hikers. By satisfying their needs, perhaps you will be able to learn new skills that will further enhance your current Indian food preparation and packaging competencies. Again, this is not an example of what would be traditionally thought of as a knowledge-based business, but it is certainly the business's knowledge and competencies that are driving its success.

I will return to the concept of core competencies later in the book. The message here is simply that putting aside notions of being part of an industry and focusing instead on examining the world markets for opportunities to apply and enhance core competencies can really pay dividends in terms of the MRC ratio.

## What Do Current and Future Clients Want?

Once you've identified your market opportunities, the key to success is to constantly listen to all your clients and industry contacts and try to determine what their underlying and nonverbalized needs really are. As Hamel states, you need to develop an organization that leads clients where they want to go (but don't know it yet) and creates revolutionary strategies (18). Any salesperson can visit clients, listen to them express their needs, write down the order, and send it in to their company. On the surface, the sales job has been done. However, today it is necessary to go further and seek to identify a customer's underlying needs. What is the client really looking for that perhaps they have not even consciously thought of? What can you provide for the client that, in hindsight, will make them think, "How did I ever do without this?" How can you help the client run a better company or offer them an improved product or service? What will they need in three to five years' time?

In the past, sales positions have tended to attract extroverts with "excellent communication skills." Unfortunately, "communication skills" was generally a synonym for speaking rather than listening skills. These individuals were trained not to hear or accept "No" to their sales pitch, and often made the sale by wearing the client down through sheer persistence. In addition, salespeople were not necessarily well informed regarding the operations of their own company and were rarely involved in strategic issues or even product development. The end product would simply be given to them to sell.

These days, the person who is in regular contact with the client is seen as (and is often called) an "Account or Client Service Representative" and can offer the client significant added value. Many highly educated and well-trained individuals now work in sales positions and represent a vitally important part of the value chain. These people are in a position to observe what is happening in the client compan-ies, build strong personal relationships with individuals in the client companies, identify opportunities for new products and services, or troubleshoot product problems. Every salesperson now needs to be a great listener and observer and needs to use reflective and unrestricted questions to make the client open up, talk, and express their needs. Many frontline salespeople are the main vehicle for communicating what a company stands for and they may spend up to eight hours in a day with the same client. Indeed, many suppliers now assign staff full time in client companies to solve problems, work on collaborative projects, and observe how the client's needs are evolving. This opportunity, to exploit the information that salespeople, customer, or technical salespeople acquire through interaction with the clients on a continual basis, is worth a thousand market studies.

## Avoiding Chasms

Many new products and services take advantage of new technological innovations, adding another dimension to the salesperson's job. Innovative technology means that deadly "chasms," as defined by Geoffrey A. Moore, are everywhere, in between each stage of the produce life cycle (see Figure 5.2). What's a chasm? It's the gap or dissociation that exists between any two psychographic target markets—between the early adopters of a new technology and the early majority, for example. The early majority would have a great deal of difficulty purchasing or adopting a product that was packaged, advertised, promoted, and sold in the same format as it had been for the early adopter purchaser. People in different groups just don't relate; in fact, they may even have an intense dislike for each other.

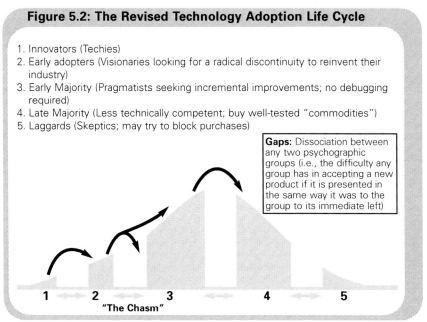

**Figure 5.2: The Revised Technology Adoption Life Cycle**

1. Innovators (Techies)
2. Early adopters (Visionaries looking for a radical discontinuity to reinvent their industry)
3. Early Majority (Pragmatists seeking incremental improvements; no debugging required)
4. Late Majority (Less technically competent; buy well-tested "commodities")
5. Laggards (Skeptics; may try to block purchases)

**Gaps:** Dissociation between any two psychographic groups (i.e., the difficulty any group has in accepting a new product if it is presented in the same way it was to the group to its immediate left)

1   2   3   4   5
"The Chasm"

Source: Geoffrey A. Moore, *Crossing the Chasm*

In past eras, although the psychological profiles of early adopters and late adopters were certainly different, given the extended time span of the product life cycle, new users always had time to familiarize themselves with new products and it was rare that new products were propelled into the market through technological innovation. In the majority of cases, any new product simply replaced the old one without any major change required in user skill level, usage method, and infrastructure. Often there was no need for a technical user manual. Today, the life span of any product has certainly shortened; no sooner has a user become proficient at using one product than another one with new logic, commands, or peripheral equipment is launched. The early adopters have turned into techies who adore playing with new technology. Members of the late majority find the barriers to new products increasing, as they want little to do with troubleshooting, tome-like technical manuals, and help lines. They want their products to work easily the first time and they don't want to take a training course to learn how to use them. Most of all, they want the final version of the product to be released.

After any stage of the product life cycle, there is now a significant risk that a product will not make it to the next stage: it can easily fall into a chasm and die. The only way to avoid this fate is by focusing on the client's needs, psychological characteristics, reference points, and the message they want to hear. Salespeople therefore need to be psychologists and consultants and have great listening skills, good internal communication tools, and solid networks for passing on changes in client needs. They do not necessarily have to be great talkers. Horizon scanners must prepare the product and the salesperson to be "chasm wary."

## Who Should Be Scanning?

Despite the flat nature of many knowledge-based organizations or the length of the marketing reports a salesperson prepares, no one should know the (underlying) needs of a client as well as the person who is in contact with that client throughout their working day. Filtering the information so that it arrives on the VP's desk in a two-page format (otherwise they won't read it!) once per quarter may seem an effective use of the VP's time, but it is a poor way to create strategy or to empower the people on the frontline. There are only two choices: let the salesperson practice VIP Leadership (horizon scan for the organization's sales division and be involved in the strategy-making process and the design of the complete product package) or make the president or vice-president spend eight hours per day with clients. Some may quite rightly say that the salesperson's skills and point of view are too short-term to perform VIP Visionary horizon scanning work well. This may be true—particularly if they are paid on a commission basis and are just focused on making a sale. If your salespeople are too focused on the short term, you have two choices: change their objectives and remuneration system or have someone with a more strategic viewpoint spend time with your clients.

In the same vein, production personnel should be scanning for trends, opportunities, and threats in the production area; Human Resources (HR) staff should be scanning for new opportunities in recruitment, career management, and remuneration packages; and executives should be focusing on the larger strategic issues and creating an environment propitious for people to effectively and efficiently horizon scan.

## Product Life Cycles and Sigmoid Curves

Having mentioned product life cycles, lets look at this traditional model and see how it applies today. In days gone by, once a new product or service was launched, you could often sit back and idly watch the product life cycle sales chart grow before your eyes. Providing you could get those early adopters to use and appreciate your product, the rest was simply a matter of following the generic recipe. Occasionally a competitor would introduce a new product that would cut the "milking the cash cow" days short, but in general you did not have to be thinking about introducing any new product until the previous product sales started to slip into decline. In fact, you could often hold off on introducing new innovations until everyone had bought the old version—then they would all have to buy the new one too! Life was fun then, and an example of supplier power at its best.

Unfortunately for manufacturers and service providers, this is no longer the case. The product development, innovation, or "version X" pipeline is now in permanent flow with the incorporation of one new value-added function being closely followed by another. First-mover advantage is often vital because it's now a winner-takes-all game, particularly in technology markets. The product life cycle is now measured in months rather than years. Instead of a leisurely one-horse long-distance race, there is a never-ending full-blown gallop among several products, all of which have new versions already in the works.

## *Sigmoid Curves*

Sigmoid curves are a favourite of mine and follow nicely from the never-ending race metaphor above. Charles Handy and several others have written in detail about the S-shaped curves we've come to associate with learning curves and market, industry, and product life cycles. I believe that it is only now possible to see the traditional industry or product life cycle S-curve as being made up of a series of smaller S-curves (see Figure 5.3). Each individual S-curve represents the introduction of new functionality, new packaging, new delivery methods, or perhaps a major release of a new product version. No unaltered product can possibly make it along an entire life cycle curve, partly because it takes different versions to meet the needs of the different personality types who will buy the product through its life cycle, and partly because without upgrades, the product will be overtaken by the competition.

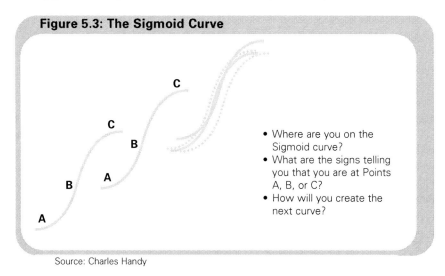

**Figure 5.3: The Sigmoid Curve**

- Where are you on the Sigmoid curve?
- What are the signs telling you that you are at Points A, B, or C?
- How will you create the next curve?

Source: Charles Handy

As you build your life cycle curve from the series of smaller sigmoid curves, the importance of the relationship that has been built between salesperson and client becomes even more important. You need to be planning for the next sigmoid curve, be it the introduction of a radical new technology or a simple version upgrade. The client tends to have a good idea of what other products or innovations are threatening yours; they are also aware of current R&D or development projects that could change their needs regarding suppliers; they can also serve as great "guinea pigs," letting you know whether potential innovations being proposed within your company will be acceptable.

The time to start thinking about the next sigmoid curve is the very moment you begin to feel comfortable in the middle section of the existing one (Point B). Planning at Point C is way too late. Point B is the time when you are familiar with the current game; you are starting to generate some cash flow and have money to invest, ensuring you lead the birth of the next curve.

The challenge is to create and choose the winning sigmoid curve. Unfortunately for the incumbent, history shows that rarely is it the market leader on one sigmoid curve who leads the next one. When trying to make a decision, you may have to choose among any one of three or four different and mutually exclusive sigmoid curves. And there is no guarantee that the one you choose to invest in and develop will be the winner. A competitor may choose a different one and develop it into the winning S-curve.

> *The more devastating S-curve will come from another industry; hence, you really need to be vigilant.*

For example, there were several companies who invested enormously in developing new products assuming Sony's Beta video technology would be the next S-curve. In fact, VHS became the next S-curve and the companies who chose to develop product with that technology continued up a large S-curve while the Beta manufacturers incurred major losses. At the moment, automobile manufacturers are investing in many types of theoretically superior, environmentally friendly fuels: solar power, natural gas, hybrids, and fuel cell technologies abound. Companies like Ballard are literally betting their company on the fuel cell—no hedging of bets is allowed. If solar technology suddenly materializes, or even if another competitor achieves a major commercial breakthrough first, Ballard's stock price will tumble, development will stop, and the company could very well close its doors. Convergence in the telecom/cable/computer industry is likely to spark a new major sigmoid curve at any time and there are numerous technologies that could be at the base of the winning curve. Investors are now gambling on which one will prove dominant—and companies are doing the same. Multinationals with resources hedge their bets by investing in several competing technologies. Everyone else generates optimistic and pessimistic scenarios and tries to build a "big win" strategy for one technology and, if possible, a defensive "hedging" strategy for the others.

Another great example of how sigmoid curves can affect a market is the music industry. The music publishing business thought of itself as an industry, one that controlled its own future. Developments generated by new small sigmoid curves were released or held back according to the life cycle and profitability of existing products. If company executives believed it was more profitable to delay releasing new technology, they could and would do so. Although there was some indecision among industry insiders as to which technologies would demonstrate sufficient added value to the consumer to warrant major investment in new equipment, the industry generally felt secure. Meanwhile, however, the giant sigmoid curve representing the growth of the Internet and its many small but radical S-curve developments were starting to converge towards the music scene. Suddenly, MP3, sound cards, and bandwidth technology made "free" music available on the Internet to be played through speakers attached to computers. Music artists suddenly realized that they could repatriate much of the power lost to music publishers by experimenting with releasing their own music on the web. The jury is still out regarding the winning S-curve, but it is clear that what was once considered a mature oligopoly is now an industry going through a shake-out. It will probably resurface in an embryonic and fragmented format as the battle of telecom convergence expands to content providers.

So what should you be doing in order to be well positioned for the rollout of the next sigmoid curve? The more devastating S-curve will come from another industry; hence, you really need to be watching new macroenvironmental trends, market developments, and technology innovations that could be transferable to your business and markets. You need to be constantly talking with clients, as they may be watching or developing new technologies for their own businesses. You need to be investing in R&D and constantly generating best- and worst-case scenarios for your business and markets.

Obviously, in all this work your hope is that it is your company that will hit the motherlode: you will be the one to reinvent the industry or reinvent the way that clients are satisfied by creating, or being the first to capitalize on, the next S-curve. You want to be the one to find the unique and defendable strategic position to deliver tenfold more value at reduced cost to your clients so the old way of doing business becomes obsolete overnight.

# Horizon Scanning in the Strategic Planning Process

Henry Mintzberg has written about the need for both a formal strategic planning process and a means by which "emergent strategies" can be adopted (26). The latter, unplanned responses to changing circumstances not discovered during the formal planning process, are often a product of the salesperson listening to the customer and management listening to the salesperson. With constantly changing market conditions and customer needs, such emergent strategies have a tendency to be more powerful and a company must have the means to incorporate these strategies into its operations. How can such strategies emerge if the salesperson is not allowed to be an entrepreneurial VIP leader?

Even if you are an "industry leader," you must always be preparing to reinvent yourself; as mentioned in Chapter 2, renewal is a key part of continued personal and corporate success. Many leading brokerage houses have taken the initiative (or have been forced) to create Internet e-brokers to compete their own traditional organizations, perhaps putting them out of business. You must always be ready to create a new, more effective product or service that offers the client additional value. If you do not, someone else will.

So even as you are constantly adapting to changes in the macroenvironment and new sigmoid curves, avoiding chasms, and trying to maximize your MRC, the valuable information gleaned from horizon scanning must be circulated to all those people who can gain value from it. Most importantly, that information must be fed into the strategic planning process.

## Managing the Process

It would obviously be ideal if you knew for certain which strategic positions and core competencies will be needed in the future. Because that is not possible, you have to manage and build a core competency portfolio that will allow you an occasional error in your judgement of the marketplace's future needs.

In a sense, your strategy will be much like that of any other portfolio manager. There are high-risk scenarios and low-risk scenarios and you have to choose which one(s) best suit you and your organization while, if possible, always hedging your bets to enhance the possibility of having a winning hand and diminish the risk of having a losing one.

Hugh Courtney, Jane Kirkland, and Patrick Viguerie help to solve this challenge by out-lining some of the options available to you. They describe four discrete levels of uncertainty, one of which you will have to deal with when planning for the future:

- ⟳ **A Clear Enough Future.** In this situation you are pretty sure about the likely out-come and you can generate scenarios knowing that a particular event is likely to happen and standard business tools were designed for such an environment.
- ⟳ **Alternate Futures.** Here the possible scenarios are clear but the "winner" could be one of several which are nevertheless already well defined. Game theory, decision analysis, and option valuation models can be used as analytical tools.
- ⟳ **A Range of Futures.** Here there is a limited range of possible scenarios but those scenarios are not easy to isolate and study.
- ⟳ **True Ambiguity**. In this situation, there is no real basis for forecasting what will happen. Pattern recognition and nonlinear dynamic models can be used to make guesses and estimate probabilities. (11)

As you look at various markets, sigmoid curves, your strategic positions, and core competency portfolios, one or more of those elements may fall into one of each of the uncertainty conditions. But as you try to predict your future and reduce your risks, you do need to make some best guesses as to what will happen and how you should prepare for it.

The best idea is to prepare a limited number of alternative scenarios (irrespective of whether you see "alternate futures" or "true ambiguity") and to combine a practical approach with your intuition. The real danger is in throwing your hands in the air and doing nothing because the future appears too uncertain, and then relying solely on intuition and reaction to whatever occurs.

Courtney et al. provide this advice:

1. Develop only a limited number of alternative scenarios (four or five maximum).
2. Avoid developing redundant scenarios that only instill panic and fear.
3. Make sure each scenario offers a distinct picture of the future environment for your business.
4. Try to work with probable rather than possible scenarios. (11)

Having examined the various possible outcomes in your different markets and possible future core competencies that you may require, you have to make a decision about how you will respond. In other words, you must develop your strategic posture.

You basically have four options here. You can be a future shaper, an adapter, a reservist, or engage in "no play." Your choice depends on your current project portfolio and all the elements (structure, resources, strategy, environment, and especially management preferences) of the Diamond-E.

## Future Shapers
Adopting this posture means that your organization intends to be at the forefront of the introduction and advancement of the market or of technological change. You intend to be a leader in terms of carrying it forward and implementing it, and you must ensure that you have the core competencies required to deliver it. As mentioned earlier, Ballard is a good example of a shaper.

There are several reasons why you might choose to be a future shaper. If you are reasonably sure of the future of a technology, product, or service and its importance to you and your clients, you may be willing to take on a little more risk. Adopting this strategy could also be a defensive posture: you may need a technology to become the dominant one to ensure your survival. Alternately, you could already be a leader in a market and you may need to be a shaper in order to maintain that position and continue to work with your leading-edge clients who have staked their future on the technology and who would switch to a competitor if you were to adopt a reservist or no play position. Finally, you may already have core competencies in the area and it may be natural for you to continue in that direction.

## Adapters

Some organizations are masters at adapting and taking more of a "follower" role in the change process. They monitor where the market is going, who is doing what, and only move quickly once the risks are reduced and the scenario has become almost a "clear enough future" situation where it is obvious what will happen. Microsoft has mastered this position. A few of the core competencies this type of organization needs are flexibility, open architecture, rapid adaptation, and learning capability.

## Reservists

Reservists reserve the right to play at a later date. Particularly relevant when the future is vague and ill defined, larger companies sometimes play this role when they allow smaller companies to be the future shaper. They will perhaps partner with the smaller company during the early stages, form strategic alliances, or simply acquire them once the outcome is clear. Ballard's large corporate investors represent companies interested in being reservists in the fuel cell game.

## No Play

Companies always have the choice to not participate or to withdraw from particular markets or businesses when appropriate—that is a valid play. It is probably much better to withdraw completely than to participate half-heartedly and waste funds. After all, there is an opportunity cost with every choice—that is, the money invested in one project cannot be invested elsewhere. Hence, at different times you may have to make no play decisions that could pay off or cost you enormously later if you're shut out of a major new market or if you have to buy your way back in. However, levels of risk, poor horizon scanning, an excess of great opportunities, and a portfolio of projects that are simply too risky mean that a no play decision can be the toughest but most prudent one to make.

Finally, under each of these postures, you obviously have a choice as to the amount of risk—or investment—you are willing to make. Occasionally you will see companies that literally wager their future on a certain scenario and invest everything in that outcome. Any company acting as a future shaper in the technology area often has little choice but to do that and hope their chosen hardware or software becomes the market leader. Keeping options open requires smaller investments but allows for larger ones should the opportunity develop. No regrets–type moves mean that, irrespective of the outcome, you may have increased your knowledge, developed a new core competency applicable in other areas, or changed your image or reputation with your clients.

For example, by managing a diversified portfolio of five projects or opportunities in a selection of business units or markets you may:

⮱ place a large big bet as a shaper when you know there are alternate futures;
⮱ have two markets with a range of futures in which you play the role of adapter; and
⮱ have two potential markets with truly ambiguous futures in which you adopt a reservist posture.

Alternatively, you may be in an organization that is making a large bet as a shaper in a new market. Your strategy will depend on all the aspects of your Diamond-E Framework, your mission, and the level of risk you like to take.

The material covered in this chapter constitutes the essence of the work of the VIP Visionary as horizon or future scanner. The horizon scanner must be looking at global opportunities, emerging macrotrends and how they could affect business; they must be scanning different markets and new technologies, and examining business or technological developments far removed from your current markets in case they are sigmoid curves that represent a breakthrough opportunity or a daunting threat; they must be analyzing the strategic role of the shaper, adapter, etc., ensuring there is a good fit with the Diamond-E.

Obviously, the type of scanning being done will differ according to the position the scanner holds and their level within the organization. However, the important thing is that each person applies the principle tasks of the role to their particular area of expertise.

## Key Points in Chapter 5

⊃ All business is global.
⊃ Horizon scan for macroenvironmental changes that will affect your company, competitors, and markets.
⊃ Fill the blanks and the white spaces.
⊃ Maximize your return on capabilities (MRC).
⊃ Assess your position on the current sigmoid curve, try to create the next one, and check for other possible future S-curve winners.
⊃ Plan in detail how you will cross the chasms—not fall into them!
⊃ Feed pertinent information from your horizon scanning into the strategic planning process.
⊃ Manage your business strategy through portfolio risk management dictated by your Diamond-E.

## Questions to Consider

⊃ What macroenvironmental forces are driving your market's and clients' needs to change?
⊃ How much time does your organization's executive team spend horizon scanning? How much time do they spend on operational issues? How much time do you spend horizon scanning?
⊃ Is your company examining all possible opportunities to apply its core competencies in order to maximize return on capabilities (MRC)?
⊃ How can you repackage your competencies in order to serve other markets and fill blank spaces?
⊃ Where are you on the current sigmoid curve? Which new curves are on the horizon? How are you preparing for their arrival?
⊃ What roles do you play in your markets? Shaper? Adapter? Are there markets that you should not being playing in?
⊃ What "imaginary" competitor to do you fear most? Brainstorm!

As a Visionary, you have already defined what it is you want to do and have established a process for defining your mission and continually scanning the horizon for macroenvironmental trends, opportunities, and threats. The tasks remaining for the Visionary are defining the value proposition you will offer, determining the strategic positioning you are going to adopt in the market, and creating a strategic intent. It is also important to analyze your competition and ensure that you are creating economic value within your organization.

Having looked at the factors that might influence a business in the previous chapter, it's now time to decide the following: (1) Whom are you serving? and (2) What needs are you satisfying? The third question, How will you do it? (that is, how will you design and build an organization and strategic system that can deliver your product and service to the client), will be answered by the Implementor.

## What: *Perceived Value and Value Proposition*

Every organization's challenge is to offer the highest possible perceived value to clients while incurring the minimum cost to do so. Perception, here, is very much in the eye of the beholder. Value can be time saved (waiting to have your car repaired on the spot) or time lengthened (receiving a thorough massage); it can be an essential guarantee (a several-year warranty on a big-ticket electronics item) or one that the issuer knows you may never use (a lifetime warranty on a hammer); it can be shopping at home or purchasing the same item shopping in a very expensive store. After all, what you perceive as value may not be what I perceive as value. Value is subjective and it depends on what the client wants and what they perceive as being valuable for your particular product or service. For example, if you sell software, your target customer may perceive value as low prices; a central location; 24/7 service; availability of support or training on new programs; or options for credit, leasing, payment terms. Your challenge is to identify exactly what your particular chosen client perceives as value and then to offer it to them. This offer is your value proposition. In the ideal situation:

| Perceived Value  | Value Proposition  | Strategic Position |
|---|---|---|
| (in the eyes of the | (that you offer to | (how you're posi- |
| client) | your client) | tioned in the |
|  |  | marketplace) |

## *Perceived Value: Some Basic Strategic Options*

In 1996, Michael E. Porter returned to some earlier work he'd done on business strategy and proposed that there were essentially three possible value propositions, or three possible strategic positions that he defines as follows:

- ⟳ **Variety-Based Positioning.** Here a company offers a narrow choice of products or services to a clientele who have a specific need. The strategic system is then designed to uniquely deliver this service. Companies following this type of strategy are usually offering one unique and specialized product or service. This could be a specialized muffler shop, a bagel factory, or White Shirts & Black Socks (which sells only these products to business types). A business-to-business (B-2-B) example would be a particular company—let's say Company X—that supplies only one specific part or module. Clients use Company X because of its high-quality product or reputation. Another supplier may carry a similar part in their large, assorted product range, but Company X's value proposition is superior, making it worth dealing with them separately.
- ⟳ **Needs-Based Positioning.** Companies that adopt this positioning attempt to satisfy all the needs of a particular group of clients; it's the concept of "one-stop shopping" (think IKEA, where you can get all your home furnishings or Bureau En Gros, where you can get all your office supplies). In this case, the organization's strategic system is again designed to uniquely deliver this service. B-2-B examples include companies that offer to do all your manufacturing or to manage all your Human Resources (HR) or information technology (IT) needs.
- ⟳ **Access-Based Positioning.** These types of companies build a value chain designed to deliver a product or service for a specifically located or specifically sized client. Examples include a company operating a network of small-town cinemas and business service centres offering photocopies, administrative services, and meeting rooms for people running home-based operations. (29)

It's not always easy to classify existing businesses into one of these three types. It's important to note that different people in different circumstances will place a value on each of the three types of offerings and will be ready to go out of their way to buy from your business because you're satisfying a particular need that they have. However, the categories certainly serve as guidelines and the message is a simple one: you must make a choice. You can't be everything to everybody.

Michael Treacy and Fred Wiersema propose three value disciplines and these are more relevant and useful than Porter's in the knowledge-based business arena. Treacy and Wiersema recommend that a company choose to excel in one of the following disciplines: operational excellence, product leadership, and customer intimacy.

Hence, if you decide that your target clients really perceive value in paying low prices, buying the latest in product functionality, or paying for a higher level of personal service, you can choose your value discipline accordingly. Then you can build your strategic system—your decision-making criteria, value creation processes, management structure and culture—so that your Diamond-E is in harmony with that choice. You obviously cannot afford to ignore either of the other two value disciplines, but your main focus always remains on maintaining excellence in your chosen one.

The following is a brief overview of Treacy and Wiersema's value disciplines and their characteristics (34).

## Operational Excellence: *Execute Extraordinarily Well*
Companies that focus on operational excellence offer a middle-of-the-road product at the best price or with the least inconvenience—or both. Examples include Wal-Mart, Dell Computer, Club Price, Future Electronics, GE, and Southwest Airlines. Their focus is on maintaining excellence in their processes and in supporting the activities of their value chain.

Typical characteristics of a company focused on operational excellence include:

- Supply chains and services that are optimized and streamlined to minimize costs and hassles.
- Operations that are standardized, simplified, tightly controlled, and centrally planned, leaving few decisions to the discretion of the rank and file.
- Management information systems that are focused on integrated, reliable, high-speed transactions and compliance to norms.
- A culture that abhors waste and rewards efficiency.
- A business that is managed in order to secure large, consistent volume throughout the day, week, or year.

## Product Leadership: *Pushing Product Performance Boundaries*
Companies interested in product leadership focus on introducing radical and incremental innovation and new functionality into their products. Examples include J&J, Nike, 3M, Bombardier, Motorola, Sony, HP, Intel. Their focus is on research and development (R&D) and the design stages of the value chain.

Typical characteristics of a company focused on product leadership include:

- An emphasis on the core processes of invention, product development, and market exploitation.
- A business structure that is loosely knit, ad hoc, and ever-changing to adjust to the entrepreneurial initiatives and redirections that characterize working in unexplored territory.
- Management systems that are results-driven, measure and reward new product success, and don't punish the experimentation needed to get there.
- A culture that encourages individual imagination, accomplishment, out-of-the-box thinking, and a mindset that is driven by the desire to create the future.

## Customer Intimacy: *Generating Specific Customer Solutions*
Companies that focus on this value discipline offer not what the market wants, but what the individual customer wants. Examples include IBM, Johnson Controls, McKinsey, and many top service companies and small consulting companies. Their focus is on customer service or on the sales activities of the value chain.

Typical characteristics of a company focused on customer intimacy include:

- An obsession with helping the customer understand exactly what's needed and ensuring the solution gets implemented properly.
- A deep knowledge and insight into a customer's needs, business, and underlying processes.
- A business structure that delegates decision making to employees who are close to the customer.
- Management systems that are geared towards creating results for carefully selected and nurtured clients.
- A culture that embraces specific rather than general solutions, and thrives on deep and lasting client relationships.

## Which Disciplines To Choose?

But how do you decide which of these disciplines you should choose? In fact, it should not really be a difficult decision, as your customer's clear preference in terms of what they perceive as value will determine in which area you need to excel. If you are unclear or if you have a choice between targeting two different markets, each with a different perception of value, the following series of questions is a process you can use to determine which value discipline is most valued by your clients and which one is the best for your company today in terms of its Diamond-E factors and competitors' positions.

### Step 1: Locating Your Business

- What are the dimensions of value that the customers care about?
- For each dimension of value, what proportion of customers focus on it as their primary or dominant decision criterion?
- Which competitors provide the best value in each of these value dimensions?
- How do you measure up against the competition on each dimension of value?
- Why do you fall short of the value leaders in each dimension?

### Step 2: Brainstorming for Theoretical Options

- What can be done in the future in the different value dimensions so that you can theoretically become the leader in each of the three disciplines?
- What minimum level of threshold value will the market require in the two unselected disciplines?
- Have you already achieved those standards? If not, how can they be attained?

### Step 3: Making a Decision and a Detailed Design

- Which of the three disciplines will you choose to excel in?
- How will the model produce superior value?
- What is the potential market and the business case for choosing this option?
- What are the key success factors that can make or break this solution?
- How will you design the core processes, management systems, structure, and other elements of the required operating model?*
- How will your company make the transition from its current state to this new operating model over a two- to three-year period?*

*Indicates work to be done by the Implementor (the *How*)

## *The Consequences of Your Choices*

The previous sections gave you some tools with which you can identify what potential clients and target markets perceive as value. This process sends the message—which can never be reinforced enough—that the choices you make vis-à-vis the strategic position you will adopt is a function of the environment you choose to work in and your own management preferences as expressed in your personal and corporate mission. The choice of strategy then dictates the resources and the structure (and everything included therein) that you will need to develop and implement in order for your Diamond-E to be in equilibrium.

It's also important at this time to highlight three crucial considerations for planning your strategy:

1. ***One value discipline, one strategic system.*** It's clear that the strategic system required to ensure the success of White Shirts & Black Socks is unique to the delivery of that particular product. The moment the company tries to offer another type of service, the optimum value creation process will be compromised. Hence, keep in mind that the optimum processes or structure designed to deliver one particular product, one specific positioning, or one value discipline will not work for a different choice. If you end up trying to focus on both product leadership and customer intimacy or produce both needs-based and access-based products, you will probably not be at optimum effectiveness or efficiency for either—and in the knowledge-based markets of today, you will pay a heavy price for that!

2. ***Unique products and services.*** You only gain a sustainable competitive advantage if the means for producing your positioning—that is, the optimum set of activities (the organization or strategic system) that produce the product or service—turns out something perceived as being different by the marketplace. For example, all business types know that continually having to go out and buy white cotton shirts and black socks is a chore they'd rather do without. However, if it's not easier, quicker, or cheaper to purchase all my white shirts and socks from White Shirts & Black Socks, then I will go elsewhere for that service (unless I receive better or equal quality of product). That means White Shirts & Black Socks or a B-2-B supplier of a single product or service has to be offering me something unique—preferably through a unique strategic system—that other companies with their structure, resources, and strategy cannot.

3. ***Image and branding.*** You need to decide what your product, service, or company will stand for. In today's marketplace, it's clear that your image, your brand, needs to be cultivated, managed, and protected in the same way as any other critical asset. Once you make a decision about positioning, you need to ensure that your offerings, your activities, and your public profile are consistent with that image and positively reinforce and enhance it in the minds of your stakeholders. A positive image is an asset that will only increase in value in today's e-world.

# Who: *Finding a Target*

How do you actually decide whom you will target? If the business is a new start-up, the target clientele is determined by the founders and owners who have a very clear purpose and opportunity in mind. If an organization or business unit already exists and you've taken it over, it may already have a certain image, existing products or services, manufacturing and distribution systems, and a marketing campaign already in place to target a particular market. Or you may have developed or acquired a certain professional expertise or have developed a new technological or knowledge-based product or service and you are seeking to commercialize it. Where do you begin?

There is often an iterative or parallel process between asking yourself whom you will serve and performing an analysis to determine whether you can actually deliver that value proposition. There may be several potential clients that you can target and some may perceive more value to your offering than others. Plus you will need to take into account your ability to deliver and the competition. But the process can be simplified by undertaking the process described below with several potential target groups.

## *The* Who *and the* What

For knowledge-based businesses, I do not think there is a better way to determine whom your clients should be or what you should offer them than with Geoffrey A. Moore's "target customer characterization" process. Although Moore deals solely with the marketing of technology products in his books, his methodology is valuable when applied to all knowledge-based products and services. His basic message is that you have to get "under the skin" of your target client and see how they view your product or service and your value proposition.

With "new" knowledge-based products or services, you are often in the same situation as an organization marketing new technology, as there are no large volumes of market studies available for you to analyze in order to create hypotheses and form well-founded assumptions. You have to begin at ground zero.

Building on Moore's ideas (28, pp. 90–109), I've created the following ten steps to help you define your value proposition and strategic positioning.

### 1. Create a personal profile of the target individuals.
This profile should be as complete and detailed as possible and should include the individual's goals, values, etc. It should be a psychographic profile of whom you are targeting to buy your product or service. The better you understand your client and their situation, the better prepared you will be to offer an appealing product or service for them to purchase.

As he does with his concept of the chasms that exist between the different stages of the product life cycle, Moore characterizes buyers as a function of the product life cycle. With technology products, he knows that the first people to adopt them are technology enthusiasts who just love playing with new toys. They want to be the first users and "in the know," and they will help the company with its debugging process; manuals are not required for these clients. In contrast, if the company wants to sell a technology product to me—a "conservative" technological illiterate—it should also be aware that a manual is not needed, but that's because I won't read it. The fact the supplier thinks it's required only undermines my confidence that it's a product for me; I want the product to be so easy to use and bug-free that a manual would be redundant.

## 2. Assess the available infrastructure.

Many knowledge-based technological products require a specific infrastructure; if the potential client doesn't have the infrastructure, they can't use the product. Here's a simple example to illustrate the point: it's not wise to market your new long-lasting electric light bulbs to people living in the country who have no electricity and still use propane gas lights. Hence, make sure that all the required infrastructure and complementary products required for your product to deliver its maximum value are available.

## 3. Consider a day in the life of your target client (before they've used your product or service).

Describe in detail multiple (and possible) scenarios in the target person's day when they could use your product or service—if it were available. Where are they? What are they thinking? What are their needs? What are their frustrations? What are the available alternatives (i.e., what does the competition offer)? What are they really trying to do? What would be their ideal solution?

## 4. Create a definition of your market(s).

Having gone through the day-in-the-life step, you will now know whether there is one or several different markets for your product ("markets" as defined by Moore in Chapter 5). If you now have identified two or more different markets, then you should continue the remainder of the strategic positioning exercise for each different market.

## 5. Consider a day in the life of your target client (after they've used your product or service).

Repeat Step 4 but now do it assuming the client is using your product. What do they do now? What are they thinking? What are their continued frustrations? How much time/energy/money have they saved? How has their work changed or pleasure increased?

## 6. Think about your product or service's "must have" qualities.

Which category will your product fall into according to your client:

   a. Unusable (and hence redundant)?
   b. Usable (but with no obvious benefit)?
   c. Nice to have (but simply a replacement for a competitor's similar product)?
   d. Should have (but the objective can still be achieved by other means)?
   e. Must have (and nothing else can give the same results)?

It goes without saying that you need to aim for a "must-have" product offering for your chosen markets (i.e., value proposition). If your product or service falls into a category closer to the first one, the motivation for a client to purchase your product or service obviously diminishes.

## 7. Determine what your product needs to satisfy your target client.

When looking at your value proposition, you have to look at what Moore calls the "whole product model." He breaks down the whole product into the following components:

⊃ **Generic Product.** This is what is shipped in the box and appears on the invoice. With knowledge-based products and services, this seldom represents what the purchaser is actually buying.

⊃ **Expected Product.** This is the product the purchaser thought they were buying (e.g., a computer with a monitor and with software). Delivery of this product represents the minimum chance of the buyer being satisfied with the purchase.

⊃ **Augmented Product.** This is the expected product fleshed out to provide the maximum chance of satisfying the purchaser (e.g., a computer with software, a printer, training, a help hotline).

⊃ **Potential Product.** This represents the potential market for growth of add-ons, ancillary products, and customized enhancements.

Organizations seeking to offer value and satisfaction to their clients obviously need to be focusing on delivering at least an augmented product to a client, with an eye to potential product sales in mind.

Questions you can ask yourself include: What are the generic, expected, augmented, and potential products offered by my product or service? What do clients expect to receive when they purchase my product? Is that what they get? Are there possible add-ons that I should be examining? These sorts of questions posed early in the product design process can mean the difference between black or red ink.

## 8. Put your product or service through the "Elevator Test."

This test is popular with presidents of start-up companies. They imagine that they have thirty seconds alone in an elevator with a venture capitalist and need to "sell" their product/company as an investment. Basically, if you cannot sell the benefits of your product or service in thirty seconds to your target client (in an elevator or not!), you may have to question whether the benefits are sufficient to warrant the potential client making the purchase. Is your product really a must have? If so, why can't you express it succinctly? If not, will there be a market for your product with this particular clientele?

### The Elevator Test Phrase

Fill in the parenthetical details about your product or service:

⊃ *For* (name target customer)
⊃ *Who* (state need or opportunity)
⊃ *The* (give product name) *is a* (give product category)
⊃ *That* (state one key benefit, the compelling reason to buy your product).
⊃ *Unlike* (name primary competitive alternative)
⊃ *My product* (state primary differentiation).

### Example Elevator Test Phrase for *Growing People, Growing Companies*

⊃ *For* aspiring but frustrated leaders in the knowledge-based economy
⊃ *Who* are seeking a new model of leadership and behaviour that will facilitate their personal leadership development
⊃ *Growing People, Growing Companies* is a leadership model and a set of tools
⊃ *That* covers all aspects of leading intelligent people in knowledge-based companies.
⊃ *Unlike* all other books and models that deal with only one aspect of leadership in traditional business environments
⊃ *This product* empowers readers to take control of developing their personal and professional lives irrespective of their environment.

### Why is the Elevator Test important?

Without it:

- ➲ Your value claim cannot be transmitted by word of mouth.
- ➲ Your marketing communications will be vague and diffuse.
- ➲ Your R&D will be unfocused.
- ➲ You won't be able to recruit allies and partners.
- ➲ You are unlikely to get financing from anyone with experience.

## 9. Identify what will motivate your target to purchase your product.

What incident, circumstance, or particular frustration will make me, a consumer, purchase your product or service? When are the conditions ripe to make the sale? Where will I be? How will I want to purchase it? When will I want to receive it? How will I want to pay for it? Everything must be designed correctly to ensure that the purchase process is as easy as possible.

## 10. Build a body of evidence.

You now know an enormous amount about your target clients. Most importantly perhaps, you have defined why they will use your product, what they will gain by using it, and what will motivate them to actually make the purchase. Your task now is to amass the evidence a client will need to believe your claims!

Obviously this will differ according to the type of consumer and the needs they are seeking to satisfy. However, it may include such items as design awards for the product, positive product reviews in magazines or trade journals, or endorsements from financial analysts (if you're a start-up). Additionally, it may require partnering with large companies to prove your validity; it may need some top companies to adopt your product and endorse it; or it may need third-party certification, accreditation, or coverage in the mainstream press. The evidence required will depend on potential clients' psychographic profiles and needs (see Figure 6.1), but you will have to obtain it before their orders will flow in.

If you can force yourself to go through this detailed exercise and hopefully work closely with your potential target clients or with objective observers to keep you honest, you should have a very good idea about how you need to strategically position your product. You'll know your target clientele almost on a personal basis—all their thoughts, beliefs, fears regarding buying new products and services, and exactly what they want from the product and how it will change their life once they've purchased it. Hence, your strategic positioning is almost done.

To quote Geoffrey A. Moore: "The fundamental rule of engagement is that any force can defeat any other force—providing that it can define the rules of engagement" (28, p. 136). This process allows you to do just that: stake out your strategic positioning as an irresistible must-have proposition for your potential life-long consumer.

## *Treating Clients According to Their Life-Long Value*

Understanding and behaving according to the simple paradigm of valuing a client is ostensibly the basis of sales and customer relationship management today. However, clients are often valued in the same way company presidents value their employees: they talk about it constantly but their actions betray their real beliefs. The idea is simple: reaching a new client and making a first sale to them requires an incredible investment in time, energy, and money. Yet, having worked hard to obtain clients, organizations often disappoint them with the whole product they offer and after one or two sales, customers move on to other suppliers who promise something better.

## Figure 6.1: Positioning: The Evidence Required

| Visionaries want: | Conservatives want: |
|---|---|
| • Benchmarks | • Revenues and profits |
| • Product reviews | • Strategic partners |
| • Design wins | • Top-tier customers |
| • Initial sales volumes | • Full product line |
| • Trade press coverage | • Business press coverage |
| • Visionary endorsements | • Financial analyst endorsements |
| *Product Information* | *Company Information* |
| *Technology Information* | *Market Information* |
| **Technology Enthusiasts want:** | **Pragmatists want:** |
| • Architecture | • Market share leaders |
| • Schematics | • Third-party support |
| • Demos | • Standards certification |
| • Trials | • Applications proliferation |
| • Technology press coverage | • Vertical press coverage |
| • Guru endorsements | • Industry analyst support |

Source: Geoffrey A. Moore, *Crossing the Chasm*

Irrespective of whether you are selling a ten- or million-dollar product, you should look at what the client—if satisfied—really represents to you: a life-long customer requires little or no additional advertising or sales costs. Imagine the scenario of a life-long client making only a $10 purchase every week. That individual really represents an important client making a $5,200 purchase ($520 multiplied by ten years). Do you treat the client as such? Do you take them for granted? Perhaps it would be better to treat them as an important client worth $5,200 from the moment you contact them. As an added bonus, life-long clients tend to be happy; as a result, word-of-mouth referrals often start knocking at your door.

## The Competition

While going through the process of identifying the *Who* and *What*, you will also glean an enormous amount of information about your competition. That material may consist of documentation your competitors have published about their own products or it could be industry publications, market studies, or trade journals concerned with your market. Of particular importance are the comments you receive from your potential clients (your competitions' current customers) about competitors' whole product offerings and why your proposed product or service is a nice to have, should have, or must have.

There are a few different ways in which you can analyze this information, your markets, and your competitors. Remember that you're interested in learning about what your competition does well, but also what it does poorly, so you can avoid the same mistakes and attack them where they are vulnerable. Don't forget that your objective is to ultimately offer targeted clients a must-have value proposition that you will deliver to them through a unique and difficult-to-copy strategic system of core competencies and interrelated activities.

## Analyzing the Competition: A Tool Kit

The following is a selection of tools that should be useful to you in terms of helping you to fit the market and competitive information you gather into models that will allow you to easily interpret the data and gain useful insights from your analysis. Some frameworks and models have been around for many years, others are relatively new. They all, however, are applicable in today's knowledge-based businesses.

### Approachs to Market Segmentation

Although I prefer to use Moore's definition of a market, it is useful to employ additional tools for analyzing your competitors' approach to market segmentation and the products they choose to offer in different segments. Henry Mintzberg offers a complete range of approaches companies can take with regard to segmentation (27, pp. 89–91).

1. **De-segmentation Strategy.** "One size fits all": companies ignore any segmentation with their product offerings.
2. **Segmentation Strategies.** Companies using a segmentation strategy have two options:
   a. *Comprehensive Segmentation.* Companies develop products and services for all identified segments.
   b. *Selective Segmentation.* Companies only offer products and services in chosen segments.
3. **Niche Strategy.** Companies produce a product or service targeting only a single selected segment.

4. **Customizing Strategies.** Companies try to develop a product or service to satisfy each individual customer's needs, thereby targeting numerous "markets-of-one" (i.e., they offer a specific product to specific individuals). There are three ways to deliver such product offerings:
   a. *Pure Customization.* Companies design each product for each customer from ground zero.
   b. *Tailored Customization.* Companies modify a basic design for each client (e.g., prefab housing and medical implants).
   c. *Standardized Customization.* Companies build a product from a modular design of standard parts (e.g., choosing your automobile on the web and choosing the memory for your computer's hard drive).

How are your competitors segmenting the market? Why? What advantages/disadvantages does that give them? What opportunities/threats does that mean for you? What can you learn from their successes or failures? How should you position yourself vis-à-vis their offerings?

### Approachs to Differentiation

Figure 6.2 demonstrates the possible ways that a company can differentiate its products and services. How do your competitors differentiate themselves? Do they offer 24/7 support? Better pricing? Is their quality or basic design better than their competitors'? Are they "copy cats"? Does their differentiation strategy fit well with the value sought by the client? How can you differentiate your own product from the competitions'? How should you differentiate your product to the client in order to present a must-have value proposition to your target market?

**Figure 6.2: Mintzberg's Differentiation Strategies**

Not fundamentally different, just better

Offers different or even unique features

Quality | Design

Feigns differentiation where it doesn't exist

Support

Image

Offers extra sales support, service, add-ons

Price

"Copy cats"

Charge a lower price with a standard design

Source: Henry Mintzberg and James Brian Quinn, *The Strategy Process*

## Whole Product Comparisons

It's also very interesting and informative to examine what each of your competitors offer as their whole product. What are their generic, expected, augmented, and potential products? Do they satisfy the client? How does your whole product compare with the competitions'?

## Value Chain or Strategic System Analysis

When scouting your competition, it is useful to analyze their value chains in order to see how they create value, where their core competencies are located, and what methods they use to keep their value creation costs low. (A detailed description of the value chain concept appears in Chapter 7.)

## Global Thinking and Competition

As discussed in Chapter 5, every company or organization has the opportunity to use global factors to their competitive advantage, and targeting well-chosen global markets can offer extraordinary potential to companies. Are your competitors exporting their products sold in your geographic region to other countries? Doing something as simple as taking a product currently only available in the UK or Japan and making it available in the US or South America may be possible at little additional cost. And it may offer your competitors economies of scale that you cannot achieve. Alternatively, the product might have required extensive and expensive redesign in order to interest US consumers and your competitor may be losing money. Will you?

Is their apparent commodity product being sold at a premium elsewhere in the world because it's highly differentiated from local products? You need to ask yourself how you can maximize value and reduce costs through targeting global markets, achieving global economies, using global knowledge or global skills, or employing other global resources. (See Chapter 7 for more on global thinking as related to creating a value chain process.)

## Michael E. Porter's Five Forces Model

This model remains extremely useful for analyzing the competitive forces at work on any business. During horizon scanning, companies should be looking at (1) rivalries with other companies, (2) buyer power, (3) supplier power, (4) the threat of new potential competitors, and (5) the threat of substitute products or services, all of which can undermine their business profitability and viability. The power your suppliers and customers hold over you and your rivals is easily identified by observing who has the strongest negotiation position in the business process. Endeavouring to tip that balance of power in your favour by changing the competitive environment is a major challenge for all businesses. Both your suppliers and your customers may be major stakeholders who need to be satisfied, but strong fences do make for good neighbours!

There are some who say that there is now a sixth force at work. The additional factor they name was mentioned earlier in the discussion of Moore's work: complementary products—their availability and lack thereof. An easily identifiable example is the computer industry, where the existence or absence of things like compatible software and maintenance capability can mean the difference between a manufacturer's success or failure. Other examples include the lack of natural gas (NG) filling stations for NG vehicles or the lack of digitally produced programming available for digital TV sets. This kind of lack severely hampers the acceptance of the technology in question. If one competitor succeeds in generating complementary products (e.g., when IBM allowed everyone to provide software for its hardware while Apple did not), it obtains what can be a major, if not determinant, advantage over competitors.

In general, rivalry increases (and profitability decreases) in an "industry" when:

⊃ the number of competitors increases and competitors become more equal in size and capability;
⊃ market growth begins to plateau;
⊃ price cuts are used to boost volume sales;
⊃ switching costs for purchasing one company's products over another's are low;
⊃ firms are in trouble and need to survive;
⊃ exit barriers for leaving the business are high;
⊃ new companies enter and revitalize a stable market; and/or
⊃ product life cycles are compressed.

In practice, many companies are very knowledgeable about rivalry and buyer/supplier power, yet the threat of potential competitors—particularly substitutes— receives little attention. Today, however, substitutes are the biggest threat. If you're a start-up company with a radically different service or new technology, this is very good news! Your potential competitors are probably not horizon scanning outside of their current markets. Just make sure that you continue to horizon scan so that you notice new potential entrants. Barriers to entry that may discourage new entrants—and you— from entering new markets include:

- Economies of scale (small entrants cannot compete on a price basis).
- The need for specialized know-how (a company possesses core competencies that are difficult for anyone else to obtain).
- The presence of steep learning and experience curves.
- Customer loyalty and strong brands (customers are unlikely to change to entrants for their purchases).
- The need for specific, scarce, or difficult-to-obtain resources to make the product.
- Lack of access to suppliers or distribution channels.
- Regulatory policies that restrict who can compete in an industry.

Once in a market, your strategic objective must be to determine if entry barriers can be created to prevent others from serving your customers.

## Competitive Position Maps

Two-dimensional, four-quadrant grids have long been a favourite tool for strategic planners. It's been cynically suggested more than once that irrespective of the axes, you just know that you should be in the top right-hand quadrant! When positioning your organization and all your competitors on competitive position maps, the quadrant you're in is less important than interpreting the patterns or groupings of organizations and deciding whether those organizations are successful or not. The exercise requires you to think strategically and creatively in order to brainstorm what parameters you should use for your X and Y axes.

The process is as follows:

1. Think creatively and identify possible characteristics that differentiate firms competing in your marketplace. Examples include price/quality, differing geographic markets, degree of vertical integration, distribution channels, choice of value discipline, value chain focus, degree of service offered, generic business strategy, standard or customized products, etc. It's important to go beyond simple marketing or advertising positions; you are really looking to identify what characteristics successful companies share—and what you should avoid doing because it does not work well in your market.
2. Draw up a number of two-variable maps using pairs of highly differentiated characteristics as the axes. You are not trying to find the defining diagram here; the idea is to have perhaps ten to twenty different permutations of diagrams with different axes.
3. Assume for the moment that there are just four competitors in a new market you are considering entering. You need to decide what measure of their relative success is important to you. Perhaps it is their market share, profitability, economic value creation, revenues, or return on investment (ROI). You may have to choose measures that are not exactly what you are seeking, but sometimes a certain element (profitability in private companies, for example) can be hard to obtain. Then allocate the size of the circles for each competitor on that basis and start plotting the four competitors on the different sets of axes. You will have four circles of the same size on each diagram—they just happen to be arranged differently according to the axes used (see Figure 6.3 for an example of six such diagrams).
4. Your objective now is to analyze the diagrams and determine what patterns emerge. Can you assign firms that fall approximately in the same strategic space to the same strategic group? What are the patterns? Who is strongly

positioned? Do industry-driving forces and competitive pressures favour some strategic groups over others? Who are you competing with directly? Which factors appear to be predeterminants of success? Are there cause-and-effect relationships? Is your value proposition already taken? Can you identify any key success factors, any attributes that you must have?

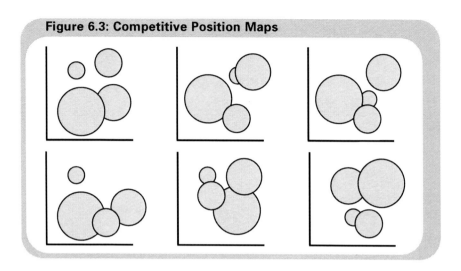

**Figure 6.3: Competitive Position Maps**

Drawing competitive position maps can give you insight into which characteristics can make you successful and which typically will not work. They can show you who is occupying your proposed competitive position and what their weaknesses may be. Ideally, they may show you something that you can do that your competition is not doing—or cannot do—something that will give you a huge sustainable competitive advantage.

Having examined who your clients should be, what they need, and how the competition behaves, you are now ready to select your strategic position—preferably a must-have value proposition that is clearly differentiated from competitors.

It is important to emphasize once again that the most important issue in terms of strategic positioning (and your strategic systems) is deciding which position to adopt and then remaining loyal to that one particular approach. You cannot and must not try to pursue different basic strategies with different clients—unless you create completely independent strategic systems to serve them. Trying to use the same strategic system to deliver products with different generic product types in today's market will result in failure. Disaster awaits organizations trying to offer a low-cost, mass-produced product to one client and a high-quality, differentiated product to another.

If you do your horizon scanning and competitive analysis well and thus define your sought-after strategic position correctly, the challenge for the Implementor is delivering that unique value proposition by assembling a unique combination of core competencies within your strategic system. The system should be optimally and integrally designed to deliver that one strategic position while offering the highest value at the lowest cost.

## Possible Competitor Reactions to Your Launch

Let's quickly look at your competitors and see what choices are open to them when you arrive on the scene. First, they can ignore you—which hopefully they will—and their clients will quickly become yours when you offer more value at a lower cost. Assuming, however, that your competition chooses to respond, they really have three choices: (1) adopt a new strategic position and create a new value chain that creates even more value at lower cost than yours, (2) radically change their organization to try and imitate your positioning and strategic system, and (3) adapt their organization to copy your strategic system and match your new position while maintaining, in parallel, their current positioning and value chain.

The first option rarely plays out as many established companies are hampered by organizational inertia, previous commitments to other strategies, and an unwillingness to reinvent themselves—particularly when they may be in a crisis mode due to your swift arrival. They may follow your lead and try to assume you strategy, but that is still difficult to do considering you are using a unique, fully integrated value creation process. Trying to copy someone else's model usually produces a poor reproduction of a winning organization.

Many organizations respond by maintaining their current positioning and strategic system and trying to add some of the visible features of your new offering. This may appear to work for a while and will certainly buy the competitor some time, but the price will probably be some red ink, as add-ons to existing systems are rarely as effective or as economic as a system designed from scratch with only one end in mind. It's like a manufacturer of ten-speed road bicycles trying to produce off-road bikes using the ten-speed's basic design. It can introduce an additional process to add brackets here, change wheels there, or put on new handle bars and forks, but the basic manufacturing process and bike design will always reflect a bicycle meant to travel at high speed on level, asphalt-covered roads—not one meant for careening over tree stumps on muddy mountain sides. The adapted bike may work, but its performance will never equal that of a bike designed exclusively for mountain trails. And the cost involved? Even the cost of the original ten-speed will increase because of bottlenecks and additional overhead costs incurred by producing the off-road bike.

Apart from the strategic system itself, it is often a company's image that will stand in the way of its adapting current products. To continue the example above, a bike manufacturer known for its expertise in ten-speed road racers may have difficulty selling itself as a mountain bike manufacturer; in fact, advertising itself as such may even hurt its old image as a top-quality road racer manufacturer. Particularly in niche markets, image is very important.

Finally, employees who bought into the mission of building the best road racer may be confused when they are suddenly asked to start making hybrids or mountain bikes. They may not have the right expertise, they may not be interested in the new market, and experiencing the new focus on off-road bikes may make them question their continued presence at the company. Seeing the costs, delivery schedules, and perhaps the quality of the ten-speeds suffer will not help the employees welcome the "straddling" option with open arms.

One last advantage to your having a tightly integrated strategic system is that it creates a constant motivation to improve any weaknesses in the system. Even small weaknesses may hurt the system and hence, you cannot afford not to deal with them. This also means that organizations with such highly interrelated activity sets and strategic systems need to be built and operated efficiently. You have to execute well on all levels to ensure a successful result.

## The Last Step: Are You Creating Economic Value?

If profit is the oxygen that keeps your organization alive, creating economic value represents the lungs that assure the oxygen flow. One of the major concerns for your financial stakeholders is your ability to be more effective with their money than any other investment they could make with equivalent risk.

As Roberto Goizueta, CEO Coca Cola in 1993 stated, "We raise capital to make concentrate, and sell it at an operating profit. Then we pay the cost of that capital. Shareholders pocket the difference." This difference is the economic value generated—it's profit that your organization has produced over and above the return that would have been earned elsewhere on the capital used.

There are many methods for calculating economic value creation; a favourite tool is the now famous EVA™ that many top North American corporations use to evaluate their corporate performance and assess their situation before they make new investments. Without going into too much detail, I think it's important that you be aware of the concept and analyze your organization's financial performance accordingly.

Simply put, economic value creation for any project is positive when the operating earnings minus any taxes paid minus the cost of the debt and/or equity used to finance the project is greater than zero. If it's less than zero, it really means that your project or organization is destroying value! Such financial analysis can be done in great detail on a computer or more casually on the back of an envelope—the choice is yours. But it's important that it get done—and that your organization or team is creating value. Otherwise, you may

> *If economic value creation is less than zero, it really means that your project is destroying value!*

find yourself growing your sales and organization while destroying value, and that will mean any astute financial stakeholders will soon be moving on to put their cash into other more attractive value creation investments.

## From Who and What to How

At the beginning of the chapter, three different questions were posed in order to determine the *Who*, *What*, and *How* of your product or service. Having completed the Visionary work, you are now in a position to fix your value proposition: precisely *What* product or service you will offer to *Whom*. You hopefully possess a must-have whole product offering, you know how it will change or benefit the life of your client, and you know when and why they will buy it. Your value proposition is perfectly aligned with the mission and values of your organization. You have purpose.

This almost completes the work of the VIP Visionary; it's now time for these results to be passed on to the VIP Implementor and VIP People Manager, both of whom work on the *How* in the following ways:

- ⊃ The VIP Implementor takes up the challenge of building the unique and optimally designed processes that allow the required value proposition to be offered. The VIP Implementor creates the processes (the strategic system) that help you realize your purpose.
- ⊃ The mission, vision, and values of the organization will be communicated to the employees by the People Manager. Working with people within your organization is the only way to realize your purpose.

These two messages are communicated by developing strategic intent and by issuing corporate challenges, which are both steps on the road to achieving your mission and strategic positioning.

## *Strategic Intent and Corporate Challenges*

These are two terms that Gary Hamel and C.K. Prahalad have coined, which serve to translate the mission created by the Visionary into something more concrete for the Implementor and People Manager to use as a means for motivating and leading their people. Even though the mission should not need further refining to be clearly understood by employees, its long-term nature and lofty aspirations mean that it often needs to be repackaged and transmitted in other more readily accessible messages and shorter-term goals—normally of five to ten years (or shorter depending on the industry and the company concerned).

I like to see strategic intent and corporate challenges treated as "advertisements" that encourage employees to realize that they are making the difference. The message is that the company is at a certain level at the moment, but it needs to move upwards in order to achieve the mission—everyone needs to go for it! There is always an implied "gap" to fill or a corporate and individual "stretch" forward required to reach both a strategic intent and a corporate challenge. To achieve either, it may mean refocusing efforts, energies, and competitive actions on developing new or more competencies, finding new ways of working, introducing more innovation, obtaining new resources, etc. As happens with most advertising, the messages are focused on the aspects of the 4Ls that differentiate you from your competitors.

Strategic intent can simply be seen as a giant stepping stone on the way to achieving your organization's mission. It is normally established for the entire organization or for a division, and hence it is created by individuals at the top of the organization. It is created by the Visionary as a means to communicate and achieve the mission.

In turn, corporate challenges serve as stepping stones on the way to achieving the strategic intent. Corporate challenges may be issued in the form of a goal for the entire organization to work towards. However, as you will discover later in the book, if an organization is to be truly entrepreneurial, corporate challenges should be established as short-term targets for different divisions, business units, or work teams and be set by the respective leaders of these groups.

## Strategic Positioning

According to Hamel, messages of strategic intent should contain a sense of direction, discovery, and destiny. Possibilities include, "To become the dominant leader"; "To overtake the current leader"; "To move up a notch in the industry rankings"; "To be among the top five in each business sector"; etc. Some past industry examples include Canon's strategic intent to "Beat Xerox"; Wal-Mart's desire to "Overtake Sears"; and Honda's pledge of "We will crush, squash, slaughter Yamaha." At 3M, the company simply increased its own already ambitious target of 25 percent of its revenues from products introduced in the last five years to 30 percent in the last four years, and then all its employees' energies were focused on achieving that objective. This strategic intent obviously was always leading them towards their mission.

Personally, I don't think it's necessary—or perhaps even wise—to establish a strategic intent relative to the performance of your competitors or your market position. Providing it serves to motivate your employees and to stretch the company towards achieving its mission, any phrase or expression can be coined and used.

Corporate challenges need to be almost personalized messages to individuals or teams in which the employee is asked to help the company, perhaps by questioning the way things are done in the company or their department, generating new ideas, introducing new innovations, or reducing expenses. Examples of corporate challenges include reducing production or new product introduction cycle times by 25 percent; improving productivity by 20 percent; improving quality by 10 percent; etc. Corporate challenges should be win-win in nature such that if the company wins, so do the employees. Later in the book you'll see how corporate challenges, in the form of personal challenges, can be set for each individual in the organization in order to ensure that everyone's work contributes to the company's achieving its strategic intent and its mission. This is accomplished using the Balanced Scorecard™ approach throughout the organization.

The terms "strategic intent" and "corporate challenge" are not really important; you can call them goals, objectives, challenges, or something else to your liking. The important thing is that they serve the Visionary, Implementor, and People Manager in translating the mission into manageable chunks with the purpose of accelerating the progress of the company towards its mission while the employees have more of their 4Ls satisfied in return.

# Key Points in Chapter 6

- ➲ The most important task is to identify a value proposition that matches what your target client perceives as value.
- ➲ Develop a description of a day in the life of your client before and after they purchase your product or service.
- ➲ Examine your value proposition as a whole product offering.
- ➲ Always seek to offer the client a must-have value proposition.
- ➲ Use competitive position maps to better understand what makes your competitors successful or unsuccessful and to identify market opportunities.
- ➲ Ensure that financial stakeholders are satisfied by making sure that your organization and any new projects create economic value.
- ➲ Offering unique products in a different way does not give you a competitive advantage unless your value proposition cannot be offered by competitors through their existing value chains.
- ➲ Establish an ambitious strategic intent and corporate challenges that will move you towards achieving your mission.

# Questions to Consider

- ➲ Can you see the opportunities and weaknesses in the competitors' offerings?
- ➲ How should you position yourself vis-à-vis the competition?
- ➲ Can you create a compelling reason to buy?
- ➲ Have you written an Elevator Test Phrase?
- ➲ Do you have the right evidence needed to convince your particular client to purchase your product?
- ➲ Are there global market opportunities for your products?
- ➲ Are you creating economic value?
- ➲ Is there an opportunity to deliver your value proposition using a unique strategic system that others do not have?
- ➲ What does your brand say to people now? What do you want it so say? Is your strategic system supporting that brand image?
- ➲ Where does your organization or team need to be in five to ten years' time? How can you package these objectives into a motivational strategic intent or corporate challenges?

V

I

P

**Part 3: The Implementor**

## Chapter 7

**The Value Creation Process**

The Visionary's role is to create purpose for the organization and to define the strategic position it will adopt or the value proposition it will offer to selected clients. In terms of the Diamond-E, the Visionary looks outside of the organization and identifies the "ideal" strategy signalled by the environment. The challenge for the Implementor is to create the "masterplan" for how—through which processes—this will be done. In the language of the Diamond-E, the Implementor determines the resources, structure, and management preferences a company will need to create and adopt in order to pursue the strategy. If you're working for an existing organization, a Diamond-E analysis will also show you what resources, structure, or management preferences you are lacking for a certain project and show you that you may have to recruit new people and find new competencies or resources before you can proceed.

The how-to masterplan consists of the design for your organization's strategic system: the arrangement of interrelated activity sets, selected core competencies, outsourcing, and organizational structure that includes each and every aspect of the value chain or value creation process. The organization you design will determine the results—as the saying goes, "Every organization is perfectly designed to get the results it gets, good or bad." The challenge is to determine what you need in order to deliver your value proposition and what unique arrangement of the strategic system "jigsaw" you can design and implement in order to create your desired strategic position. Once in place, your strategic system will ideally produce the value proposition you want to offer to your clients while incurring the lowest possible cost to do so. This is the Implementor's first challenge.

# Creating Maximum Value at Minimum Cost

The essence of the Implementor's work is to design and implement business processes that create the perceived value sought by your clients. Figure 7.1 illustrates the value creation challenge in a very simple way.

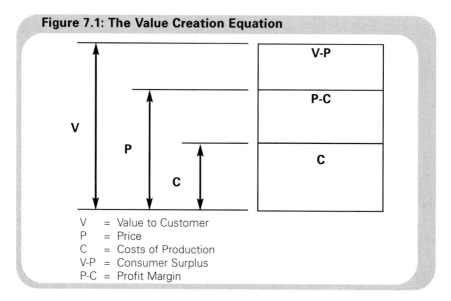

**Figure 7.1: The Value Creation Equation**

V  = Value to Customer
P  = Price
C  = Costs of Production
V-P = Consumer Surplus
P-C = Profit Margin

V is the perceived value of your product or service to your consumer. Now, you obviously want to use every means possible to maximize V in the eyes of your customer—that is, offer the must-have value proposition. As discussed in the previous chapter, this may be exclusivity, low price, product performance, warranty, colour, feel, look, etc. according to the identified needs of your client and your selected value proposition. The Implementor's challenge is to build your strategic system so that you deliver this value at the lowest possible cost (C). The more that you can maximize V and minimize C, the greater the room for profit making, the more flexibility you have vis-à-vis competitive pricing, and the higher value/lower price ratio that you can offer in order to motivate the customer to make a purchase.

Figure 7.2 shows a typical value creation process (based on Figure 1.1 shown on page 8). Raw materials enter the organization already representing a certain value and having a certain cost attached to them (their purchase price). Examples include raw lumber, semi-finished parts for assembly, or information required by your business. As the raw materials move forward through the value chain, certain stages of the value creation process add a greater or smaller amount of perceived value and cost to your developing product or service. By the time your work-in-progress becomes finished product at the retail stage, it represents $V_{max}$ of perceived value and $C_{min}$ costs have been incurred throughout the process.

At each step of the value chain there are four generic ways by which you can either increase V or decrease C: by being more innovative, by improving product quality, by being more efficient, or by being more responsive to your customer's needs. For example, during the design phase, employees can be more innovative by adding more functionality to the product or by introducing a new multifunctional design team; they can improve the quality of the product by refining the designs they pass onto the manufacturing team; they can be more efficient by speeding up the design process; they can increase value to the internal customer by addressing manufacturing concerns in the assembly process. Every stage—and every individual working within an organization—must maximize value while minimizing the costs of doing so.

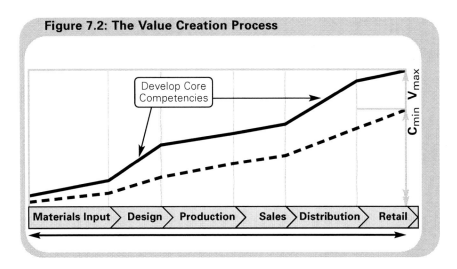

**Figure 7.2: The Value Creation Process**

## *Strategies for Creating Value*

There are two apparently conflicting models of strategy that we need to examine before proceeding further. Both have already been mentioned, but now its time to look at the strengths and weaknesses of each one in more detail.

### *Activity Sets*

Michael E. Porter states that "the essence of strategy is in the activities—choosing to perform activities differently or to perform different activities than rivals" (29, p. 64). The Implementor's task is to find a new value creation process that consists of a unique combination of value creation activities that allows an organization to achieve its strategic positioning at the lowest cost—and it's the term "unique" that is of particular importance here.

Let's assume that you "benchmark" against other organizations who are either trying to produce the same product or service as you or are using the same processes as yours in their organization. If everyone is trying to optimize the use of the same processes and activities to generate and deliver the same or similar strategic positioning, everyone will ultimately be delivering the same product by the same processes at exactly the same minimum cost. In other words, everybody will be operating at optimum performance using an identical strategic system. Each competitor will effectively cancel the others out—and the consumer will literally be spoiled for choice by having too many companies offering an identical product. They will have enormous buying power to negotiate better prices and terms and will probably become quickly bored with the product. A company caught up in this situation certainly doesn't fulfill my vision a world-class knowledge-based organization. Instead, it should seek to create more perceived value at less cost, and that means offering a unique value proposition through unique activities—or activities in an unique combination—in a way that it is difficult for competitors to copy.

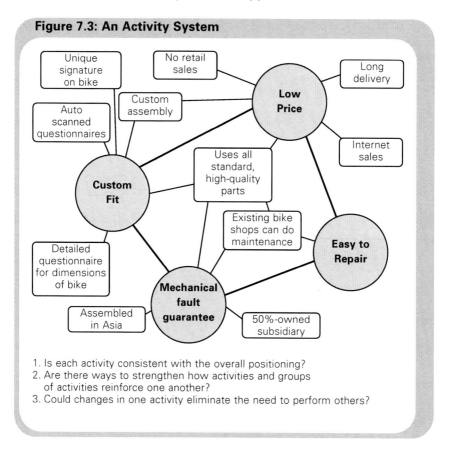

**Figure 7.3: An Activity System**

1. Is each activity consistent with the overall positioning?
2. Are there ways to strengthen how activities and groups of activities reinforce one another?
3. Could changes in one activity eliminate the need to perform others?

Perhaps the bicycle manufacturer example from the previous chapter would be useful again here. Imagine that you want your company to enter the still-growing mountain bike market. The current market leader has a good standard product with four different sizes to choose from, a bike frame made in-house from the latest composite materials, eighteen automatically changing gears, and sales that are made through specialty retail outlets. Your personal mission has always been to build and market mountain bikes and your horizon scanning and customer characterization research shows that there is an opportunity for you in that same market. What strategy will you pursue? What will maximize your chances for success? Should you copy the strategic system and activities of the current market leader? Or should you try to find a new and unique way of building, designing, and marketing your own bike that increases $V_{max}$ and decreases $C_{min}$? The market is still growing so there may be room for two companies producing similar products with similar cost structures. But aren't your chances of long-term success greatly enhanced if you can find a unique way to deliver the $V_{max}$—particularly if you employ a strategic system that the present market leader will have difficulty adopting?

## The Value Creation Process

Assuming that you decide to look for a new way of doing things, what might be some of the key activities you could do differently in your mountain bike business?

Imagine that you want to offer a high-quality, low-price, and guaranteed product that is uniquely designed for each individual user. Quite the challenge. But from your research as a Visionary, you feel very confident that there is a market for such a product—if you can deliver it.

Figure 7.3 shows a section of an activity sets diagram for our hypothetical bike manufacturing company. It demonstrates that in order to offer the value proposition, you need to create a custom bike from high-quality but standard parts; allow customers to measure themselves and send their measurements by fax, Internet, or e-mail; transmit information from questionnaires to all parts of the value creation process; ensure that bikes are repairable by existing bike repair shops; and not offer quick delivery (something not valued by your customers anyway). The diagram shows how you work backwards from the value proposition you want to offer so that you can determine exactly what unique activity sets you need in order to offer more value at lower cost.

This example illustrates the idea that every activity needs to be focused on delivering the promised service or strategic position. The more one activity fits, combines, interrelates, and interlocks with others the better—the more valuable it is and the harder it is to copy!

According to Porter, there are three types of activity fit:

- ⊃ **First-Order Fit:** *achieving simple consistency*. This first order of fit means there is, at minimum, consistency between the activity and the chosen strategic position; that is, if you're pursuing a low-cost strategy, each activity required to create the product or service is also low-cost.
- ⊃ **Second-Order Fit**: *reinforcing activities*. This second order of fit sees one activity automatically leading to or complementing another. It's more than consistency—it's synergy! You can see how having clients enter their measurements on scannable questionnaires allows you to avoid using expensive retail outlets; allows the required standard parts to be ordered from suppliers in real time; allows you to plan production; and ensures the high-value, unique customer signature applied on each bike can be obtained at no additional cost. With activities that reinforce each other, value is added, the strategic positioning is constant, and the costs of operating all the activities alone are markedly reduced.
- ⊃ **Third-Order Fit**: *optimizing effort*. This third order of fit is achieved when coordination and information exchange across activities eliminates redundancy and minimizes wasted effort. This is simply the optimal arrangement of reinforcement. It's as though you are killing three birds with one stone!

Obviously, the higher the order of fit and the more interrelated the activities, the more value is created for the lowest cost. Equally important, however, is that a complicated system of interlocking activities is difficult for competitors to copy or imitate. If you can design an organization with as much second- and third-order fit as possible, many of your competitors will have difficulty discerning what is really happening within your organization—they'll wonder how you manage to do what you do! Some competitors may see certain visible aspects of your service and product and copy it, but reproducing one activity will not in itself make a large impression on competitiveness. It may even cost your competitor much more to offer the service simply because you have designed such high orders of fit into your activities. For example, a competitor trying to add a unique customer signature to each bike without your information scanning system would find it prohibitively expensive.

It's clear that if you are designing an organization in an interrelated manner down to its smallest but still vital activity, your strategic position must have been carefully chosen and you must be ready to become a future shaper and place a huge wager on your idea working; once the activity sets and strategic system are put into place, it is very difficult, expensive, and time-consuming for you to change them.

## Core Competencies

Although not the first to visualize a company in this fashion, Gary Hamel and C.K. Prahalad were the first to expand on the concept of managing an organization as a portfolio of core competencies. They define core competencies as the "well-integrated skills" or "collective learning" of an organization (17). They suggest that an organization's challenge is to exploit these competencies in as many different industries, businesses, markets, or product areas as possible. Hence, as an organization grows, does more projects, applies its competencies in different areas, and learns, it continually acquires a greater depth of skill and expertise and thus continually builds up and renews its competencies. In addition, by horizon scanning, new applications for core competencies can be found and the organization can identify new core competencies that it will need to serve current markets or enter new markets in the future.

Hamel and Prahalad extend the logic of core competency management to suggest that anything not "core" to a business be subcontracted out to someone for whom it does represent core business—they can do it better, cheaper, or quicker because it's their area of expertise. Obviously, core competencies—although partially captured and saved on disk or in the form of patents—principally reside in the organization's employees, usually in its core members. It is your employees, your people, who actually own them—the real competency or capability is contained within their heads. So if you want to invest in competencies, you need to invest in growing and developing your people.

In their work, Hamel and Prahalad offer three tests for identifying core competencies. In their view, a core competency

1. provides potential access to a wide variety of markets;
2. makes a significant contribution to the perceived customer benefits of the end product; and
3. should be difficult for competitors to imitate.

James Quinn and Frederick Hilmer also outline the essence of core competencies, but take the definition even further. They suggest that core competencies are

1. skills or knowledge sets in the value chain and not products or functions (they are often skills that cut across traditional functions);
2. "flexible, long-platforms" of capability, useful for many applications and products, on which more product-oriented skills can be built;
3. limited in number (most authors suggest between one and six competencies per company is normal);

4.  unique sources of leverage in the value chain;
5.  areas where the company can dominate;
6.  elements important to customers over the long run (Quinn and Hilmer state that "at least one of the competencies should normally relate directly to understanding and serving its customers"); and/or
7.  embedded in the organizations systems (competencies cannot be particular to one or two people—they must be spread throughout a team or throughout the company). (30, pp. 45–47)

Bearing all the above in mind, in the past I have successfully used the following simple list to define core competencies. A core competency is

1.  something (a skill) we do really well;
2.  something not easily lost;
3.  something that forms a part of a key benefit (value) to our clients; and
4.  something not easily duplicated by other companies.

Examples of core competencies that we might possess include a strong capability in the design and manufacturing of engines and power trains, which could be applied to cars, trucks, or even lawnmowers. We might have competencies in managing large, overseas projects and in constructing large buildings, which could be exploited by seeking large-scale construction projects around the world. Alternately, we might have competency in stripping old furniture and in household design, which could be used to make home office furniture or imitation antique furniture. The possibilities and combinations are limited only by your imagination—and the skills of your employees.

As shown in Figure 7.3 (see page 124), areas that create the most value for your clients are the obvious places to build up your competencies. Strong competencies represent the key to building up a sustainable competitive advantage over your competitors. If you're a global multidivisional organization, you may find that some competencies are shared throughout the organization, while others are required only in certain product divisions or parts of the globe. Your core competency strategy should be built accordingly.

## Managing Core Competencies

Figure 5.1 (see page 87) shows some of the questions to ask yourself as you lead and grow your business and plan the development of your core competency portfolio. As well as using your competencies to deliver your current value proposition, opportunities to offer new products in the blank spaces by simply rearranging your existing portfolio of competencies need to be continually investigated. These markets represent great opportunities to maximize your return on capabilities (MRC) ratio.

When looking at future markets, you need to be continually horizon scanning to ensure that you will have the appropriate core competencies in place in five to ten years' time for maintaining and building your current businesses—it may even take that long to develop them. You also need to be verifying if there are opportunities to acquire or build competencies that will let you enter new "mega opportunities" markets such as biotechnology, information technology, the Internet, etc.—the markets of the future that could offer huge potential returns.

In summary, the key to operating a company as a portfolio of core competencies is ensuring that you are building your existing competencies for the future and seeking out new competencies that you will need to incorporate into products in the short-, medium- and long-term future. Therein lies the beauty of focusing your thinking around your organization as competencies rather than products: it's rare that you cannot build on your competencies over the long term. On the other hand, products tend to become obsolete very quickly.

As you grow, it may be feasible to acquire new competencies through the acquisition of smaller, more research-oriented organizations. For many large companies, such acquisitions are an important part of their knowledge and competency development function and a way of making "small bets" or playing the reservist role. However, as I mentioned earlier, many high-tech entrepreneurs are focused on being acquired by such large companies; the knowledge they possess is very mobile and their loyalty and motivation to remain with the new owners is not always to be taken for granted. It is crucial to assess cultural fit and verify that the new employees have a desire to be part of a large organization before executing any acquisition strategies. Many companies ignore this step and that is one of the many reasons why the vast majority of mergers and acquisitions do not create value.

## Reconciling Two (Conflicting?) Points of View

> *The challenge for the Implementor is to create the "masterplan."*

Viewing an organization as the management and marketing of a portfolio of core competencies has always been considered contradictory to the concept of building an organization with a fixed strategic position and a tightly interrelated strategic system. Supporters of the core competency approach say that you should simply focus on excelling at a few of the most important value creation activities and subcontract the things that are not crucial. The disciples of strategic positioning and systems say that it's important to choose your value proposition, remain with it, and remember that it's the way all activities—even the smallest ones—are combined that is key. Hence, they see subcontracting—even subcontracting what may seem like a minor activity—as a potentially fatal error. What happens if a competency in an as yet unimportant area eventually becomes crucial to your success? If you have subcontracted certain activities, you may have lost all your skills and knowledgeable people in those areas long ago.

It's a common notion that the core competency approach can work better in faster-moving markets and that an activity sets viewpoint is better suited to more slowly evolving markets. That may be so. But having an organization in which every small aspect of the strategic system is crucial to delivering the value proposition is probably better in all situations—providing it can be easily and quickly changed as the environment evolves. So can the two models be reconciled? I think they have to be; there is certainly a lot of value in each. Here's a list of key points that, when considered with an open mind, do not conflict with either model:

⊃ It's important for an organization to acknowledge its mission and stake out a long-term strategic position in the marketplace.

○ The design of an organization's strategic system, including relatively minor activities, can be a source of significant competitive advantage, even in an organization that may lack even a single real core competency.

○ There is no reason why the very outsourcing of certain activities cannot be built into an organization's strategic system. After all, partnerships and strategic alliances are a key weapon in most knowledge-based organizations' arsenal and are in themselves an activity and a facet of the strategic system that is very hard for existing competitors to copy.

○ Even within a tightly integrated strategic system there are some skills that need to be particularly well developed in order for an organization to compete successfully. Hence, all organizations need to actively develop and manage key areas of expertise—areas that can be called core competencies.

○ If an organization possesses competencies or expertise and wants to grow, create economic value, innovate, and be entrepreneurial, it needs to encourage itsemployees to identify new opportunities—in the present and the future—that the company can exploit. It should continually scan to determine what expertise is needed to remain competitive in the future. If it identifies opportunities that can be exploited (taking into account the existing mission and strategic system), it should do so. If not, it should spin out a new company or let the employees leave on good terms to start their own venture. If the organization does not develop such a culture, the people will leave anyway, either to move to competitors that are more entrepreneurial or to start their own businesses.

○ When new market opportunities are identified, a strategic position should be selected (through customer characterizations, etc.), possible activity sets should be generated, and a strategic system should be designed to uniquely deliver that value proposition. Once those tasks are accomplished, there may be excellent opportunities to generate additional and sustainable competitive advantage by building small value creation activities around core competencies to serve other markets—which is surely the objective of both strategic positioning and activity sets enthusiasts (e.g., Porter) and core competency supporters (e.g., Hamel).

For the VIP Implementor, the message is that ideally, everything should matter. By putting together unique arrangements of activities, companies can build up distinctive, fast-growing, and highly competitive businesses—even when they do not possess a single core competency. In addition, when it's obvious that an element of the value chain is creating substantial value to clients, you should seek to build your competency in that area. And once you've done so, all opportunities should be fully explored and exploited to increase your MRC ratio—even if you need to create subsidiaries or new divisions in order to build up the appropriate activity sets around a competency that will allow you to be truly competitive in each market.

## E-Business

The decision about doing e-business with your clients, be it business-to-business (B-2-B) or business-to-company (B-2-C), is ultimately determined by whether the client perceives added value if you do so. Defensive moves to counteract a competitor's e-offerings may become necessary, but the decision as to whether you and your competitor are simply wasting money through such a project depends on the client's perception of the offering's value.

However, even if you do not have an e-interface with your clients, you need to fully exploit the potential of technology within your strategic system in order to ensure that your effectiveness, efficiency, and costs are optimized.

Imagine if you could

- ⟳ reduce the number of people required to deal with 35,000 international employees' expenses to 2 by using technology;
- ⟳ receive 80 percent of incoming resumes through the web;
- ⟳ have 80 percent of your customers' FAQs answered by their visiting your web site;
- ⟳ achieve an additional 30 percent in sales from geographic areas not targeted by your marketing staff as a result of traffic on your web site; and/or
- ⟳ access pertinent information required for your job in real time at your workstation.

By building technology into activity sets and strategic system, the above (and additional) efficiencies and savings have been achieved by existing companies. Now imagine that you're trying to compete "the old way" with a company that is achieving the efficiencies described above. Who is more likely to win? Taking full advantage of technology to reduce costs and to free your people up to do their work more efficiently is an option that is not longer an option—it's simply a necessity.

## Outsourcing: The Big Dilemma

At some point, a decision has to be made about which activities an organization should do in-house and which should be subcontracted or outsourced. If the source of a company's competitive advantage is the possible combination and interaction of activities, it is impossible to accept the philosophy that everything but core competencies could or should be subcontracted. However, doing everything in-house sounds like a recipe for high costs, inefficiency, and perhaps poor quality. Under what circumstances is it best to keep an activity in-house? When should it be purchased from outside?

> *Taking full advantage of technology to reduce costs and to free your people is a necessity.*

Geoffrey A. Moore suggests that a company subcontract all activities that don't increase share price. The challenge with this philosophy is knowing in advance which activities will meet that criterion in the future.

The standard argument used to be that transaction costs—those costs arising from doing business with another company—often outweigh any advantage gained by outsourcing. With the advent of the Internet, electronic data interchange (EDI), e-mail, etc., and the growing culture of collaboration and partnerships, today the difference between dealing with an outside company versus another part of your own organization (which may be located on another part of the globe) is negligible. The costs and benefits are probably roughly the same; in many cases, "strong fences do make for good neighbours." And knowing that an important client can find an alternate supplier if they are dissatisfied can be a useful lever when dealing with outside suppliers.

## The Value Creation Process

According to Quinn and Hilmer, "the key strategic issue in insourcing versus out-sourcing is whether a company can achieve a maintainable competitive edge by performing an activity internally—usually cheaper, better or in a timely fashion, or with some unique capability—on a continuing basis. If one or more of these dimensions is critical to the customer and if the company can perform that function uniquely well, the activity should be kept inhouse" (30, p. 48). If we change this statement only slightly and substitute "any arrangement of activities" for "an activity" in the first sentence, I think it provides us with a guideline that fits with the proposed approach.

Some so-called virtual companies have gone to the extreme and have subcontracted many, if not all, parts of their value chain to organizations that are the best in their field. Thus, outsourcing itself becomes a key competency, a part of their difficult-to-copy activity sets—particularly useful when competing against highly unionized organizations with high fixed labour overheads.

Below I've slightly adapted Quinn and Hilmer's guidelines for what you should bear in mind when considering the insourcing/outsourcing decision:

1. What is the potential for obtaining competitive advantage from this specific activity set today and possibly at any time in the future?
2. Is this activity critical for defending a core competency or is it integral to an activity set or the strategic system?
3. What is the worse-case scenario that can result from outsourcing? How can this risk be diminished?
4. If a function is outsourced and subsequently becomes a critical part of an activity set, how can the expertise be reacquired?
5. Do you really want to do the activity (set) internally in the long run?
6. Can you license technology or buy know-how today that will let you develop best-in-the-world capability in the near future? Can you acquire and manage a best-in-the-world supplier to achieve competitive advantage?
7. Can a joint development program be established with a knowledgeable supplier that will ultimately provide the capability to optimize activity sets?
8. Can the item be purchased on a long-term basis as an off-the-shelf product or service from a best-in-the-world supplier? Is this a viable long-term option as volume and potential complexity grow? Is this adequate for your needs?
9. Does it make economic sense to outsource, taking transaction costs into account?
10. Can controls and incentives be established to reduce transaction costs below those of producing internally?

There are obviously many other issues you need to think about when considering outsourcing any activities: loss or gain in flexibility, shorter or longer design cycle times, loss or gain of specialized knowledge, loss of innovation capability, loss or gain of important information, corporate cultures and individual relationships—the list goes on and each opportunity must be considered on a case-by-case basis. However, the most important factor you will be taking into account when you outsource is that you are unlikely ever to be able to rebuild that competence internally to a level where it can be strategic in the future. You are therefore betting against that function ever being a key part of your value creation process. Given the radical changes that you see in business, this is the toughest factor to determine.

# The Strategic System

## Activity Sets, Competencies, and Outsourcing: The Process

So what is the best method for designing your unique strategic system? Although it appears a painstaking process, beginning with activity system diagrams (see Figure 7.3, page 124) is by far the best way of making sure you get everything right. In fact, it is probably the only way to see how everything interrelates and to make sure everything is coherent. Always remember: it is easier make changes on a computer screen than it is when the foundations are in place and the building is half finished!

Here's how to make your map:

1. Review the strategic position the Visionary has determined that you should to adopt.
2. Make a detailed list of everything that the client will perceive as maximum value (functionality, service, etc.) given the strategic position (the $V_{max}$ in the value creation equation).
3. Identify all the activities that you will need to incorporate into your strategic system in order to generate $V_{max}$. Use Post-it® Notes or software to arrange activities onto an activity map and start brainstorming about the possibilities of first- to third-order activities that would deliver $V_{max}$ at the lowest possible cost ($C_{min}$) and with the highest order of possible fit.
4. Identify the core competencies you will need in order to excel at exploiting this strategic system today and in the future. Which do you already possess? Which do you need to acquire or generate?
5. Which activities can you or should you outsource?
6. Ensure that everything is coherent with the strategic positioning and either supports or enhances it.
7. Do a second round of brainstorming about changes you need to make due to a lack of resources, structure, competencies, etc. and about how to raise first-order fit to second-order, second-order fit to third-order. The more interrelated and the higher order the fit, the better it is for you and the worse it is for your competitors.

Having developed the activity map, the work of the Implementor is just beginning. The major process still has to be developed—the value chain itself. How will you organize processes and activities into an organization?

## Building an Organization from an Activity Map

Having determined the activity map or activity sets, you now have to design the strategic system or the organization that can contain and facilitate these activities. In a sense, you are trying to design and build a new organizational jigsaw puzzle from scratch; you will design the shape of the pieces and the ultimate image (or vision) that the jigsaw will create (see Figure 2.4, page 38).

The strategic system consists of (for the sake of argument), "named pieces" or functions such as research and development, production, marketing, information systems, human resources, materials management, alliances, training, and reward and recognition systems. But even those can be changed! The focus is on developing innovative and advanced new pieces (around the processes or activity sets we've just identified) to deliver the strategic position as defined by the Visionary. Like a jigsaw, all the pieces are almost meaningless alone; yet each attaches snugly to perhaps three or four other pieces and together, they fit perfectly to make a whole, coherent image—your vision. If one piece is in the wrong place, no amount of forcing, bending, or snipping will make the whole picture come together.

Obviously, as shown in the diagram, the activities designed within the strategic system will determine the results that the organization will achieve. The strategic system must be superimposed on the required activity sets to facilitate the smooth and efficient generation of your value proposition. The activity sets can be monitored against predicted results and adaptations and improvements can be made, but it is essential that the principal design of the strategic system be correct at the outset during the planning stage. To reiterate an important point, errors are expensive to correct once the company is operating, even if they're spotted during start-up phase.

Questions you need to ask yourself at this point include: What makes the best sense in terms of creating entrepreneurial units? managing processes? reducing costs? optimizing communication? giving priority to Human Resources (HR)? creating synergy? taking advantage of location economies? building core competencies? I will return to this challenge in the next chapter.

## Crib Sheets for Value Creation

Before leaving the topic of value creation, it's important to have a last look at value creation on the organizational level. Are there universal mechanisms for generating both perceived and economic value creation that we can count on and use on an ongoing basis? The answer is "Yes." These mechanisms are largely the work of Yvan Allaire, someone who helped develop my personal interest in strategy while I was at the Université du Québec à Montréal (UQAM). Below is a modified version of Allaire's value creation thrusts. I believe that by focusing on these somewhat aggressive value creation drivers, an individual and an organization can go a long way to ensuring that they create economic value on an efficient, effective, and long-term basis—providing that they are applied with a win-win philosophy in mind.

### Value Creation Thrusts: Operations

1. *Improve/maintain the market position and economic efficiency of each business.* For example, segment your markets and seek out scale and scope economies wherever possible. Focus on improving customer services, examine the pros and cons of vertical integration, signal actions to warn competitors, and continually emphasize product and process innovation. Try to build switching costs into your offerings and, wherever possible, introduce barriers to entry into your markets.

2. *Invest in the business's (a) tangible and (b) intangible assets to maximize yield.* With your tangible assets, create new businesses to tap unused assets and seek out partners/clients to use assets that are being underutilized. Focus on managing time: speed up processes and cash inflows, slow down cash outflows, and implement just-in-time (JIT) delivery and EDI, etc. For intangible assets, ensure that you fully lever the client base and maximize "share of customer," client knowledge, and the value of your brand name.

3. *Build up your strategic system to reap the full economic potential of each business.* For example, optimize the organizational structure, the planning process, and the information technology systems. Eliminate all duplication and establish the appropriate motivational recognition and reward systems. Build an organizational culture focused on high performance and build up your competencies.

4. *Protect strategic resources (intellectual capital and core members) that are critical to the growth and survival of your business.* For example, erect barriers to the exit of key personnel (e.g., ensure benefits and incentive programs offer deferred rewards). Control the flow of key information and diminish the importance of individual people by ensuring you have depth in key areas. Wherever possible, use strategic but limited proprietary systems and train people with firm-specific skills that are not easily transferable to competitors. Try to locate strategic resources deep within the organization to reduce employees' exposure to competitors.

## Value Creation Thrusts: Financial

1. *Aim for an optimal capital structure.*
2. *Seek out yields greater than the cost of capital.* For example, only authorize capital investment projects with yields greater than the cost of capital (adjusted to the risk of each business within the corporation).
3. *Minimize the cost of funds through innovative financing instruments.* For example, use sophisticated financial management techniques; try to gain access to low-cost funds unavailable to others; minimize your financial transaction costs. Work closely with the investment community in order to minimize their perception of organizational risk.
4. *Minimize the effective tax rate by using careful fiscal planning and corporate strategies.*

## Value Creation Thrusts: Corporate

1. *Carry out restructuring moves: spin-outs, sell-offs, management buy-outs (MBOs).* For example, management should have information, expertise, and the will to quickly and energetically build value creation activities and transform or remove "value drag" operations. Economic value creation is crucial and time is money!
2. *Plan mergers and acquisitions based on realistic value creation principles.* Ensure that economic value will actually be created through mergers and acquisitions. Ensure that the planned synergies or cost savings can be obtained.
3. *Manage relationships with financial markets, investors, and other stakeholders.* For example, management's good relations in investment circles may translate into substantial value for the firm's shareholders.
4. *Set up high-performance governance structure and systems throughout the corporation.* Establish the correct balance of monitoring and autonomy; build appropriate information system and networks; establish remuneration incentives linked to creation of economic value; develop an effective strategic planning process.

These extremely useful and practical thrusts can be used on a continual basis as guidelines as you build and operate your organization.

## Key Points in Chapter 7

➲ The Implementor's objective is to design and implement a unique strategic system to deliver a unique value proposition.

➲ A strategic system is a complete organizational design superimposed on an arrangement of interrelated activity sets, a selected number of core competencies, and outsourcing.

➲ Develop $V_{max}$ while incurring $C_{min}$.

➲ Activity sets are arrangements of unique activities or unique arrangements of activities. Design them on paper first—it's much cheaper!

➲ Exploit the appropriate use of technology to its full potential.

➲ Core competencies are skills we do really well and form part of a key benefit to our clients. They are not easily lost and are difficult for other companies to duplicate.

➲ Outsourcing can be an integral part of a unique activity set.

## Questions to Consider

➲ Is your strategic system really delivering a unique value proposition that no one else can deliver at the same cost?

➲ Have you maximized the level of the order of fit?

➲ Can you eliminate some activities by redesigning your activity sets?

➲ Do you have a core competency agenda mapped out?

➲ Are you a technophile or a technophobe? Are your competitors exploiting the value of technology better than you are? How can you improve your organization's performance using technology?

➲ Are you outsourcing appropriately?

➲ Does your company recruit for a position based on the type of intelligence required?

➲ Do you take advantage of all Allaire's value creation thrusts?

## Chapter 8

The work described in the previous chapters, needed to build up an organization's mission, value proposition, strategic system, and core competencies, will all go to waste if the Implementor's final task is not accomplished. And that task is to create a culture and environment of entrepreneurship within an organization—regardless of its size. To create such an atmosphere in a start-up company is a relatively straightforward challenge—it almost comes naturally—but trying to implement "intrapreneurship" in an existing and perhaps large and stagnating organization is one of the most difficult challenges facing a VIP Leader.

Why is the creation of an entrepreneurial culture so important? Because all organizations must now operate in the fast-changing, highly competitive macroenvironment described in detail in Chapter 1. To flourish and succeed in that environment, all organizations need to be responsive, flexible, and working at optimum performance levels. They need every employee to be creating and delivering value, horizon scanning, satisfying stakeholders, building core competencies, etc. To achieve this, each individual must have the authority, flexibility, resources, and responsibility to deliver their results—and this cannot be done in a culture of rules and procedures, rigid controls, bureaucracy, layers of approval processes, and paperwork. Too many of today's organizations are still structured for Compliance, Control, Contract, and Constraint (Christopher Bartlett's 4Cs) rather than for Purpose, Process, and People (the VIP 3Ps) and the Ten Criteria for Success, which allow leadership and innovation to flourish. To succeed today, the "feel" of an organization must be one of flexibility, empowerment, creativity, teamwork, and open communication. In other words, there must be a culture of entrepreneurship and synergy, not one of dependency and control.

The objective of the Implementor is to create an aggregation of small entrepreneur-ial business units that are linked or networked together by an effective system of communication and information exchange. The overall performance of the organiza-tion is a function of the strength of each component unit and the effectiveness of their synergistic integration into the organization. The performance equation is simi-lar to the one presented in Chapter 2:

$$\text{Organizational Growth and Development} =$$
$$\sum (\text{Unit Growth and Development})^m = \sum (\text{Individual Growth and Development})^n$$

In the equation, $^m$ is the power of the synergy created between units due to the entrepreneurial culture, communication, and information networks created by the Implementor.

The challenge is analogous to the process of designing the mountain bikes described in the previous chapter. Several different teams may be involved in the design of the various component parts: the brakes systems, suspension, frame, gears, etc. The teams have to assume full responsibility and have the resources and authority to ensure that their particular part is perfectly designed. However, each and every part is also an integral part of the overall bike design and cannot be created in isolation. Different design parameters will be required from other teams, the design of many individual components may need input from external professionals, and there may be secondary value creation services set up to offer assistance in several areas. Most importantly, however, the individual parts will have to be designed in close collabora-tion and communication with teams working on the design of other parts; if they aren't, a perfectly designed gear system will simply not fit with the overall bike design.

The collaborative efforts with other teams may require many forms of interaction, from face-to-face meetings, e-mail communication, and teleconferencing, to the use of common databases, intranets, and software that allows concurrent tasking. For other parts of the process, someone on another unit may not be at all interested in hearing about the methodologies, problems, or reasons behind design or manufac-turing choices—they simply want to be confident that the piece will do its job once it's designed. With clearly defined deliverables, each team will be empowered to and responsible for the delivery of their particular contribution to the overall design; each team will be entrepreneurial in nature, but effectively integrated into the overall unit.

So what are you seeking to do here? At an organizational level, you need to create a company that decentralizes responsibility and pushes it down to the entrepreneurial units. At the same time, you have to make sure that there are simple but clear guide-lines in place to ensure that each individual in the units is empowered yet aware of the strategic objectives and guidelines that they must follow. Information networks, value chain support services, and reward systems must also be put in place to ensure that synergy is created between all individual units. Each unit needs ambitious per-formance targets—specific corporate challenges—for which they alone are responsi-ble and held accountable for achieving; yet these challenges must be perfectly aligned with the organization's overall strategic intent and corporate challenge. Under this scenario, the units feel and become a part of a larger and integrated whole and the shared vision, values, and mission act as behavioural guidelines that empower employees without a need for mechanisms to control their behaviour. At the unit level, your responsibility is to create such an environment among your work teams. Building such an exciting and motivational working environment is the final challenge for the Implementor.

# The Ingredients of an Entrepreneurial Framework

Christopher Bartlett and Sumantra Ghoshal have written extensively on the process of creating an entrepreneurial environment in large companies. They argue that the process of transformation and renewal into an entrepreneurial organization has three crucial steps: simplification, integration, and regeneration (the entire process occurs possibly over a number of years).

# Simplification

A synthesis of Bartlett and Ghoshal's work reveals that the following conditions must be in place to create an entrepreneurial culture: (1) senior management accepts that small entrepreneurial business units are the real building blocks of the overall organization; (2) the business units are broken down into small entrepreneurial entities; (3) together, senior management and the entrepreneurial unit heads devise appropriate performance and reward systems; and (4) each unit develops its own mission and values and runs as an individual, but interconnected, VIP organization (8, p. 136).

In fact, many large and successful organizations already operate as a network of entrepreneurial units. Bartlett cites examples such as 3M, ABB, GE, and Corning to illustrate how entrepreneurial-style businesses can function. Obviously one of the most important prerequisites for such organizations is the senior management's belief that breaking the company down into smaller entrepreneurial units is the way to move forward. Management has to adopt a bottom-up approach and accept that their organizations are literally disaggregated and built from a portfolio of interconnected entrepreneurial units.

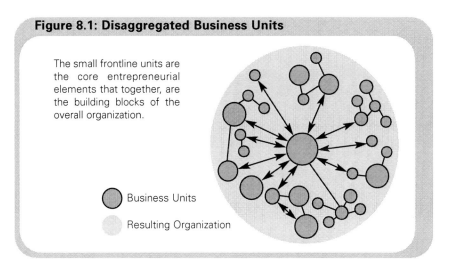

**Figure 8.1: Disaggregated Business Units**

The small frontline units are the core entrepreneurial elements that together, are the building blocks of the overall organization.

Business Units

Resulting Organization

Figure 8.1 shows the network of collaboration between different disaggregated units and the several bunches of units represent groupings that work to serve similar markets, share core competencies, or have operations or geographic areas in common. These units work more closely together than with others while maintaining separate unit missions, strategic intents, and corporate challenges. The resulting organization represents the tangible and intangible infrastructure—supplied by the corporate or organizational office—that supports the units' efforts. This paradigm is a very difficult one for many 4C organizations to accept. In these organizations there's a grave danger that breaking large units into smaller entrepreneurial parts will be done in name only; the real motivation is to maintain tighter control so that the senior administrators at head office can know exactly what each group is doing. This only causes greater harm to the organization.

> *There's a grave danger that breaking large units into smaller entrepreneurial parts will be done in name only.*

To achieve true subsidiarity, the roles of senior executives and middle managers have to evolve too. They must learn to spend more of their time providing guidance, support, and coaching to their unit leaders. This is obviously an enormous challenge for individuals who have focused their careers on exercising power and developing their management, administration, and control skills rather than leadership skills. In the case of the new leaders on an entrepreneurial unit, they will need to develop and fully use all the skills and expertise of the Visionary, Implementor, and People Manager if their unit is to be a success.

## Co-Missioning in Entrepreneurial Units

Is it appropriate for an entrepreneurial unit to go through the mission and stakeholder analysis process, to examine its strategic positioning, activity sets, and strategic system? The answer is a resounding "Yes"; this process is fundamental to the philosophy of VIP Leadership and to the development of a successful organization, irrespective of size. When a unit is part of a greater organization and goes through its own stakeholder analysis, it must remember that the most important stakeholder is its parent organization. What does the parent expect of the unit? That is the most important question for the unit to ask itself—and to ask the parent. Obviously all units must help the parent achieve its mission and strategic intent, to build its core competencies, and achieve its financial goals. The units must then ensure that this particular stakeholder is fully satisfied.

Going through the co-missioning process helps all of a unit's employees to build and buy into their own particular mission, which may have different stakeholders to consider and may elaborate different guiding values (although not conflicting ones) than the parent's. Providing nothing conflicts with the parent—and nothing should, as the parent is one of the main stakeholders that needs to be satisfied—the process can only be beneficial. As mentioned before, co-missioning is as much about going through the process as it is about the content of the final mission statement. As a result of the process, the employees should feel like an important asset and integral part of both their unit and the parent company.

## Establishing Performance Standards

In addition to carrying out its own VIP Visioning, each entrepreneurial unit needs to establish performance standards for itself in collaboration with the organization's executives. Clearly the overall organization must achieve certain standards of performance. The obvious one is that it probably has to achieve a certain level of financial performance or return on investment (ROI) in order to satisfy its shareholders. Performance review, however, needs to be more than a simple financial evaluation. There should be other factors or indicators that the unit and the parent measures, evaluates, and rewards. These could include such items as entry into new markets, development of new competencies, decreased turnover of employees, or a certain percentage of projects completed in collaboration with other organizational units. Targets set need to create a "stretch" for the unit—and must be in line with its strategic direction and mission. Recognition and reward systems also need to match the desired objectives, creating a "win" for all parties concerned—from the floor sweeper to the unit head.

Having jointly established criteria for performance with executives, the unit head should then be given the latitude to propose the means by which to attain them—a true entrepreneurial challenge. This may mean devising new strategic positions or new systems, or may entail requesting additional resources, be they financial, human, or technical in nature. Operational budget preparation would be carried out by the entrepreneur in close collaboration with the central office and capital allocation budgets would be incremental and flexible, but extremely rigorous. The reporting system should also be rigorous but simple enough so as not to create an administrative burden for the unit.

The problem is that although evaluating financial performance is one good way to indicate past performance, it is not a great indicator of what a unit's future performance will be. Is there an alternate way to ensure that all units contribute to the future development of the organization by establishing performance targets that are coherent with a culture of entrepreneurship?

In short, yes. One way to approach this question is to combine (a) the Balanced Scorecard™ approach, developed and popularized by Robert Kaplan, with (b) a model of delegation like Stephen R. Covey's DR.GRAC model. Let's look first at the Balanced Scorecard™.

## The Balanced Scorecard™ Approach

Throughout, this book argues that organizations can only expand through the growth and development of their employees. Now it is true that, sooner or later, most organizations must face up to some sort of scrutiny regarding financial performance. This may happen upon publication of the annual report, when the bank checks to see if the organization has achieved its projected results using borrowed money, or when the owner of the company realizes that there is a hefty tax bill to pay. Either way, some sort of financial performance evaluation is carried out.

It is certainly reasonable to argue that there are really only two ways to improve future financial performance: through increased revenue or improved productivity. The former is achieved by increasing customer satisfaction and the latter by improving business processes. Increasing customer satisfaction is also generally dependent on improving business processes, be it sales, marketing, or customer management methods; design processes to improve product functionality; or manufacturing processes to reduce costs or allow for customized manufacturing. The question is, how do you improve these processes?

It's hard to deny that the only way organizations can improve their business processes is by employees continually seeking to improve the existing ones or by introducing new, significantly better ones. Employees can improve processes or create new ones only if they are being creative and innovative, and are applying their learning gained through training or additional on-the-job experience. If you accept the preceding argument, it would appear that the only way for an organization to improve its financial performance is through the increased learning of its employees—the growth of its intellectual capital. This logic is shown diagrammatically in Figure 8.2.

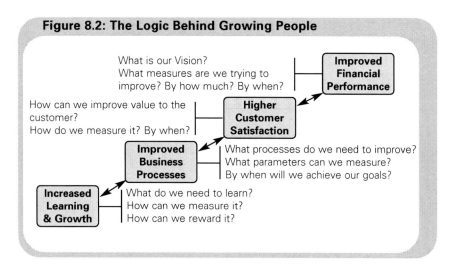

**Figure 8.2: The Logic Behind Growing People**

Kaplan takes the above logic and proposes that if you take four parameters—financial performance, customer satisfaction, business processes, and learning and innovation—set targets (or in VIP terminology, corporate challenges) for each, and measure the results, you should obtain a superior financial performance and a more balanced organization (25). This represents the essence of the Balanced Scorecard™ approach. What's more, if you have selected corporate challenges for each parameter that are indeed steps towards your strategic intent and delivery of your value proposition, you will ensure that all your activities are firmly fixed on your strategic objectives and mission; you are less likely to be poorly focused and too opportunistic. This all seems quite logical, but how is it accomplished in reality?

## The Balancing Process

Let's assume that you are in a corporation that consists of three different business units. The corporate office and each of the three units have already been through the co-missioning process and have developed mission statements. Corporate office has just outlined its longer-term strategic intent and is in the process of setting some corporate challenges to stretch itself forward towards attaining it.

To adopt a balanced approach that ensures the corporate challenges are successfully achieved, you need to examine what new levels of financial performance, customer satisfaction, business process improvement, and learning you will have to attain. To that end, you have to establish some key metrics for each of the four factors, which you can use to measure each of these factors as you move forward. In other words, you have to establish some key performance indicators (KPIs).

## Selection Criteria for KPIs

If you're looking to establish KPIs that will allow you to measure how well you are improving levels of customer satisfaction, processes, or learning, you need to find criteria that are:

- Specific (e.g., 5 percent improvement in customer satisfaction)
- Measurable (based on real business results used throughout the company, or results that are easily accessible)
- Challenging (difficult enough that people feel motivated to "stretch")
- Realistic (achievable enough that team members make an attempt)
- Available (are already used; can be supported by the current information management systems)
- Simple (easily understood and interpreted by users)
- Sensitive (variations are significant and easily seen)
- Mobilizing (serve to motivate employees and specific actions can be attributed to improvements)
- Relevant (pertinent, revealing, and linked to the overall success of the organization)
- Empowering (users can react based upon the results)
- Comparable (permit comparisons with competitors or industry)

Here are some examples of KPIs.

### Possible Financial KPIs

- % of revenues from high-margin clients
- # of new high-margin clients
- All traditional financial measures

### Possible Customer Satisfaction KPIs

- Target market penetration index (% of target met in volume, product, and customer mix)
- Quality index (frequency and severity of complaints and costs)
- Customer satisfaction index (customer survey of eight attributes)
- Preferred supplier ranking (% of customers that rank you in their top two suppliers)
- Product visibility index (comparison of product visibility to benchmark product visibility)
- % of on-time delivery

### Possible Processes KPIs

- % improved productivity
- % reduction in downtime
- % reduction in maintenance costs

⮑ Manufacturing product cycle time; measured from receipt of raw material through to receipt by customer

⮑ Net operating efficiency index (total finished products divided by theoretical production capacity of each unit and downtime)

## Possible Innovation and Learning KPIs

⮑ # of new techniques developed

⮑ # of pilot projects

⮑ % of revenues from new technologies or new products/services

⮑ Individual performance improvement index (improvements on annual performance evaluations)

⮑ # of continuous improvement initiatives (registered projects)

⮑ Internal recruitment ratio (# of positions filled internally divided by total recruitment)

⮑ # of new skills acquired, promotions obtained, or positions rotated

⮑ Turnover rate

⮑ Safety performance index (accident frequency rate and total lost workdays due to accidents)

Obviously the actual KPIs will be company-, unit-, and team-specific; your choice is fully dependent on what exactly you are trying to achieve (i.e., your strategic system). Each unit's KPIs should be as different as their strategic positions and corporate challenges.

Going back to our example of a corporate office with three business units, having determined the strategic intent, corporate challenges, and measures for the entire organization, corporate office should simply determine what contribution each of the three units would need to make in order for the overall organization to achieve its KPIs. Each of the three units would then establish their own strategic intents and corporate challenges and build their own Balanced Scorecards™ with their own KPIs in order to deliver their contribution.

The scorecard concept can be as in-depth and flexible as you need. It can be done on a computer and performance against KPIs can be tracked on a daily basis—many of the top management consulting companies offer corporate-wide Balanced Scorecard™ software among their profit offerings. Alternately, like economic value creation, the scorecard can be done on the back of an envelope—providing that exercise is accurate, implemented, and measures the right strategic criteria.

Different companies have played with this concept and have introduced parameters beyond the four mentioned above, ones they consider key to their organization's performance. If you have chosen to excel in Michael Treacy and Fred Wiersema's product leadership value discipline (see Chapter 6, page 101), then it might be worth developing some key parameters to measure product leadership. Perhaps your public image is something that is crucial to your success (in the pharmaceutical, forestry, or insurance business, public image is paramount); a scorecard can be used simply as a framework in which you can place any parameters you feel are key to achieving your strategic intent and success.

The real beauty of the Balanced Scorecard™ is that it can be used through all levels of an organization, from corporate to divisions to business units to teams and even to individuals. Each level contributes to the KPIs of the level above, and the message that your company is built on the expertise of its individuals is clear for all to see: your employees have proof of their contribution to the team and the organization's overall strategic objectives.

## A Visit to DR.GRAC

Having built up your Balanced Scorecard™ and established KPIs, how can you make sure that their use is fully adopted and becomes part of your organization's culture? The answer? Implement, measure, and reward their use by delegating through Stephen R. Covey's DR.GRAC model (which can also be used to create win-win agreements with individual employees as I'll explain in Chapter 10).

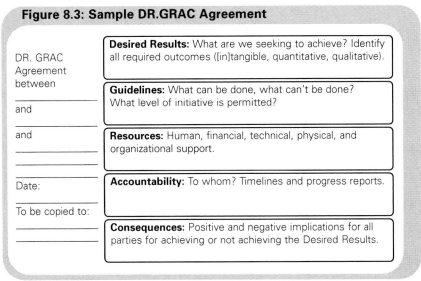

**Figure 8.3: Sample DR.GRAC Agreement**

| DR. GRAC Agreement between _____ and _____ | **Desired Results:** What are we seeking to achieve? Identify all required outcomes ([in]tangible, quantitative, qualitative). |
| --- | --- |
| and _____ | **Guidelines:** What can be done, what can't be done? What level of initiative is permitted? |
| | **Resources:** Human, financial, technical, physical, and organizational support. |
| Date: _____ | **Accountability:** To whom? Timelines and progress reports. |
| To be copied to: _____ | **Consequences:** Positive and negative implications for all parties for achieving or not achieving the Desired Results. |

Source: Stephen R. Covey

DR.GRAC basically says that for two parties to reach an agreement, they first have to agree on all the desired results (DR), which in this case are the corporate challenges (measured by the KPIs) on the four parameters of the Balanced Scorecard™. In the example of the corporation consisting of three business units, each unit would have determined its particular DRs with the corporate office. The two entities then have to discuss and determine what guidelines (G) must be followed en route to achieving the desired results and what human, financial, technological, or financial resources (R) will be made available to facilitate the unit's meeting the KPIs. Finally, accountability (A) to whom and for what has to be determined and the consequences (C) for the company, the individual unit, and its employees—whether positive or negative—need to be clearly explained. The latter item, C, includes any unit, team, or individual reward or remuneration that accompanies meeting or failing to meet the KPIs. Above is a form that you can use for initial DR.GRAC agreements.

By combining the Balanced Scorecard™ approach with DR.GRAC you can ensure that balanced targets are established and achievable for key parameters, maximizing the future financial security and performance of your organization. Every unit is clear about what is available to help achieve the results and what consequences that will follow if the KPIs are or are not reached. It's fair for everyone concerned and it's a concept firmly founded on organizational and employee growth and learning and an appropriate rewards system.

One key challenge when delegating is to ensure that the key corporate guidelines devised by the senior executives are communicated to everyone in the organization. You obviously do not want to create a lot of tight, complex rules that minimize creativity and empowerment—you're trying to get away from that. However, it is sometimes useful to implement common process rules for all teams or units so that everyone follows the same organizational rules.

Work published by Kathleen M. Eisenhardt and Donald N. Sull on this topic shows how some companies have devised "simple rules" that inform employees about the "company guidelines" regarding different business processes: what business opportunities one may or may not pursue, when and how one must communicate knowledge to others, what priority to give different clients' orders, etc. (14) The idea is to provide all employees with the same guidelines so that they have tacit organizational approval for their work and need not worry about whether they should take any particular action and suffer repercussions later.

Let's return to our mountain bike company example for a moment. Suppose this organization wants to establish some "simple rules" regarding new parts development. The rules could look something like this:

**Parts design improvements must**
- improve (a) overall bike performance or (b) lower business costs without hurting performance;
- have design teams that include one member from all other design units impacted by design change;
- have a design team with a member from manufacturing;
- be implementable within eight months; and
- generate a positive economic value creation contribution.

Adopting such rules would clearly communicate strategic guidelines to the teams' design units while leaving a lot of space for creativity in achieving the objectives.

Alternately, if the company is trying to encourage improved material sourcing partnerships, it could adopt rules for new partners as outlined below.

**New partners must**
- be ISO9000 qualified;
- have on-time delivery records of 95 percent and higher;
- have at least two working partnerships with university researchers in area of sourcing;
- offer at least a 5 percent reduction in current material costs; and
- offer at least an eighteen-month price guarantee.

Such simple and clear rules provide straightforward guidelines that people can use without needing verification. Materials sourcing people would simply use the rules as a "test" for potential suppliers. If suppliers pass, a new arrangement can be discussed; if they do not meet the criteria, the project has to be dropped immediately.

Such simple rules are often already in place on an unofficial basis and experienced staff in purchasing will already know that the company likes to do business with suppliers who are partnered with universities. The process of establishing rules just makes the process explicit and clear. It prevents wasted effort and empowers people to do their work without seeking approval at each step.

## Results of Disaggregation

The kind of disaggregation described in the preceding sections creates numerous benefits for the organization and for the individuals that populate its units.

1. Disadvantages of large, aggregated organizations such as excessive reporting, slow approval processes, slow reaction times, etc. are largely eliminated.
2. Entrepreneurs feel empowered to carry out their new role and are driven to achieve the performance target (that they helped establish) and to build and grow their units.
3. The search for new business opportunities can be initiated more rapidly and is more easily pursued.
4. Core competencies and other resources important to the unit can be better developed and managed. Continuous improvement within a unit becomes an easier process to implement and monitor. Projects such as reducing inventories, processing cycle times, etc. are not top-down measures forced on units; they are instigated by the entrepreneurs themselves to help them achieve performance targets.
5. The central office has more time to evaluate corporate strategic objectives and can better evaluate which value-adding services it should be offering to its units.
6. Former administrative personnel and middle management are refreshed and renewed as they take on new roles and learn to develop themselves in new areas. Their roles become focused on offering support and guidance to the entrepreneurial units and seeking ways to link and lever resources available across the units. They work on improving communications regarding best practices and on developing mechanisms that allow for unit-based competencies to be accessed throughout the company. They also focus on developing the organization's people. Jack Welch of GE has stated that middle managers need to see their roles as a "combination of teacher, cheerleader and liberator, not controller" (23, p. 81).

Despite all the benefits and the tools available, the disaggregation of an organization is not an easy task to accomplish. Strong centralized corporate cultures, lengthy and bureaucratic administrative procedures, and inflexible and demotivating reward and recognition systems are difficult to change and the full support of senior management is essential if disaggregation is to happen. Yet, it is the way forward for all organizations if they are to remain competitive. It is also an enormous opportunity for both professional and personal growth, for those who are interested in stepping forward to take on the challenge.

If individuals cannot adapt to the new environment, they often end up leaving an organization—some of their own accord, but others have to be dismissed. Preferably they find a new position in another organization with the assistance of your Human Resource (HR) outplacement personnel. Those who cannot or will not adapt need to find other organizations that are still in the 4C mode. Their departure is often a win-

win: they are able to find work in an environment where they feel less stress and their skills are still of use, and you are able to recruit someone more suitable to the new role and environment.

I have always enjoyed using Christopher Bartlett's butterfly metaphor regarding corporate renewal. He says, "The metaphor of a caterpillar transforming into a butterfly may be romantic, but the experience is an unpleasant one for the caterpillar. In the process of transformation, it goes blind, its legs fall off, and its body is torn apart, as beautiful wings emerge" (6, p. 14). Does it have be like that? My belief is that change is usually a painful experience—but even more so if you fight it. If you go with the flow once the process has been initiated, it can be a challenging yet still liberating experience for everyone concerned.

The usual time for organizational transformation and change is when a crisis hits; until then, inertia will often prevent any radical change from being implemented. However, as David Hurst points out, it's part of the organization's leaders' role to provoke a mini-crisis in order to start the process of organizational renewal (recall the comparison to a healthy forest fire from Chapter 2).

Many external macroenvironmental trends, particularly those observed while horizon scanning, can be conveniently used as a catalyst to justify that change is required. The arrival of a new technology (or even the threat of it), the opening of new markets, a fall in a currency, etc. can all be the spark that lights the fire. Engaging senior staff in a half-day session to analyze macrotrends always serves as a wake-up call to how quickly things are changing; they realize that they need to start preparing for a future where all the current "constants" have been changed. Launching new corporate challenges, implementing Balanced Scorecards™ and DR.GRAC agreements, and establishing of some simple rules can then serve to energize and mobilize individuals and start them moving in the new direction.

### Becoming an Aggregated Disaggregated Organization

Let's return now to Bartlett and Ghoshal's premise of three crucial steps—simplification, integration, and regeneration—in the process of an organization's transformation and renewal. Having thoroughly examined disaggregation or simplification, it is now time to look at the integration and regeneration phases.

## Integration and Regeneration

During simplification, the organization is "broken down" in entrepreneurial units and is given a simple but "stretching" corporate challenge. For example, GE's Jack Welch told his employees "to make each business number one or number two in its industry" (6). While working towards simplification, the infrastructure, the size of corporate staffs, the nonstrategic businesses, etc. can all be discarded; the primary focus is giving the entrepreneurs of the core businesses the freedom to develop new strategies and to take control of their own operations. By issuing a simple "stretch" challenge, reducing overhead and barriers to change, and offering new kinds of support and freedom to manoeuvre, the entrepreneurs become responsible and accountable for the results. Integration (the building of inter-unit relationships) and regeneration can only happen and are only sought once the entrepreneurial units are successfully operating.

One key element of any effort to integrate teams or units and to generate real synergy is the creation and management of a variety of networks linking up internal and external stakeholders.

## Communicating Knowledge, Not Information

It is clear that as organizations advance further into the third millennium, the management of all types of networks will become an increasingly prized core competence. As alluded to earlier, organizations are already becoming little more than slightly denser areas of activity within already sprawling networks and clusters. The Internet has simply decreased transaction costs to the point that integration or agglomeration offers few advantages; it is now intellectual capital (employees), branding, and network management that offer competitive advantage.

Hence the paradox discussed earlier in this chapter: as organizations are broken down into entrepreneurial units, you also need to be creating inter-unit communication networks, systems, and processes that will facilitate overall organizational learning, diffuse knowledge, and create synergy. If this doesn't happen, each of the entrepreneurial units simply acts as a well-managed individual element and would be better served by being spun out from the parent company to be completely free—a true small business.

To facilitate a strong degree of interlinkage—between individuals within a unit and between different entrepreneurial units—new communication channels and tools must be introduced, particularly in traditional 4C organizations where most communication systems tend to encourage vertical rather than horizontal communication. (If communication is favoured at all, that is!)

Sharing knowledge rather than information also poses unique challenges. In some organizations, individuals pass on enough information to cover themselves—just in case there is ever any follow-up—but not enough for the receiver to really know what it means, what is valuable, what priority to give it, or what they should do with it. Other organizations see knowledge flow freely among certain groups to the exclusion of others. In a third scenario, information is passed around in such large volume that the important items are lost among reams of meaningless numbers and reports.

> *Despite all the benefits and the tools available, the disaggregation of an organization is not an easy task to accomplish.*

Gaining knowledge implies the receipt of "know-how"—that is, after having received information, you know how to use it. Passing on knowledge as opposed to mere information usually requires that the sender "care" about whether the receiver has understood the message, knows what it means, and has learned it. It certainly takes more time and effort on the part of both the deliverer and the receiver. Entrepreneurial organizations have to take the time to build up a sense of belonging and shared mission to ensure a "caring" factor and the notion that "me helping you is me helping me."

Now that we are often functioning in virtual environments or at a distance for colleagues or clients, the communication of knowledge is an even more demanding task. Some organizations have begun encouraging the reintroduction of tea and/or coffee breaks so individuals—even those on the same team—can actually sit in a relaxed atmosphere and discuss common issues and exchange useful knowledge. During this time, they are encouraged to "think" and not to "do." However, when our colleagues, clients, or suppliers are only known by their e-mail addresses, such communication is at a premium. Charles Handy discusses companies setting up office environments similar to a coffeehouse or club where people simply drop by to "chat" and "exchange" with their colleagues rather than to do "work."

> *Passing on knowledge as opposed to mere information usually requires that the sender "care."*

David Hurst has written extensively about how the behaviour of the Kalahari bushmen, having evolved from hunters to herders, can be related to the behaviour of people in offices. He notes how companies such as GE, 3M, and Corning try to arrange—particularly in the successful research and development (R&D) departments—for workers to "chat around the camp fire" in order to release tensions and keep in touch. They have found that the best ideas are often generated during these relaxed downtimes. GE goes so far as to insist that researchers change lunch partners so that casual contact will occur between researchers from different disciplines! Hurst also states that, despite e-mails, video-conferencing, and webcasts, "real communication takes countless hours of eyeball to eyeball, back and forth. It means more listening than talking…it is human beings coming to see and accept things through a constant interactive process aimed at consensus" (23, p. 81). What's more, despite the advent of electronic communication, most senior business people or salespeople are finding that they now need to spend more time "on the road" building face-to-face relationships with the individuals they know through the Internet or via an e-mail enquiry. High-tech does need high-touch!

Given this new reality, and the fact that the management of both intra- and extraorganizational networks—with colleagues, suppliers, partners, buyers, members of strategic alliances, etc.—has become a major part of most business peoples' tasks, the management of several different types of networks has become a key skill of the Implementor and plays a vital part in any organization's success.

## *Managing Networks*

With your organization broken down into entrepreneurial units there is always the danger that communication, learning, and synergy will not flourish in the "honeycomb" because everyone is so focused on developing their own businesses. To prevent this, the first thing is to set strategic objectives that can only be achieved by units working together. Next, you need to actually reward collaboration between units. If it's not measured and rewarded—perhaps as a parameter in your Balanced Scorecard™ and DR.GRAC—then individuals will not find a very positive motivator when they ask themselves, "What's in it for me?"

One initiative that needs to be undertaken quickly is the set-up of communication and common information exchange mechanisms across the entire organization. These may be face-to-face meetings between individuals from different units or simply intranet sites where "learning" is posted. Again, the latter only happens if individuals are encouraged to post new knowledge by being rewarded for doing it or by facing consequences for not doing it.

Among the many options available for encouraging communication are:

1. Setting up shared access to a common database of technical information.
2. Holding regular face-to-face meetings between team and unit leaders to brainstorm and problem solve on specific topics.
3. Arranging meetings between specialists from different units.
4. Encouraging job rotation between units so learning is transferred and informal networks are developed.
5. Forming ad hoc multifunctional and multi-unit teams to solve particular problems.
6. Setting up conference calls, list serves, e-mails, teleconferencing, etc. to discuss issues and joint opportunities.
7. Providing simultaneous access to design software for members of different teams.

To further facilitate communication, there are three different types of networks that organizations must learn to manage.

## 1. Internal Formal Networks

It's an unwritten rule in many organizations that to get anything done, you have to circumvent the formal approval process: if you need a collaborator for a new project, you're better off finding an external partner than looking for one internally; if you need support for a new project from your peers or superiors, the only way you'll get it is by "scratching their back," bad-mouthing a colleague's project in a one-on-one with your boss, or devaluing competing projects in a win-lose–style competition. This is not a culture that encourages learning, collaboration, or synergy—yet this is how a lot of people view the formal communication and approval processes.

Managing the formal committee network is an art that must be mastered by all entrepreneurial unit managers. The "political" support of members of the formal network is often the difference between a unit's project moving forward and its cancellation. Without it, your project may die irrespective of its merits. Members of the formal network are all stakeholders in your team's future: they all need satisfying and they are all individuals. There may be a collective way of thinking that exists within any organization, but individuals all come to the table with their personal agendas. It is the job of the team's participant member to ensure that they know exactly what that agenda is—what "win" the others are seeking. The use of stakeholder maps (discussed in detail in Chapter 4) can be extremely useful for managing internal relationships and understanding exactly what it will take for colleagues to feel that they are getting a "win" and, in turn, supporting your initiatives.

Formal networks also need to be established for information exchange rather than for simply seeking project approval. Specialized technical networks and experts in marketing from different units must be encouraged to meet, share knowledge, and learn. Without evidence of the latter, participants will soon recognize that there is little value to be gained by investing in the network, so concrete corporate challenges must be established for each network—meeting for meeting's sake is not what you are seeking here.

Formal networks can also be useful when you are seeking to embed successful practices and processes into the operations of an organization. It can ensure best practices, legal obligations, regulations, ISO standards, etc. are carried out and reported. It can ensure that the information required by all stakeholders (particularly financial institutions and shareholders) is collected. However, although your formal network may provide a solid foundation for information flow and communication, the occasions are rare when it will provide a primary source of new ideas and innovation, which is what a successful company needs to encourage. Hence, you need to build and manage other networks to offer additional value to that offered by formal networks.

## 2. Internal Informal Networks

Members of these networks can make an invaluable contribution to organizational communication and learning. Members are often individuals who have little formal authority. However, they are generally leaders or key influencers and are deemed by others to be trustworthy, open to collaboration, and concerned about other people and the future of the company. Hence, they can play a major role in fostering "grass-roots" input and commitment. They can help diffuse information quickly through their extensive network and they are recognized as a source of knowledge, resources, and solutions when issues arise. They are often breeding grounds for new visions, ideas, and innovation. As a result, people confide in them.

*Formal or informal gateways give an organization a public face, a source of market, and competitive intelligence.*

The major advantage that these networks have over formal ones is the openness of the individuals, the flexibility in terms of who is involved, the methods they use to communicate, and the frequency of that communication. In a sense, the members of these networks are all "volunteers," which means they are difficult to manage (or manipulate) but can be incredibly effective. Informal networks can more easily call upon expertise from other departments and other companies; they can use e-mail and voice mail more openly as they know the discussions are not "minuted." True dialogue and discussion can take place when people feel that they are being listened to—an important aspect of communication often ignored, but which keeps everyone in touch, builds morale, releases tensions, and prevents pressure from building up and people getting fixed to their positions.

The informal nature of the network allows for an ongoing process of mutual assistance, creativity, and problem solving. Membership in these networks is obviously based on one's attitude, behaviour, and contribution—if someone doesn't contribute, is not supportive, or is proved untrustworthy, membership is easily withdrawn.

Informal networks are often the forum where potentially difficult topics can be more readily debated in a more casual context until consensus is reached or stakeholder "positions" on a topic can be identified before the issues are discussed at a formal level.

***Formal Informal Ambassadors.*** Some company presidents actually appoint "informal ambassadors" who simply rove between different parts of a unit or between units, building an extensive informal network so that they can collect, sort, and communicate knowledge that can be of immediate use in other areas of the organization. Using formal channels to communicate the same information would be ineffective, untimely, and the information would stand a good chance of never reaching the intended target in its original form. Through ambassadors, crucial operational or strategic knowledge can be rapidly diffused through a high-trust medium—something that within many organizations is in desperate short supply. The cost associated with hiring such a roving network pays dividends well beyond any financial returns providing that the individuals can move freely and build win-win relationships where they see opportunities to do so.

There is one major limitation to the effectiveness of informal networks and it is directly linked to one of the reasons why they are so effective. The problem arises when a project—or an individual involved in a project—supported by the informal network faces resistance from someone in the formal chain of authority. This barrier can be overcome if the informal network is viewed as valuable and if it is sufficiently developed so as to include members who also participate in formal networks.

## 3. External Ambassadors

Traditionally it has been the job of the organization's president, the divisional managers, or team leaders to "link" their entity with others—whether inside the organization or with external stakeholders. Today, all managers spend a lot of time cultivating and managing links or relationships with external stakeholders, which may be done by sitting on company committees, participating in multifunctional team projects, dealing with suppliers or alliance partners, or by making proposals to financiers or shareholders.

These relationships can be either formal or informal in nature. Different people have used different expressions to describe the individuals who carry out this function: gatekeepers or gateways, ambassadors, links, etc. However, all titles generally fall under the term "networking" and involve building relationships with stakeholders, customers, and potential future partners, and overseeing contact management databases of the names of people who, one day, may all be in a position to serve the needs of the organization. Because this network must be in place before it's actually needed—time is of the essence when assistance is required—various people in an organization need to fill the "keeper of the gateway" role. Often an organization will have people "specialize" in a particular gateway: a person with an interest and knowledge in technology may join a network of technology-oriented people; someone in finance may link up with the financial community; etc.

Formal or informal gateways give an organization a public face, a source of market, and competitive intelligence. Gateways are also useful for signalling to outsiders the right person they should deal with inside a large organization—there's nothing worse than trying to find the "right" person to talk to when you're dealing with a large global multinational.

Viewed from outside the organization, a valuable gatekeeper must appear (and be!) well informed and credible, and must truly represent the organization. Here, the word "trustworthy" pops up. To cultivate a relationship, people need to know that there is a possibility of a win-win arrangement somewhere down the road.

As a gatekeeper, you need to find a balance between communicating everything and nothing to your colleagues. What may be of interest, what should not or need not be disclosed—it's all up to your judgement. The challenge is to communicate just the right amount of information to the right people so they can decide how best to act on it. To do this well you need to have spent time with your different teams to really understand what they are interested in, working on, and what they'd prefer to avoid dealing with. It sounds simple, but in fact it's not an easy mandate.

## The Challenges of the New Organization

Turning organizations into interrelated entrepreneurial units is obviously not an easy change process. It demands new behaviours from staff (and perhaps new staff), the development of new skills, the relinquishing of old power positions in senior management, and the assumption of responsibility at lower levels of the organizations that many say they want, but most hope never to receive.

Trust, and the trustworthiness of each employee, is continually put to the test. Transforming your organization into an entrepreneurial one demands a lot of trust be in evidence between the senior management and the entrepreneurs—and within the entrepreneurial teams themselves. Even today, when the opportunities to work more efficiently and effectively at home abound, many people are still required to go into the office because an organization or a particular boss does not trust employees sufficiently to let them work unsupervised. In the new environment, the degree of trust that you are willing to extend to your subordinates and colleagues will probably dictate your probability of success more than anything else.

However, by setting up mission statements, Balanced Scorecards™, and DR.GRAC agreements along with value-added and easy-to-use networks, the argument for adopting the paradigm of an organization as a synergistic "package" of entrepreneurial units is very persuasive, especially if you are seeking effective ways to achieve success in the new environment and to create value for customers and stakeholders. Bringing this paradigm to life completes the work of the Implementor. It's now time for the People Manager to take over and start developing and growing your employees. The next chapter starts this process by looking at what steps need to be taken in order to create synergy between employees.

# Key Points in Chapter 8

- ⟳ Financial factors are a great indicator of each unit's past performance. But you need to focus on and measure improving customer service, business processes, and organizational learning to better ensure future financial performance.
- ⟳ Issue corporate challenges and Balanced Scorecards™ for each business unit in your organization.
- ⟳ Key performance indicators (KPIs) measure factors that are crucial to your organization or unit's strategic positioning and future success.
- ⟳ DR.GRAC agreements ensure clear understanding, transfer of responsibility, and that resources and guidelines are given for each win-win agreement.
- ⟳ Devising some simple rules for different processes in your business can provide employees with clear but simple guidelines to follow, ensuring strategic coherence and employee empowerment.
- ⟳ Knowledge is transferred when people care that the other person has received it.
- ⟳ Managing networks in an entrepreneurial organization is crucial to its success. There are three different types of networks: internal formal, internal informal, and external gateways (ambassadors).

# Questions to Consider

- ⟳ What parts of your processes are crucial to improving your unit's performance in customer service, processes, and learning?
- ⟳ What key performance indicators (KPIs) can you establish to measure your organization's future performance in all its key business areas?
- ⟳ Does your team have its own mission? Do you set corporate challenges?
- ⟳ How can you encourage inter-unit collaboration by setting up corporate challenges, Balanced Scorecards™, and an appropriate measurement and rewards system?
- ⟳ What useful and empowering simple (behavioural) rules can you set up in order to make some implicit rules explicit?
- ⟳ Can you map out your internal stakeholders using a stakeholder map?
- ⟳ Do you use the three different types of information networks? How would you rate the quality of your personal network in each area (on a scale from 1 to 5)?
- ⟳ Does your organization or unit "feel" entrepreneurial? If not, why?

# Part 4: The People Manager

V

I

P

## Chapter 9

*Give me a lever and with one finger I will lift the world.*
—based on a quote from Archimedes

With the work of the Visionary and Implementor complete, it is time for the People Manager to lead your people forward in achieving the mission you have created and making the strategic system on the drawing board come to life. The only way to do that is by facilitating the synergistic growth of your people and by allowing each one of them to be leaders themselves. Without synergy, the organization will always remain a group of individuals—it will never become a living and thriving entity. The People Manager's task is to make this dream of synergy a reality. Remember the formula:

Organizational Growth and Development = $\Sigma$ (Individual Growth and Development)$^n$

where $n$ is the synergy created between individuals due to the efforts of the People Manager.

The objective of the People Manager is to really create the lever mentioned in the quote that opens this chapter. People Managers develop a team mentality, a culture of learning, win-win situations, and enable your group of individual employees to achieve more than they ever could do alone or simply working side by side. 1+1 = 2 is not a representation of synergy; 1+1 = 3 is what synergy is all about.

This chapter explores the mechanisms for achieving synergy and explains how VIP Leaders can and must break the laws of mathematics.

# A Role Model—Who, Me?

What's the best way to change the way things are done? Start by changing yourself. There is little value to expounding the virtues of synergy, encouraging creative collaboration between colleagues, or talking about learning and risk-taking if at the same time you are acting in distrustful ways, withholding information, playing power games, or chastising people who try to innovate but "fail." You must be the one who exemplifies the way you'd like your colleagues to behave.

Unfortunately, when you're trying to change your own behaviour, it's normal that from time to time you will make mistakes and fall back on old ways—that is a natural part of the learning process. However, to prepare the ground for such occasions, the best policy is to talk openly with your team about what it is you are trying to do and excuse yourself in advance for regressing to old habits in stressful situations. Make them understand that you're trying to improve the way you do things, trying new behaviours—but you're only human and might slip up every now and again.

Obviously, by taking a risk and trying to change and improve yourself, you will leave yourself open to mockery—but once people realize that you are serious and are making a real effort, most will admire your courage and motive. If they realize they stand to benefit from the change, they may even support you in your efforts! You will probably be surprised as to how many people will be there for you; as for those who aren't, there is nothing you can do—you cannot change others. You must accept that you are changing yourself because you believe it's the only way to go in your own development, not because you are consciously or subconsciously hoping that everyone will follow.

# Building Trust to Create Synergy

Think of someone in your workplace whom you don't trust 100 percent. What happens when you have to work with that person? You are probably very selective about what information you pass on to them; you probably (quite wisely) spend energy "watching your back"; you are probably more inclined to work alone than include your colleague; you are probably more stressed, anxious, and possibly quite unhappy about working in such an environment. In contrast, in a high-trust environment, you can relax, be more comfortable, let your guard down, and invest all your energy positively. You are more prone to share information and knowledge with colleagues, to support and coach them, and, consequently, there should be more opportunites to create synergy. People want to work with each other because it's fun and stimulating, and everyone can learn something from their colleagues.

So the most crucial element that you need in place before collaboration, synergy, and learning will develop is Trust—with a capital "T"—throughout and between each entrepreneurial unit. If you or your management team are not trustworthy, if the structure and decision-making processes are not transparent and fair, if communication is not open, if the reward and recognition system is not just; if any one of these are not in place, then neither collaboration nor learning nor synergy can flourish. It's like trying to build a fire with soaked wood.

In large organizations, some of the above factors—the remuneration system, for example—have been fixed by the corporate office and unions in protracted negotiations. Your efforts need to take into account this reality: it's part of the "structure" factors to consider in your Diamond-E assessment. Should you try to change these before seeking to create a collaborative, synergistic environment within your business unit or team? No—you may be retired before that happens! But you have to recognize that there is a component of your Diamond-E that will always be clashing with your objective and the way you are running your team. However, explaining this situation to your team will go a long way to alleviating the problem and, often, there is room to manoeuvre with regards to nonfinancial rewards, which can assist in recognizing and rewarding the behaviours that you are trying to encourage.

Table 9.1 presents an extensive list of behaviours that both encourage and destroy trust in an organization. How many of these behaviours are practiced regularly within your company? How many people in your office do you really trust 100 percent? How many people in your office trust you 100 percent? Why?

### Table 9.1: Building and Destroying Trust

| Behaviours That Create Trust | Behaviours That Destroy Trust |
| --- | --- |
| ⮌ Honouring commitments | ⮌ Making commitments you don't intend to keep |
| ⮌ Delivering what you have promised | ⮌ Failing to deliver what you have promised |
| ⮌ Keeping your word | ⮌ Being irresponsible |
| ⮌ Being honest yet compassionate | ⮌ Telling lies and being inappropriately harsh |
| ⮌ Respecting others | ⮌ Disrespecting others by showing (having) prejudices; Being unethical, arrogant, a hypocrite, or on a "power trip"; Stealing credit |
| ⮌ Having the competency to do your job | ⮌ Being unreliable |
| ⮌ Apologizing when you need to | ⮌ Gossiping about, backstabbing, betraying others |

To change the situation, the only thing you can do, starting from this moment, is to cease exhibiting behaviours that destroy trust and start investing in those that build it. You must express the vision and values that you believe in and try to live by them. Once you can say that you have honestly begun to do that, you can start to explain your new behaviour to others by illustrating how your past behaviour harmed the organization and your efforts to build relationships. Most people are not naturally of bad faith; they simply adopt behaviours at work that they would find unacceptable in any other environment—but it's the prevailing culture in most organizations.

Building trust is a long-term project. It takes a long time to build and it can be destroyed easily. How many times does it take for you slip up before all your positive trust-building effort is lost? The unfortunate reality is that you only need talk disrespectfully behind a colleague's back once and the trust you have built up in the people around you will be seriously undermined. People who overhear you will wonder just what you say about them when they are not present.

Ideally, if you can create an organizational culture that values activities in support of trust-building, all you will need to do is recruit people who naturally tend towards these behaviours—and your first task as People Manager will largely be done. But how many recruiters check for "trustworthiness" when hiring? It's not an easy quality to spot on someone's resume.

Trying to be trustworthy yourself in a nontrusting environment is particularly challenging. However, it *is* possible—all it takes is for you to resolve to always exhibit this quality. Unfortunately, you may find that being trustworthy and honest will build a barrier between you and a limited number of people as they come to realize that you are "different" in a way they perceive as being threatening to them. Being a "good" person can irritate those who rely on other ways of behaving, but it's a price worth paying in order to be more at peace with yourself. Over time, the trusting relationships you build will more than compensate for a few lost "friends."

## *The Characteristics of Great Teams*

Obviously, if one plus one is to equal three, the two individuals involved in the equation must be different—why else would they need each other? Moreover, they need to be able to value the differences that exist between them. Generally, people are comfortable working with other people who show work characteristics, beliefs, and ways of thinking and behaving that are similar to their own. But if you work on a team where everyone has the same paradigms, ideas, and personalities, "group think" can quickly prevail. Creating synergy demands dialogue; you need to listen to other people's ideas, value their expertise, and consider their different point of view. By working together, listening, supporting, and being open, you can create something productive that neither of you could have generated while working alone.

Organizations need a mix—analysts working with artists, capitalists working with socialists, North Americans with Asians, etc.—if they are going to generate some truly new and synergistic ideas, processes, or products. They need to be able to work together creatively as a single unit with a common goal in order to generate maximum value creation.

Hopefully everyone has had the opportunity at some time in their life to be part of a great collaborative team. It may have been during university in a group seminar, it may have been in a temporary short-term project, or it may have been in a previous position before layoffs killed the sense of collaboration that had taken many years to develop. Irrespective of the duration or the circumstances, the vast majority of people will look back on those times with great fondness, and are probably trying somehow to create that same feeling. Or they would jump at the chance to work on a team where such a culture existed.

When a great team forms, it often feels like a separate community has been created within a workplace; you feel part of something unique in which everyone shares and cares for everyone else. I remember my early consulting days when I was a part of a young group at an organization. The eight of us were all interested in learning and proving ourselves. We were able to be autonomous while working together to produce high-quality work for our company. The atmosphere, energy, and desire to go to work and help each other was incredible! The environment was basically due to the efforts and skills of our team leader, who, despite the very difficult circumstances she had to work in, managed to make us feel part of a great team (thank you again, Sara). I'm still in touch with many of the people from that team and we still all agree that it was *the* best place that we've ever worked. And I'm still trying to reproduce that same "feeling" fifteen years later within my own work teams.

Let's look at the common characteristics of some great teams. Charles Handy and, in particular, Warren Bennis, have looked extensively at what Bennis calls "great groups" and the following have been identified as some of their key characteristics:

1.  **Top-Class People**. It's difficult to build great teams if the individual members are not great themselves. You want VIP Leaders: people with intelligence, originality, vision, a sense of mission, trustworthiness, and the ability to focus on results. You want team members with diverse backgrounds and different perspectives in order to encourage out-of-the-box thinking and ideas. However, these team members must value their differences and be open to other peoples' ideas and to the notion of personal change.
2.  **Leadership**. Each team needs a single person—the project leader—who has a vision or mission that is shared by the other team members. This person can keep people focused on the task at hand and can create an optimum environment in which the others can unleash their creativity and productivity. They can also take some of the pressure off their team members' shoulders so that they can concentrate on getting the project done.
3.  **A Sense of Mission**. Great teams believe that what they are doing is important, vital even, and that they're creating a part of their legacy.
4.  **Distinctiveness**. Teams tend to establish their own culture, style of dress, language, work habits, values, and behaviour that distinguish them from others within their organization. They create their own sense of community.
5.  **Goal Setting**. Great teams have a simple but ambitious corporate challenge that they are focused on attaining together. It must be implicit that none of the individuals can achieve it alone—they need the others to make it work. Some teams invent an enemy, a competitor, that they can focus on defeating; this often has the dual effect of also diminishing internal competition as everyone focuses on the external competitor.
6.  **Good Communication**. Internal communication and external networking are facilitated. Open communication within the group needs is encouraged through formal and informal means, through electronic and face-to-face gatherings. Networking with all stakeholders and other information sources is encouraged to ensure the group's political support and outreach. There is no room for withholding knowledge and information within the culture of the team.
7.  **A Sense of "Stretch."** Great teams are optimistic, not realistic. If they really examined the "odds" they would probably admit defeat in a second. But it's their belief in their legacy and their abilities that allows them to keep working towards their goals.
8.  **Good "Fit."** Each person is in the right job for their particular expertise. Everybody brings something unique and valuable to the team and they trust each other's capabilities.
9.  **Support**. Team members all want to learn and grow, and are open. They share knowledge (not just information) and are willing to "go to bat" for their colleagues and the team.
10. **Freedom**. Guidelines are in place and do not represent tight procedures. It is pointless to hire intelligent people only to take away the opportunity for them to be creative and synergistic. Intelligent people need flexible structures, work rou-

tines, and work processes in order to produce synergistic results. They also need to "celebrate failure"; being creative involves taking risks and even though certain team members and their project segment may "fail" to achieve the initial goal, they will have created new intellectual capital that could be crucial to the long-term success of the organization if it's recognized as such. How many products like 3M's famous Post-it® Notes have resulted from an initial project failure?

11.  **A Creative Work Environment**. It is difficult to brainstorm or produce creative work in a boring work environment. Great groups are composed of team members who are allowed to personalize their space, to jazz it up and break with the traditional environment.

A great team is little more than a great working group—but that is everything it needs to be. To use a sports analogy, each player on the team has their particular skill and many can only play one position. Each member shares a common goal—to win the game—yet they all know they cannot achieve that goal alone because it's a team sport. They need to communicate, devise a winning team strategy, help and work for each other. Each team often has its particular culture and idiosyncrasies, and each has a team manager and captain who lead and inspire the others with their vision and drive. Most importantly—and there are examples of this in all team sports—there are teams of great individual players that have been never able to produce the results that they, on paper, should have achieved. Why? Often the team never gels; the individuals can't play as a team. Occasionally members break records for individual performances (goals scored, etc.), but the team never produces synergy together!

The objective of VIP Leaders is to play their part on a great team. As Italian author Luciano De Crescenzo states, "We are all angels with only one wing, we can only fly while embracing each other."

What small actions can People Managers take to facilitate both collaboration and increased creativity among their teams?

- ↻ Have a reward and recognition system based on team performance.
- ↻ Be honest but compassionate in pointing out when individuals do not perform up to the standards of the team.
- ↻ Fight for change throughout the entire organization in order to make your challenge easier.
- ↻ Do not let others—individuals from outside the group or superiors in particular—get away without correction when they are interacting with the group and do not behave in accordance with the team standards and culture.
- ↻ Walk the talk. Be open to working with others yourself—your people are watching you!
- ↻ Assist team members in recognizing the skills of others and appreciating the differences their colleagues possess.

## *Building a Sense of Community*

Several authors have talked about the need to create a sense of community within an organization. Robert Monk, a US expert on corporate governance, has been quoted as saying, "In less than a century there is serious doubt whether the modern corporate form has become obsolete" (20, p. 52). Charles Handy states that a corporation "has now to be regarded as a community not a piece of property—although a community created by a common purpose rather than a common place" (20, p. 52).

Community is normally defined as the citizens living in a particular geographic area. Those citizens have claims on and responsibilities to that community. In this book's context, community refers to a team of people who share a mission or purpose and who feel a common bond with their colleagues. In an earlier chapter, when discussing the 4Ls, I stressed how "Love," or peoples' social needs, was one of the major drivers that employers should seek to satisfy for their employees. Employees' feeling as though they are part of a living community with a common purpose is certainly a major step that encourages open communication, caring, and, ultimately, creation of synergy. It also encourages employees to commit, invest, and want to remain at an organization.

What does treating an organization as a community mean in practical terms? Obviously it means recognizing that employees are the true citizens, or owners, and that the organization is much more than a machine for making money for shareholders. It means that employees have their rights as citizens—and corresponding responsibilities to the organization. The more people feel that they are citizens of a community, the more they will have a sense of "Love," of belonging, of joint responsibility, and the more they will share with their colleagues, be motivated to perform, "stretch" themselves, and work together synergistically.

The basic elements required to develop community are relatively simple, but when considered together, they produce powerful results.

### Keys Ingredients for Developing Community
1. Building a shared purpose or mission.
2. Developing shared values, high trust levels, mutual respect, and integrity.
3. Creating win-win agreements for all parties.
4. Developing the organization's intellectual capital.
5. Developing deep levels of communication.
6. Encouraging high levels of mutual support and coaching.
7. Obtaining commitment from all parties (senior management in particular) to a community paradigm and process.

This last factor is often the most difficult to obtain, particularly if senior executives have been shareholder- and finance-focused in the past. However, the work of John Kotter and James Heskett outlined in Chapter 4 may demonstrate to them the merits of adopting a new way of seeing things.

## *Characteristics of a Learning Environment*

At the beginning of the chapter I mentioned how creating synergy is a key factor in creating an organizational culture that facilitates and encourages learning. Not surprisingly, learning environments share many of the same characteristics as collaborative and creative environments. Any organization that views its intellectual capital and its employees as its main asset should also be structured to promote learning and many of the elements created by the Implementor, including the adoption of the Balanced Scorecard™ approach, the development of core competencies and appropriate reward systems, and the formal recognition and promotion of a culture of real learning. Remember that if knowledge is your main asset, you can only treat your current level of intellectual capital as a "cash cow" for a limited time if you do not reinvest in its regeneration.

So what do you need to do to create an environment that encourages learning?

1. A leader who has a mandate to develop each team member's professional capabilities and in doing so, facilitates the growth of the organization.
2. A leader who is constantly learning and reinventing themself. After all, if the leader is not growing, changing, and learning, it's unlikely that the other team members will listen to them "talk"—they'll be too busy watching the walk!
3. A leader who is a facilitator and not an instructor; a coach and not a manager. They must appreciate and encourage the original thinking and new ideas of others.
4. An organizational structure that is adaptive, flexible, social, motivational, supportive, and nonbureaucratic. Also, as mentioned above, it must focus on the results obtained using a Balanced Scorecard™ approach. Job rotation must be encouraged; 360-degree performance evaluations, where employees are evaluated by their superiors, subordinates, and peers, are mandatory.
5. A conviction to celebrate projects that do not achieve their original goals but that enhance the organization's intellectual capital. These projects must be viewed as successes and not dismissed as failures.
6. The encouragement of visioning, concept generation, and systems thinking. Intuition must be accepted as justification for decision-making and exploration. Individual and team initiative along with experimentation and risk-taking must also be encouraged. A sense of exploration is fostered within individuals who are encouraged to explore outside of their own particular "box."
7. Allowance for different rates and directions of personal growth. Employees are given a chance to explore opportunities and themselves. If they feel their mission is no longer aligned with the organization's, their departure should be facilitated—they may be back one day.
8. The encouragement of formal and informal networking and communication.
9. The use of constructive criticism as a means of feedback and learning (See Chapter 10 for more details).

In Stan Davis's terms, the challenge for a learning-centred organization is to shift its paradigm from the accrual and management of "data" through "information" to the growth and use of "knowledge" (13, p. 13–14). Data and information can both be stored on a disk; to date, knowledge still resides in the organization's citizens, or its employees.

## *The Learning Process*

Learning is not about simply sitting down and reading an article or a book, though that is an important means of gaining new information. Organizations need to focus on building up their intellectual capital—that is, to encourage their employees to develop new know-how, new knowledge that they can exploit, not simply store as new information in their memories.

Peter Senge has written extensively on "Learning Organizations" and uses two different yet similar models for discussing the learning process. John Dewey is another author who describes the learning process through a cycle of four stages:

1. **Discovery**: *The realization of new insights*. Discovery may occur analyzing work, reading articles or journals, attending conferences, or taking training programs, etc.
2. **Invention**: *The creation of new options for action; inventions or innovations*. This entails taking the discovery or insight and generating new applications or new personal behaviours based upon it.
3. **Production**: *The construction of the new action*. Through production you learn how to really do something, to try a new idea, to put the new action into practice the first few times.
4. **Observation**: *Monitoring and analyzing the new action, which cycles back to Stage 1: more Discoveries*. At this stage, you observe the results of the action, determine if it works, weigh the benefits or costs of the new activity, and then reassess the application or seek new insight. In effect, you observe your learning or new know-how; that is, you decide if you really "know how" to use the insight.

In the quality management movement, the motto is always "PDCA": Plan-Do-Check-Act, which is similar to Dewey's cycle.

Irrespective of the model used, it's clear that in many organizations the learning cycle is broken. Many people never dare to try new behaviours or skills and there are very few people who can afford to—or are allowed to—set aside sufficient (or any) time for true reflection to generate new insight. As discussed earlier, "doing" is still encouraged within organizations and most employees are so focused on delivering tomorrow what they promised today, that experimentation is an unrealistic scenario. The biggest complaint of most students in my university classes is that they do not have any time at work to reflect, to think deeply about a topic—never mind experiment! Worse still, in many organizations, the actual premise of observing an action to see *if* it works is unthinkable; it *has* to work or it's the end of the project—and perhaps the employee's job.

But how can an organization or entrepreneurial unit seriously measure learning? Obviously the implementation of a Balanced Scorecard™ approach rather than measurement based solely on financial performance is a major step forward (see Chapter 8 for a full discussion). That approach allows you to measure the fruits of learning: increased rates of new product launches, reduction in cycle times, reduction in time to market for new innovations, application of specific new skills in employees' work, and the rate of adoption of new technologies/software. You can also measure the number of new techniques developed and incorporated into the value chain, the number of new services introduced to clients or the percentage of revenues from new technologies or new products. These elements measure organizational learning and represent challenges that can only be solved by teams working synergistically.

Improvement in any of these measurable and vital parameters reflects an organization that is learning—one that is Discovering, Inventing, Producing, and Observing. Such measurements can easily be incorporated into any Balanced Scorecard™ model for a team you supervise or of which you're a part. In the next chapter you'll see how this same model can be used to promote and evaluate individual learning.

# Team Corporate Challenges and Balanced Scorecards™

As you discovered earlier in the book, one of the last Visionary tasks is to break down the timeless nature of the mission statement into more understandable and realizable "steps," called the organization's strategic intent and corporate challenges. In addition, the last act of the Implementor is to disaggregate the organization into numerous entrepreneurial units and to set each the challenge of creating their own strategic intents and corporate challenges, which "stretch" them forward in the direction of achieving the mission. You also saw how the Balanced Scorecard™ approach is used to provide corporate challenges for each entrepreneurial division, unit, or team.

The challenge now is to work with each group of individuals in order to set each group a balanced corporate challenge that can *only* be achieved through group learning, collaborative effort, and the generation of synergy—that is, by working together.

Let's look at a couple of examples. Imagine that one of your units is responsible for research and development; your manufacturing department could be considered its principal customer. Possible concrete and measurable objectives that could be set for the unit in terms of customer satisfaction include: a 20 percent increase in the commercialization of technological developments; a 30 percent decrease in the time taken to customize product to client orders; a 10 percent reduction in manufacturability issues (as a result of increased communication and accountability to the internal client). Process challenges could include: a 20 percent decrease in research and development (R&D) cycle time; a 10 percent increase in time spent in the laboratory versus doing administrative tasks; implementation of intranet list-serve to facilitate discussion on hot topics. Financial challenges could include: a 10 percent increase in the obtainment of government grants; a 20 percent increase in revenues derived from products developed in the last twelve months. These are just examples of group corporate challenges that could be issued—and each would require a greater collaborative and synergistic effort between colleagues.

In a Human Resources (HR) department, challenges could include: a 10 percent reduction in hiring costs; a 20 percent increase in the number of training courses taken by employees; a 20 percent reduction in the amount of time taken to actually recruit people; the implementation of a new web-based recruitment system or CD-ROM training system. Challenges have to require "stretch" without being perceived as too difficult to achieve. It's vitally important that the challenges fit with each group's mission and the method for achieving the challenges be left to each team's creativity, motivation, and initiative (this is the crucial element that will see the group form its identity, culture, and collaborative nature).

Having set balanced corporate challenges for your different teams and a system to measure their success, you now again need to use a DR.GRAC agreement to ensure that a win-win agreement is established for all teams and that they know the Desired Results (the group corporate challenges), the Guidelines they must follow, the Resources they will have access to, the Accountability they will have, and the Consequences (including rewards) for the team and for each individual member (see Chapter 8 for details on DR.GRAC agreements). An important point: If employees are to be rewarded for their individual work within the team, that reward should be very carefully established (preferably using the Balanced Scorecard™ described in Chapter 10) to ensure it does not effectively discourage collaboration among colleagues and hamper the creation of synergy.

# Encountering Resistance

Despite your best intentions there will be objections from some groups or individuals who have no desire to change the way in which they currently work. Learning, being creative, and having their performance measured in nontraditional ways that demand accountability can seem quite threatening to some and it is rare that group or team initiatives do not meet with at least one or two dissenters, stragglers, obstructionists, or saboteurs.

It's no secret that the harder you push these people, the deeper they dig in their heels. Instead, you have to talk with them, address their concerns, work with them to show the benefits of the new approach, and be honest yet compassionate—hopefully they will eventually buy in to the team-building project. Once they realize that your new behaviour is not a whim and that you are determined to change despite what others do or think, they may reluctantly begin to participate. Colleagues may even bring them on board if they are convinced of the benefits of your initiative.

There are times when you will despair, and some people may have to be released if they do not want to participate—you cannot afford to keep them if you want to compete successfully today. But it's important to remember that it's yourself that you're really interested in changing, not other people. And your own life will be all the better for it.

# Final Steps

The final and crucial factor that People Managers or creators of synergy need to consider is that the principal objective is to develop each individual within the team to their maximum potential. That starts, of course, with the recruitment of people they recognize as VIP Leaders and continues with their development and possible ultimate departure from the team or from the organization. The development of these individuals is the focus of the next chapter.

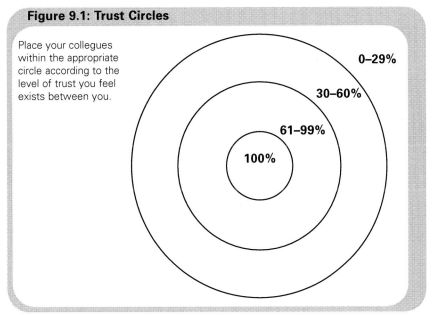

**Figure 9.1: Trust Circles**

Place your collegues within the appropriate circle according to the level of trust you feel exists between you.

0–29%

30–60%

61–99%

100%

Note: see Questions to Consider on the next page

## Key Points in Chapter 9

- ⊃ Be a great role model for the behaviour you believe in and want to see adopted throughout your team.
- ⊃ Be trustworthy! Stop behaviours that destroy trust and start practising those that build trust. It doesn't necessarily follow that because you behave in a trustworthy way that all others will suddenly develop similar behaviour. But it *is* guaranteed that if you talk about being trustworthy and expect it of others in your team without following through on it yourself, your initiative is doomed to fail.
- ⊃ Build a community with your employees.
- ⊃ Allow your employees time to learn—and to learn from their failures.
- ⊃ Implement a Balanced Scorecard™ management approach that encourages learning.
- ⊃ Use DR.GRAC for your team.
- ⊃ Ensure that the Consequences in DR.GRAC include an appropriate reward system.
- ⊃ Encourage the learning cycle: Discover, Invent, Produce, Observe.

## Questions to Consider

- ⊃ Prepare a list of all the people at work whom you trust 100 percent. (Be warned: the list may be short!) How many do you trust 80 percent? 50 percent? with certain things but not others? (Use Figure 9.1 as a guide in this exercise.)
- ⊃ How many people in your office trust *you* 100 percent? Why? Look at the behaviours in Table 9.1 again and try to judge how many of them you yourself practice. Does this explain why you don't trust more people and why, perhaps, they cannot trust you?
- ⊃ Think of a time when you discouraged an employee from learning. What should you have done instead?
- ⊃ When was the last time you tried the learning cycle? What learning activity will you commit to implementing now?
- ⊃ What criteria could you use in a Balanced Scorecard™ that would measure an increase in your customers' level of satisfaction, your work process, and learning among your team members?

In Chapter 2 I used David's Hurst's comparison of organizations and ecosystems, specifically the parallel between corporate change and a healthy forest fire, to stress the importance of continual organizational renewal. Like a forest, an organization needs the occasional "fire" to spark regeneration and keep itself in state of dynamic equilibrium. It's not surprising, then, that in this chapter on the VIP People Manager's role in growing your people and growing your company, the fire metaphor is useful once again.

In order to light the fire of change, ideally you will have the right conditions: dry ground, not too much wind, good wood, etc. However, even in the worst, wettest conditions, a knowledgeable, determined person can still succeed—it just takes more time and effort! And poor conditions are certainly not an excuse not to try; in fact, it's even more important to light a fire when the weather is inclement. You're in the same situation when you're considering whether to implement the VIP Personal Leadership model within your organization.

Having decided that you want a fire, you need to find the right starting materials: some dry twigs (just the right ones—not too big, wet, or rotten), paper, some matches. It's the same within your company: you need the right people and practices if the fire is to ignite. As your fire catches, you must carefully add properly sized pieces of wood in the right position at the right time. One wrong or careless move and you'll squash the fire and need to start all over again—often with new materials.

Most importantly perhaps, have you ever tried burning a fire with only one log? It's very difficult, if not downright impossible. You need a minimum of two logs—preferably ones that are of good quality and dry—to create a sustainable flame, and just the right amount of air to optimize the chemical reaction. Not enough wood, not the right type or size of wood, too much wood, too much or not enough air—all of these factors will leave your fire struggling. The choice of good-quality wood is particularly crucial, just as in the case of choosing your employees. If rotten wood is in the fire, you have to remove it or it will hinder the fire's combustion and capability to generate heat until the fire is out or the wood is burnt through.

Once your fire is burning brightly, you will build up a nice layer of hot embers that create a solid base for the fire in the future. Where your company is concerned, those embers are the good practices, healthy culture, good management systems, and personal goodwill that you have created. However, even a thick layer of hot embers needs attention; you always have to be conscious of the fire's needs. Even a fire that is burning brightly can suffer from exposure to a damp log; a strong breeze; or a short, sharp rain shower. In fact, if you want to keep a fire going for ten years, you must be extremely vigilant and care for it on an ongoing basis. Maintaining a lifelong flame is a lifelong task.

And that is your challenge as a VIP Personal Leader: continually monitor and feed the "fire" created from the interactions of each individual employee as they grow. It requires your investing an enormous amount of time in caring for and working with and on behalf of your employees. It means you must develop all of your employees into "guardians of the flame" too.

Consider what Christopher Bartlett says about a vice-president at ABB: "He estimates that he spends between 50–60% of his time communicating directly with his people in a process called 'human engineering'" (5, p. 136). Personally, I feel that when working with teams now, I spend most of my time in a similar manner. No one has ever said that grooming new VIP Leaders is easy work.

## *Revisiting the 4Ls*

It is widely estimated that while working, people in general only use about 10 to 20 percent of their capacities. The motivated and ambitious ones go on to pursue other activities outside of work; they get involved with community projects, volunteer with nonprofit organizations, or invest enormously in their children or family life in order to fulfill their individual potential and satisfy all their needs. Unfortunately, the vast majority of employees "plateau" early in their careers and lose their appetite and capability to learn. They accept that they must run on autopilot and, in a worst-case scenario, learn how to mentally "switch off" for eight hours each day. This sad scenario is often not their fault. Who can blame them when the system discourages people from being individualistic and creative, and prevents them from learning and risking failure?

As children, most individuals have high levels of curiosity, interest, and desire to learn. However, if the school system does not make people realize that being creative, trying new things, and challenging the rules is not always recommended or rewarded, many of the systems, procedures, and cultures of organizations will. The best and brightest people are probably the quickest to learn that it doesn't pay to challenge the system. In recruiting staff, you need to look for people who still have a desire to learn, to be creative, to challenge, and to question the prevailing ways of doing things—the building blocks described in Chapter 3.

As mentioned earlier, the initial challenge offered by working with others is to satisfy their 4Ls: Live, Love, Learn, and create a Legacy. You want to satisfy their economic, social, and learning needs, and their desire to be part of something bigger than themselves. Again, each person's 4Ls will be different. Some may focus on earning the highest possible salary. If you believe that they create sufficient value to warrant it and your company can afford it, great. If you can't, you should recognize before you hire them that they are unlikely to be satisfied at your company. Perhaps one individual is not interested in learning; perhaps another wants only a full-time job and you only have part-time positions available; perhaps the mission or the legacy a person wants to leave behind does not match the company or team's. Again, if any of these scenarios are the case, you should either not hire them or if they are already working for you, you should assist them to find alternative work that will better satisfy their fourth L—you are always in pursuit of a win-win scenario.

Knowing the needs of each of your team members also helps you coach them with regard to maintaining a balanced lifestyle. It's in your interest as well as theirs that they not be out of equilibrium for too long. At some time or another, all companies may need personnel to put in a few 80- to 150-hour work weeks to finish a project on time. In general, however, requiring that the whole team work those kinds of hours week in and week out is not a desirable work culture. That pace can only be maintained for a limited amount of time or workers are inevitably lost to burnout, moves to other companies, or termination (as they can no longer perform). Alternately, they find less stressful and more rewarding or enjoyable activities, hobbies, and relationships that take them away from their jobs. Today, companies cannot afford to develop people and intellectual capital only to have them walk away; companies should be generating organizational growth and developing their own staff and more future leaders. It is amazing how, even among students at universities, word quickly gets around as to which companies are really keen on training and investing in their employees and which are only there to "milk" their staff.

> *Maintaining a lifelong flame is a lifelong task: you must be vigilant and care for it on an ongoing basis.*

## Encouraging Life Balance

To be healthy, we need to be "in balance." We need the right mix of physical, social, spiritual, intellectual, and emotional stimulation along with sufficient rest and relaxation time. In Stephen R. Covey's *The 7 Habits of Highly Effective People*, he lists the seventh habit as "sharpening the saw": individuals take the time to "replenish their batteries" by looking after all their different needs both inside and outside of work. Each person's particular "optimum mix" of activities that will allow them to achieve their maximum potential in all aspects of their lives is different and each person must take the responsibility for discovering their own needs and seeing to it that they are met. The task of the VIP Leader is to create an environment in which individuals can do that. Without such an environment, employees will become burnt out, ill, or will leave the company when they recognize that they can no longer maintain an unsuitable and harmful lifestyle. Divorce, physical illness, and depression should not be wake-up calls that signal employees' lives are out of equilibrium.

The relationship between the company, stakeholders, and employees needs to be a win-win arrangement; everyone's needs must be met. If they are not, there will be friction, inefficiency, and a feeling of dissatisfaction for all. The Covey principle of win-win or no deal must be the driving force behind your decision-making processes.

## The Employee Life Cycle

There are three stages to an employee's life cycle within your organization. The cycle begins with the hiring process, continues with the employee's development and value creation while they're with you, and ends with the management of their departure. Each stage needs to be handled well and viewed as a crucial part of your "intelligent asset" management strategy. Let's look at each stage separately.

## Recruiting VIP Leaders: Investment or Expense?

How much does it cost to hire an intelligent person? Costs obviously include placing advertisements, using a "headhunter" or, alternately, spending a lot of time "working the network" in order to identify a few interesting candidates. After an initial triage, you must organize and arrange to interview candidates—probably on two or three occasions, including several different people in the process. Depending on the position to be filled, there may also be moving expenses and signing bonuses to be paid if you can actually find the right candidate. Even when recruiting new graduates out of university, there is a major cost attached for organizations.

However, there is a real cost to pay if after having hired a candidate, you fail to build a productive long-term win-win relationship with them and you lose them to a competitor. Then the cost really is an "expense" rather than an "investment"! Many companies seem forever willing to continue recruiting people only to have them leave after one or two years—they even build that rate of turnover into their strategic system and their model of doing business. What a waste! If you are hiring the right people and developing them during the time they are with you, their importance as a corporate asset should only be growing, and you certainly don't "give away" other (financial or equipment) assets to competitors once you've developed and built them. Why should you do it with your "human assets"?

So how can you maximize your chances of being successful during the hiring process?

### The Importance of the Human Resource (HR) Department

It's a tragic indictment of many organizations that the Department of Human Resources is more often than not positioned at the lowest level in the corporate departmental hierarchy. Departments of finance, marketing, and production almost always have more "power" than their HR colleagues. Why? In previous eras, when economic value creation focused first on manufacturing capability and subsequently on marketing or customer service levels, it was these department heads who carried the most responsibility and power. Particularly during the manufacturing era, employees were considered simply an additional "cost" required to operate the real source of competitive advantage: the machines. In this paradigm, HR was made up of mere "paper pushers" who added little value even in the hiring process where the real decisions about recruits were made by the project manager or the manager of the department seeking to fill a position. In those days, as long as *someone* was operating the machine, it didn't really matter who it was. Employees were interchangeable commodities.

Usually in knowledge-based organizations, division, product, or project managers are involved in the hiring and interview process. Sometimes—and I've heard this with my own ears—when they feel it is useful to say so, these individuals will make disparaging remarks about HR to candidates: "HR doesn't really understand what I'm looking for," or "They force us to use HR—otherwise we'd recruit you tomorrow." Such comments undermine the HR group and the status of an HR department (and HR issues) is often immediately apparent to an applicant.

HR's authority becomes particularly clear at the lower levels of an organizations where project managers and supervisors can be tempted to resist releasing their subordinates for training, job rotation, even for vacations, so that they can meet deadlines. This may be understandable in the context of the demands placed on them, but it's a practice that a strong and well-respected HR department needs to counteract.

In many organizations today, HR, employee evaluation, and employee training is still seen as a "value-less" activity, a cost-centre, and a part of the company's bureaucracy and administration rather than an essential part of maintaining or enhancing an organization's most crucial activity and value creation capability. How many managers still try to avoid doing their employee appraisals and are allowed to do so by their organizations? Providing that their paycheque is not a day late, many supervisors still prefer to hear as little as possible from HR.

> *HR must have the power to ensure human resources are the main focus of an organization's growth strategy.*

Due to past stature, the reality is that in some organizations, the HR department really does offer very little that is of real value. Due to their previously elevated profile and importance, the more powerful organizational functions such as production, finance, and marketing have traditionally attracted the best personnel into the professions. Hence, although I am glad to say that there are a growing number of exceptions, HR departments are traditionally viewed as unattractive places to pursue a career and have been staffed by individuals with less ability, ambition, and motivation. I want to emphasize, however, that this is changing as both individuals and companies start to realize that the key to their success is the hiring and development of staff.

Bill Gates, for example, recognizes that from among the 120,000 resumes Microsoft receives each year, there is only a small percentage of applicants who can make "the difference" in keeping his organization on top. He thus encourages his existing staff to invest time into identifying them and encouraging these key individuals to join the company. Many high-tech companies recruiting at universities for young engineers now fight over the top 20 percent of students. In fact, I believe *all* companies are starting to realize that success depends on attracting the very best; many are spending a lot of time on campuses raising awareness about their organizations and meeting and interviewing potential candidates. They know that the cost of making poor recruitment choices far exceeds the cost of making good ones.

HR must have the authority, autonomy, and power to ensure that the development of human resources is the main focus of an organization's growth strategy. And it goes almost without saying that if the development of your company is a function of the development of the individuals therein, the person in charge of that function should be highly qualified and possess an excellent staff and the corresponding authority. Otherwise, you're simply inviting poachers to steal your employees away!

## Emotionally Intelligent (EI) Organizations

Robert Cooper has done a lot of work in EI cultures and basically suggests that organizations treat their employees as human beings and not simply as brains designed to produce. For example, he suggests we take "strategic pauses" of fifteen to thirty seconds every half-hour or so to refresh ourselves. How many people become so engrossed in work at their computer that they "wake-up" two to three hours later with stiff backs or necks from not having moved their bodies, taken some water or food, or focused their eyes on something further away than their computer screens? I used to focus intently on work for hours at a stretch and would "come to" with a feeling of malaise throughout my being. I know from personal experience that by taking brief pauses, drinking more water, and doing stretches during the working day I'm more effective when I am at the computer and therefore gain more time away from it!

Cooper also gives credence—from a scientist's point of view—to the value of people listening to their "gut feelings" and their hearts, which is an essential action for People Managers. He discusses how a new stimulus is really first *felt* in the intestines (thus the proverbial "gut feeling"). This theory stands in marked contrast to the way that stimuli, information, and communication have been viewed in the past—as entities detected in the brain through rational thinking. In fact, stimuli pass from our intestines to our heads via our hearts, where we again have a scientifically proven reaction to them. Cooper therefore suggests that we in fact have three brains: one in our intestine, a second in our heart, and a third in our cranium. It's interesting to learn that in making a decision based on a gut reaction, you are still "using your head"!

As mentioned in an earlier chapter, Cooper's research studies have also found that "the only statistically significant factor differentiating top leaders from the worst was *caring*" (10, p. 2). When people do not feel recognized, respected, and valued, they mentally and emotionally quit their positions, even if they are still physically present and you continue to pay them. The message here is that you can be a brilliant Visionary and Implementor, but if you don't care about your staff (or you can't express your caring) and you can't be a good People Manager, your efforts are doomed to fail.

## Mission Matching

Assuming that you are trying to recruit someone to join your existing team, an essential factor is that their personal mission statement be coherent with the organization's (see Chapter 3 for a complete discussion). People who focus on money should join an organization that focuses on maximizing its money-making potential; those interested in saving the environment should join eco-friendly companies or ones that focus on developing new environmental technologies. Therefore, it is important to match vision with vision, values with values, and desired legacy with desired legacy. If there is no match, it's better to know that before hiring an individual. Going through the process of finding out may be time consuming, but it means that you will save a lot of trouble down the road and there is an enormous return on investment (ROI) when you recruit the right candidate.

## *Length and Terms of Employment*

A few decades ago, when a new employee was hired, it was done with the idea that they could remain with the organization for their entire career. Today, all companies shy away from the very suggestion of such a vision and many are focused on hiring sufficient staff simply to fulfill the current contract. Whether they will need or want to keep the employee at the end of that contract is often not even considered. Many employees, or at least the contractuals, have had to adjust to this situation and for some, it fits their own needs and objectives perfectly. But if you are trying to build up the company's assets—that is, its intellectual capital—then it's obviously advantageous to retain most of your employees for as long as you can, or for as long as both employer and employee see substantial benefits from maintaining the relationship.

In today's world, an organization's need for certain types of expertise constantly changes and opportunities abound for individuals who are prepared to learn, travel, or develop themselves. Consequently, for the agreement to be win-win, you should really plan for an employee to be with an organization for a finite length of time and you should ensure that both parties know and agree to the arrangement before hiring occurs. Both parties can then make the appropriate plans for the end of the relationship.

What does that mean exactly? Basically, the employee should know that they will be highly employable and will possess top-level skills in their field at the end of their tenure. For the employer, it means planning for a successor, a new team member to take the departing person's position. In this context, Charles Handy suggests the idea of granting a type of temporary membership or citizenship to your work community.

### Granting Community Citizenship

Just like the inhabitants of a geographic community, recruits or citizens of an organization are proud to have a sense of belonging and to feel that they have certain responsibilities to assume within the team, while also knowing that they have certain rights afforded to them in exchange. Consider the form of citizenship used in the armed forces. Is such citizenship offered for life? No. In most cases recruits sign up for either five or ten years, knowing that they are going to learn skills that will make them very employable upon their discharge. In exchange, the army knows it has a recruit who believes in the mission of the forces and on whom it can count for five or ten years. It is a win-win scenario.

Is there any reason that this kind of contract cannot be used within an organization after the employee's period of probation? I don't believe there is. The employee contributes to the mission or purpose to which both they and the organization are committed. The organization commits to fair remuneration and reward and also ensures that the citizen's assets—that is, knowledge, expertise, abilities, etc.—are fully developed so that at the end of their tenure, they are marketable or have high employability.

Could there be a possibility for the contract's renewal? Certainly. If the mission, objectives, and needs of the two parties still match at the end of the contract period and both feel it is in their best interest to extend it for another five or ten years, why not? However, bearing in mind that the average job tenure in the UK is now 5.7 years and even less in the US, a 10-year period would be beating the odds.

With such arrangements, both parties gain from knowing the terms of the employment contract at the outset and providing that an organization fulfills its obligations, remunerates fairly, and allows the citizen to improve their skills and assets, it will likely have a stream of qualified, motivated candidates applying to join.

# Developing VIP Leaders: Growing Intellectual Capital

Having hired the right people, how do you manage their professional development and growth? How do you continually improve their Visionary, Implementor, and People Manager skills? How do you make sure they achieve their ambitions and create their legacy? Once hired for what they thought was going to be an exciting career opportunity, too many people find themselves using only a small percentage of their talents. I will always remember, many years ago, being hired for my one and only job as an engineer. I was recruited mainly for having just obtained a Master's degree in the magnetic separation of minerals. Having been hired by an iron ore processing company, having seen their magnetic separation operation, and having been told that they lacked expertise and needed my help in that area during the interview process, imagine my surprise when during the one year I worked there I never once even saw the magnetic separation plant!

During my time at this company—and in several of the posts I've since occupied—I have been ripe for being poached to work in other organizations. Why? Because I never felt like my employer's most important asset. Through my own efforts, I have usually been able to find win-win situations while in someone else's employ, but it's only been on very rare occasions when I have felt like my employer or supervisor truly cared about my well-being. Usually I felt that they were only looking to ensure they obtained their own "win."

Headhunters are always approaching intelligent people in key positions. There is simply not enough supply to satisfy demand and so it is essential to make employees feel like they belong and that they are a major asset. Have one-on-one meetings with them every couple of months to make sure that they are satisfied with their work and to plan for their future development and their work schedule.

But in order to communicate effectively with intelligent people (indeed, with all people!) there are two key skills that you must first learn: listening and talking.

## The Hardest Skill: Listening to Intelligent People

Although there are many communication skills you need to develop if you are to become a good People Manager, one of the most important—and least recognized—is the art of simply listening. Children are taught throughout their school days to read, to write, to make presentations, and yet I rarely have seen courses offered in "listening." But being a good leader and coach probably derives more from that particular skill than any other.

## *Really* Listening

Some people rarely listen. They are usually too busy trying to think of a way to make you accept their point of view; they don't actually take the time to listen to what you are saying.

Listening is something you really have to concentrate on—not just to hear the words, but to try and understand the feelings and emotions *behind* the words. How many times have you tried talking to your boss with the knowledge that all they want is to get out of the office because they're late for their next meeting? How many times have they just given you the same reply without ever hearing what you've really said? How many times have you done that to others? While the other person is talking, are you listening to them or preparing your answers? Do you pose empathic or reflective questions? Do you answer the phone or accept other interruptions when you're meeting to discuss something important with a member of your team? Do you really try to put yourself in their shoes and appreciate their point of view? Or do you force them to see the issue from your point of view so you can move on to more "important" things?

> One of the most important communication skills—and least recognized—is the art of simply listening.

### Some Tips for Listening Well

- ⮑ Actively concentrate on listening—focus on it!
- ⮑ Listen on three levels: (1) the facts as told; (2) the emotions behind the facts; and (3) the true intentions, motives, and desires—what does the speaker really want?
- ⮑ Ask for clarity when you need to verify that you understand.
- ⮑ Remain neutral and withhold any judgements.
- ⮑ Pre-empt your question with the phrase, "If I were to play Devil's Advocate I might say…" when you feel a person's opinion needs to be challenged.
- ⮑ Use reflective questions or phrases like "I understand" or "I see" to show a person that they are being listened to.
- ⮑ Ask questions to find out how someone feels about an issue rather than to gain more facts.
- ⮑ Do not formulate your views or opinions until you know all the facts.
- ⮑ Avoid the phrase "If I were you…"; you are not and never will be!
- ⮑ Lead someone to make their own decision. You do not want to be responsible for their actions—they should be. This encourages them to grow.

Listening is where People Managers succeed or fail, mainly because most people have never learned the skills required to listen—they've only learned the skills to ensure they are being listened to! Employees will accept that you make a lot of mistakes during your own learning and development if they feel that you are listening to them and understanding them when they talk to you.

By listening you will learn what your employees really want: what their 4Ls are; what their concerns are; what they need from you; why they're really upset, angry, happy, looking to leave the company or your team, or why they want a promotion. This information is vital if you are to make informed win-win decisions.

## Learning to Talk to Intelligent People

Just as intelligent people have to be led and not managed, so the language of leadership must change from command to open persuasion. Open persuasion is a process that convinces people to buy into your idea while you remain open to their suggestions about changing or improving it in order to reach an even better idea. Open persuasion creates synergy.

Jay Conger outlines four essential steps in the art of persuading:

1. **You establish credibility (on a given topic) with your audience**. Hopefully you already have established a broad base of trust and credibility within your team. However, sometimes you should acknowledge that you have no expertise or knowledge in an area—it builds trust if you admit the truth. "Skating" (i.e., pretending to be well versed in a subject) is an art form that is too easy to see through and too stressful to play. Paradoxically, credibility may be established through admitting your lack of knowledge—particularly if you bring someone with expertise into the discussion to represent you.
2. **You frame your goal in a way that identifies common ground with your audience's**. If you have been actively listening and seeking a win-win agreement, you should find it normal practice to frame your suggestion in a way that appeals to your audience by touching on their objectives, and showing that you are considering the needs of all stakeholders.
3. **You reinforce your position by using vivid language and strong compelling evidence**. Using examples, stories, metaphors, and analogies in order to paint a visual image of your position is much more effective that using statistical data. Use the latter only to support your positions.
4. **You connect emotionally with the subject and the audience**. You need to show that you believe in your position and in finding a win-win solution. If people believe that you are only saying the right things to win their support, they will consider you manipulative and untrustworthy. Connecting emotionally with your subject should come naturally as you should only be proposing ideas or suggestions in which you believe. (9)

Presenting your position is an art. Following these brief but succinct points will ensure that your position receives a fair and hopefully positive reception. If you then practice active and empathic listening, you may well end up creating real synergy—that is, achieving an ideal solution that neither you nor the other party(ies) could have developed alone.

## Individual Balanced Scorecards™

Having had a real dialogue with an employee—that is, having listened to and understood them and then expressed yourself in order to be understood—you can once again use the Balanced Scorecard™ approach with DR.GRAC (see Chapter 8 for full details on using each method), an excellent way to ensure that win-win agreements are created with all employees on an individual level.

The types of personal challenges that can be developed for individuals in the four areas of the Balanced Scorecard™ will vary markedly according to their position, but possible general themes include the following:

1. **Customer Perspective**. Depending on an employee's position, several stakeholders may be viewed as their clients. It may be one of their colleagues, someone in another department, or one of the organization's external clients. Factors that may be measured include: improved results on customer satisfaction surveys; contact time with clients; amount, quality, and timing of product delivered; reduction in complaints; improved results on a good 360-degree assessment (i.e., an assessment from all internal/external clients or stakeholders).

2. **Work Processes**. Parameters to measure here may include: reductions in time needed to accomplish tasks; incorporation of new technologies or new ideas into their work; elimination of wastage; improved team leading, organization, or participation skills; increased productivity; more billable hours; less organizational infrastructure and support required.

3. **Learning and Innovation**. Factors to measure here include: new skills applied on the job; job rotation activities; contributions to multifunctional teams; training courses taken and passed; improved communication skills, soft skills, or behaviours through 360-degree assessments; improved technical capabilities; the transfer of skills to other team members.

4. **Financial Perspective**. Parameters to measure include: more sales generated from their department; more productivity from their team; less wastage of materials or time; increased economic value delivered to the organization.

These are just a few examples of the sorts of challenges that can be set for individuals. Because we're using the same Balanced Scorecard™ model at each level of the organization (be it for the business unit or for the team or group), individual employees should be able to see how their efforts are contributing to the achievement of their group's objectives and the organization's objectives. When coupled with the sharing of the common mission and values, this feedback should give each team member an enormous sense of contribution and belonging as they see for themselves that they are making a difference. When this is the case, all employees feel vital to the success of the organization, even if they are hired at its so-called "lower" levels.

## Individual DR. GRAC Agreements

Before drawing up DR.GRAC agreements with individual employees you need to decide the level of delegation you want to allow for any given task. The concept of situational leadership—particularly the work of Paul Hersey and Kenneth H. Blanchard (see Figure 10.1)—has shown that you should not adopt a style of supervision that suits you; rather, your leadership in any given situation should change as a function of the needs or "state of readiness" of your subordinate to accomplish any given task (22, p. 745). This could mean that you might need to be more directive and focused on the task itself with an employee in one situation while you may play more of a coaching role with that same employee when they are faced with a different task. Another employee doing the same tasks may have completely different needs and hence your style of supervision would change accordingly. The message is simple: give the employee what they need rather than what best suits you.

Stephen R. Covey provides a simple but effective "release" tool for analyzing this scenario so that you can increasingly allow greater empowerment as employees gain knowledge and experience and develop themselves. As an employee's trustworthiness and level of initiative increases, you can delegate responsibility to them as follows:

- ⊃ Employee waits until they are told to act (Level 1)
- ⊃ Employee asks before acting (Level 2)
- ⊃ Employee receives recommendations for action (Level 3)
- ⊃ Employee acts and reports immediately (Level 4)
- ⊃ Employee acts and reports routinely (Level 5)
- ⊃ Employee acts (Level 6)

This process is a great tool to help you move from a paradigm of managing people to one of leading them. Intelligent people want to be led and not managed, but your team may be used to being managed by you or by others, and it is important to talk openly about the changes you are adopting and explain how one of your tasks is to make sure that you develop a "win-win" agreement with each of your employees.

The essential components of a DR.GRAC agreement with employees including the following:

1. **Desired Results**. The results you are seeking should be clearly spelled out using any combination of the four components of the Balanced Scorecard™ you have drawn up for the employee. If you are concentrating your focus on just one initiative or learning activity, then it may be something narrower or more specific. The objective here is to make sure both parties understand each other's objectives and expectations. What do you want to achieve here? What does the employee want and expect?
2. **Guidelines**. In this process you are seeking to empower the employee to take responsibility and to use their intelligence to achieve desired results—not to give them the solutions (i.e., to do the intelligent work yourself). You do not want to give the employee detailed procedures to follow. You want to provide guidelines for what level of release or empowerment they can operate on for this particular project. What can they and what can't they do?
3. **Resources**. Most projects given to an individual cannot be accomplished alone. It might take access to other people with different skills (including yourself); to information; to equipment, new equipment, or financial resources for the employee to realize the agreed upon results. There is nothing more demoralizing than to be given an exciting project only to be asked to do it under impossible conditions. One thing that I always make clear is that I am always there to help team members when they need it. But I also emphasize that they are responsible for the project and they have to ask me for assistance if they need it; otherwise, by the terms of the contract, I assume they have everything under control.
4. **Accountability**. The employee must understand that they are now accountable and responsible for achieving the desired results. As mentioned above, I am always available to help, and I'm sure my superiors will see me as being accountable should something go wrong, but I have to put my employee fully in charge of achieving the goal. My boss might not know (or care) about that—but I will if things go wrong.
5. **Consequences: Results, Rewards, and Recognition**. The results and their direct consequences for all stakeholders from any project should be spelled out so that the employee understands the motivation behind the challenge. It helps them to understand how they will be contributing to the larger picture of the organization's strategic intent and helps them appreciate the importance of their work.

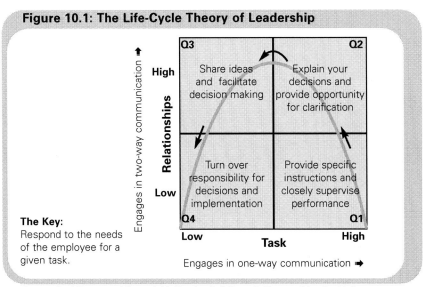

Figure 10.1: The Life-Cycle Theory of Leadership

Source: Paul Hersey and Kenneth H. Blanchard, "Life-cycle Theory of Leadership"

The reward or recognition received by the employee for successfully completing a project could simply entail being offered another similar one—or a different one. It could be a financial bonus. It could be recognition within the team or organization. It could simply be the satisfaction of taking another step forward in terms of skill level and achievement on a resume. The consequence of not achieving the agreed results should also be spelled out. It could be having to do the project or a similar one again, taking a step back on the release scale, or even to being released from the team if the project is the "last chance" effort with this particular employee.

Before doing a "debriefing" at the end of a project that has been part of a DR.GRAC agreement, it is important that the employee rate themself on their performance before doing a review with you. The desired results, the guidelines, and the resources were all agreed upon by both parties before the project began so the employee can easily self-evaluate (and experience shows that employees are often tougher on themselves than you will ever be). It's through the "observing" part of the learning cycle explained in Chapter 9 and having done their self-assessment upon meeting with you that employees learn make their own suggestions about how things should proceed or be improved upon in the future.

While an employee is working on a project, your task as a VIP Leader is to create an environment that is free of bureaucratic procedures, administration barriers, reporting processes, etc. so that the employee can achieve results. It is unfair to set ambitious but ultimately unattainable challenges when you know that you have not done your Implementor work in order to create an entrepreneurial environment in which employees can succeed. The process of moving from "V" to "I" to "P" is important here!

## *Avoiding the Plateau: Treating Work as a Craft*

In increasingly flat knowledge-based organizational structures, employees need to know that they can move forward, grow, and develop—that they have not "plateaued" at the age of twenty-eight! However, as there is now very little "room at the top," where can they move? How can they develop themselves?

It's strange, but even when there were more levels of hierarchy and middle management to pass through, workers still felt uncomfortable with the system. As people rose, they found themselves doing less and less of the valued work that they had chosen as a career, trained to do, and often loved to do. Rather, they found themselves doing more and more administration or project management work, more time moving paper than working in their real area of interest. People often did literally rise to their level of incompetence: they were working in areas in which they'd simply not been trained in and in which they had little interest. For example, great teachers often move through the ranks to Department Head, Deputy Headmaster, and then Principal. But in making those moves, that teacher will be doing less teaching—the very thing they are good at.

Is there anything wrong with a great teacher who wants to continually upgrade their skills, try new techniques, improve their communication methods, learn more about children's education, and constantly seek to improve their students' grades? Is it wrong not to want to rise to become even the Department Head? Is it healthy to want to stay put, focus, and hone and apply core competencies? Family, the education system, and society would probably think it odd or strange—a lack of ambition that such a teacher would want to remain in the same job. But by constantly improving, that teacher is always moving forward, advancing their depth of expertise and craft.

Resisting a rise through the ranks can be a sign of someone who knows their mission, the legacy they want to leave behind, and their capabilities. They won't buy into what they "should do." Does this describe one of your employees? Encouraging people to overcome their fears of taking on more responsibility and to aim for a promotion is laudable, but only if it's going to benefit both the company and the individual. If it is not to the individual's benefit, they should be encouraged to remain where they are. The alternative? You lose a great asset in the position in question and gain a poor one in the new position—it's a lose-lose situation. What's more, because demotion or a return to an old position is often culturally unacceptable within organizations, you will often lose the employee to a competitor where they can re-establish themself in their old position.

The moral of the story? A good People Manager recognizes an employee that can best develop in their current position rather than being promoted.

# *Facilitating Exits*

Although mission statements are usually timeless, there may be occasions when the owners of your intellectual capital will want to move on. Sometimes this will be to your mutual benefit, other times to your loss or gain. Irrespective of the consequences, the exit process should be as healthy and smooth as possible, always leaving the door open to a possible future rehiring.

There are many reasons why an employee might wish to leave a company and many of them might not reflect negatively on their relationship with you or the company. A spouse's relocation is an obvious reason in these days of global organizations and working couples. The arrival of a child or the return to an "empty nest" environment can also mean that people's needs and circumstances change. In addition, no one knows how missions, corporate or individual needs, and "wins" will evolve, and it is in no one's interest for there to be lingering negative feelings following someone's departure. Perhaps it is simply the time for both parties to say goodbye at the end of an employment contract or when missions start to diverge. The employee may simply want to learn and gain experience in an area in which your company does not work. Strategic alliances and expanded networks can always result from having a good relationship in place with an ex-employee working in a different organization. Also keep in mind that it's usually also viewed very negatively if the remaining employees see a departing colleague being treated poorly by the company.

Individuals released by the organization should always receive help in finding a position that suits their skills, needs, and personality. Providing this service is an ethical way to work and exhibits a win-win mentality. It also is incredibly sad to see individuals staying in positions and in organizations where they obviously do not fit, but where they feel secure. Helping these people find a new position can be rewarded many times over by the goodwill promoted in fellow employees and by the removal of the friction caused by having a "square peg in a round hole."

Finally, exit interviews should be held, as they are a crucial way to gather "objective" information that can help to improve the organization. In my experience, these are seldom conducted. I never had one in the four times that I have left organizations—and each organization missed a great opportunity to gain some feedback from someone who was intimately familiar with it.

## Key Points in Chapter 10

⮑ Make sure that you and your employees lead balanced lives. It pays off for everyone in the long run.

⮑ Treat employee recruitment as you would a financial investment.

⮑ Make sure the HR department is well staffed, adds value, and has the necessary prestige and power.

⮑ Start running EI-smart work places.

⮑ Learn to listen and learn to persuade.

⮑ Implement individual Balanced Scorecards™ and DR.GRAC agreements with your team members.

⮑ Provide opportunities that will benefit your people's development.

⮑ Encourage people to treat their career like a craft.

## Questions to Consider

⮑ Do you know the 4Ls of each of your team members?

⮑ How many of your employees would you consider to be leading lives that are "out of balance"?

⮑ How is HR viewed with respect to other departments within your organization?

⮑ Do you give your employees the guidelines and resources that they need, make them accountable, and spell out the consequences of their work?

⮑ What level of delegation has each of your employees achieved?

⮑ Do you hold exit interviews? If not, why? Do you help employees who do not fit into your organization find other positions?

**Part 5: Conclusion**

## Chapter 11

**Making It Happen**

Having now gained a full theoretical understanding of the VIP Leadership model, you can look back at the Ten Criteria for Success (see Figure 2.5, page 39) and see that adopting the model ensures each of the criteria will be satisfied. Re-examining the Diamond-E diagram in Figure 1.4 (see page 12), you can see that building up your organization's strategy, structure, and management preferences in harmony with a team of (human) resources with a VIP Leadership paradigm will allow your organization to constantly realign itself with its ever-changing environment. But even with a good theoretical understanding of the VIP model of strategic leadership, the thought of implementing it within your organization may seem quite daunting at first.

In fact, you are likely applying many parts of it in your work already. However, you will not gain the full benefits of the model until you start applying it in a thorough and systematic way—that is, when it becomes your paradigm, the way you do things, your way of thinking. For example, you may already have established corporate challenges for your people, but you may have been concentrating on financial and customer service objectives and not dealing with processes and learning. You may already have analyzed your value chain for perceived value creation in the eyes of the customer, but without checking if your projects are creating economic value. You may already have concentrated on defining and communicating a vision and mission, but have not established a short-term strategic intent in order to make them more meaningful and motivational for your team. In isolation, each of the VIP activities in themselves do have value—but it is when they are all tied together that you really begin to create synergy between initiatives and see order of magnitude improvements in individual and organizational performance.

In order to explore the VIP concept more closely, the first part of this final chapter looks at some examples of the sort of work individuals must do as VIP Leaders within the different levels and functions of an organization. The second part of the chapter discusses how you can start introducing the VIP paradigm into your own operations. Finally, the chapter presents some activities and exercises that will give you a launching pad for the development and application of your own personal skills as a VIP Leader.

## *The Daily Life of a VIP*

The amount of time spent doing Visionary, Implementor, or People Manager work varies according to organizational level. The type of work done in each role also changes quite markedly depending whether you are a CEO or a small team leader; a CEO's activities or Balanced Scorecard™ challenges will never be the same as those of a team supervisor on the shop floor.

Historically—and unfortunately this still remains the case in many companies today—presidents or CEOs were expected to spend more time on Visionary activities than perhaps floor supervisors; the latter were expected to spend more time on Implementor or People Manager activities. As I've argued throughout this book, that mindset and practice cannot continue if an organization is to be successful today.

> *As an individual making a career choice, you should choose the position that best suits your 4Ls and your skills.*

A CEO can no longer be expected to do Visionary work that affects a production line—they no longer have the expertise to do so. A CEO must rely on the production manager or supervisor to scan for new production technologies or new materials to be used in the process. People at each organizational level have to do their share in each of the VIP roles. Though it may be true that individuals will always be stronger in one of the three roles, an organization cannot afford to hire individuals who do not have the skills to engage all three in their work. While it is possible to hire assistants to pick up the slack in an individual's weak areas, this strategy means that you need two people to do the work one person could or should be doing. Few organizations can afford such luxuries.

As the type of Visionary, Implementor, or People Manager work required at each level of an organization differs depending on your abilities and preferences, you may choose to work at a particular level in an organization—that is, at a level where the need for your best skills is most pronounced. For example, a CEO Visionary would probably need to have a more holistic or general view of the world in order to scan the horizon for possible competitive threats or opportunities for the business as a whole. A production supervisor probably has less general business knowledge and in their Visionary activities would spend more time scanning around more focused materials handling issues; they should find scanning for changes in this area interesting, fun, and straightforward. The CEO would probably find this work uninteresting and energy-sapping, and could easily misunderstand the potential impact of a new development in the production process. It's the same role, but different skills and interests are required at different levels.

As an individual making a career choice, you should choose the position that best suits your 4Ls and your skills. You do not need to be higher up the organizational ladder in order to have a fulfilling working life and be a success.

The descriptions below recap the key activities that Visionaries, Implementors, and People Managers undertake. They give specific examples of what sorts of activities four different positions in an organization may engage. Those positions include: a CEO, a division leader, a manufacturing team leader, and a salesperson.

# VIP Visionaries

## Recap
Visionaries have two main tasks:

- ⊃ They use their knowledge and expertise to horizon scan and analyze trends in the macroenvironment and opportunities in the global market in order to determine the strategic positioning the organization will adopt.
- ⊃ They refine the vision of the company; facilitate the definition of a mission statement, strategic intent, and corporate challenges; ensure all stakeholders are fully satisfied; and communicate values (behavioural guidelines) that are shared and employed within the company.

The Visionary's role is to give the organization *Purpose*.

## VIP Visionary Activities

### The CEO
The CEO is focused on identifying any macroeconomic sigmoid curves that might affect the entire organization. These might be political events, economic trends, or new technologies that might serve to enhance or threaten the organization's core competencies. Some of these trends might be passed on to the divisional leaders for closer and further examination. The CEO is consistently asking themselves, "How does all of this fit together?" and "How might it affect my organization?" The CEO also questions how such possible changes might require them to change the portfolio of divisions they possess, which ones to build up and which are no longer strategic, how they might better distribute the organization's global sales or business activities, and how to generate more value for clients at lower costs. The challenge of identifying new sales, new businesses, new partners, new human resources, and to improve existing and develop new core competencies is continually on their mind.

The CEO also focuses on how the needs of all the organization's internal and external stakeholders are evolving and how they can ensure that those needs continue to be fully satisfied. They are also responsible for ensuring that the strategic positioning of the various divisional units is unique, competitive, and coherent, and that the positioning is durable given potential changes in the macroenvironment.

Finally, the CEO continues to communicate their vision of the organization's future and its values, and develops the overall strategic intent and corporate challenge–type goals for division leaders, ensuring that they can achieve the organization's strategic intent and corporate challenges too.

## The Division Leader

The division leader focuses on identifying macroenvironmental trends that might impact on their particular business unit. Their trend analysis tends to be more focused on their markets, the geographic regions they operate in, the market gaps to fill, and the development of existing and possible new core competencies. Their business and technological scanning will focus more on improving the existing value chain and finding new ways of satisfying all stakeholders—which includes the CEO.

The division leader's main responsibility is to ensure that the strategic positioning of their personal business unit is unique, at an optimum, and sustainable over the long term. If they have several products under their direct supervision, it is their responsibility to ensure that each has the appropriate strategic positioning. If they are responsible for product managers, they should work with them to ensure that each develops unique offerings.

They will also develop a mission statement for their particular unit that is coherent with the organization's. This statement, along with their vision and values, will be consistently communicated to their employees, and a strategic intent and corporate challenge will be created and issued for their division.

## The Team Leader (Manufacturing)

The team leader has a much greater level of knowledge in their particular field of expertise—production—than either the division leader or the CEO. They therefore need to be continually horizon scanning for new sigmoid curves that only they can identify as potentially impacting the operation. This process is more likely to be of a technical nature and involve new production techniques or software, new sources of raw materials, new delivery systems, or new materials handling equipment. They ask questions like, "How will this affect my production costs?" and "How can this eliminate time, tasks, or wastage?"

The team leader looks at the manufacturing-related competencies that their team needs to acquire or improve and whether these can be developed by existing team members or if they must hire new members.

A team mission statement aimed at satisfying all of manufacturing's stakeholders should be adopted. It should also include the values and behavioural guidelines that the team believes in must be coherent with the mission of the particular division. Manufacturing's own strategic intent and corporate challenges should also be launched.

## The Salesperson

Each individual salesperson also must do their own horizon scanning. This work may include reading industry journals (and others sources outside the traditional area of sales) to learn about new trends and keep up-to-date regarding structural industry changes, competitor moves, and new innovations that could adapt current sales techniques and tools.

But perhaps more importantly, the salesperson needs to be an expert in the macroenvironmental changes that may possibly affect their clients so they can report back to their superiors and the company can proactively change or improve its product or service offering. They may also be able to identify potential new clients or new sectors that may be interested in their company's products. They can certainly report back client satisfaction rates and new competitor moves (e.g., possible new whole product offerings) and should anticipate requests for electronic invoices, add-ons, support services, and new value creation opportunities. The salesperson, be it through telephone sales, e-sales, or face-to-face meetings, is in a privileged position to actively scan for any changes that will be needed to keep one of the organization's major stakeholders—the client—fully satisfied.

# VIP Implementors

## Recap
Implementors create and manage the unique work processes required to allow the organization to deliver the strategic position developed by the Visionary. They design and implement Balanced Scorecards™ and build up the core competencies that will be needed in order to exploit the selected strategic position and to ensure that the strategic intent and corporate challenges are achieved now and in the future.

Implementors have three main challenges:

- ⊃ They build and manage the unique activity sets. They turn technology and networks into work processes and a strategic system that achieves the required and distinctive strategic position.
- ⊃ They manage and operate the intra- and inter-unit information and communication networks and ensure that synergy between units is created.
- ⊃ In addition, they produce a flexible structure suited for a culture of entrepreneurship in which People Managers can achieve the desired results through the growth of their people.

The Implementor's role is to give the organization *Process*.

## VIP Implementor Activities

### The CEO
The CEO is responsible for the design of the organization's global strategic system and activity sets, and the means of generating value creation across its divisions. They create an entrepreneurial environment for their division leaders, allowing them to develop their own mission statements and strategies, and then give them performance measures and the authority, resources, and climate needed to achieve them. They are involved in the development of Balanced Scorecard™–type key performance indicators (KPIs) for the entire organization and the individuals units, and they support divisional leaders in their efforts to achieve their particular objectives.

The CEO develops the organization's network and their own personal informal networks and manages them for the organization's well-being. They also assist the division leaders by establishing the required reward systems, information management systems, and communication networks and by encouraging the growth of formal and informal communication networks. They seek out and negotiate partnership agreements or strategic alliances with other "best-of-breed" organizations in the network. They decide which core competencies the organization should be developing as a whole.

### The Division Leader

The division leader must focus on developing and implementing the detailed activity sets and strategic system for their particular division. This entails developing "unique" means of creating value and an appropriate organizational structure to support the adopted strategic positioning and activities.

Within the framework of Balanced Scorecard™ and corporate challenges established in partnership with the CEO, they ensure that new and existing core competencies are build up and developed, and that learning flourishes. They work with their own teams to establish and achieve Balanced Scorecards™.

The division leader also develops and manages their own network (which could include several different partners or suppliers in the value chain) and their personal and informal network.

Within their own division, they also create an entrepreneurial culture in which their people can be creative, "stretched," and performance driven.

### The Team Leader (Manufacturing)

The team leader operates in the entrepreneurial environment created by the division leader and should have the liberty and responsibility to create their own processes and activities to achieve Balanced Scorecard™ targets. Once again, they will have to devise the activity sets and build up the required networks that allow their team to achieve its goals.

In turn, they must create an entrepreneurial environment in which their team members can flourish.

### The Salesperson

The salesperson will have their personal Balanced Scorecard™ challenges to motivate them and all four factors should serve to improve their sales performance for the organization. As an Implementor, they will focus on improving the sales process, whether that entails looking for better ways to lock the customer into the organization's products or services, developing an easier reordering process, improving delivery, providing new means for clients to obtain more information on products, establishing an electronic means of monitoring inventory levels, or facilitating electronic payments.

The salesperson has their own personal information and communication networks, which may include rivals, customers, suppliers, etc., so that they can stay aware of the latest market, competitive, or technological developments.

## *VIP People Managers*

### Recap

Companies grow through the development and growth of their people. People Managers' work focuses on two principal tasks:

- ⊃ They oversee the professional and personal development and growth of each individual employee.
- ⊃ They develop synergy and a sense of community, growth, and learning in their group, team, or entrepreneurial business unit.

The People Manager's role is to lead the organization's *People*.

## VIP People Manager Activities

### The CEO
The CEO ensures that the culture of the organization favours a strong role for the Human Resource (HR) department and a focus on the professional and personal development of all employees. They set an example by encouraging the development of the people who report directly to them and by ensuring that training, employee evaluations, and balanced lifestyles are not set aside as productivity and work levels increase.

They establish a high level of interpersonal trust among the organization's vice-presidents, ensure that honesty (delivered with a healthy dose of respect and compassion) is encouraged and rewarded, and trust-destroying incidents are dealt with in a swift and appropriate manner. The CEO must be 100 percent trustworthy.

The CEO establishes Balanced Scorecard™–type performance evaluations for each direct report and should encourage 360-degree assessments—including an assessment of their own performance. Where individual work is required it should be rewarded, so where teamwork and collaboration is appropriate, rewards should also be put into place.

### Division Leader and Team (Manufacturing) Leader
In terms of the People Manager role, the work at both the division leader and team leader level is more or less identical to that of the CEO, except that each one takes responsibility for the role within their own division or team. This simply means that trust must be built and collaboration, learning, and innovation must be encouraged, facilitated, and rewarded. Each person's foremost responsibility is to develop their people and the major asset of the successful organizations of today: capital intelligence.

### The Salesperson
Like all other individuals in the organization, the salesperson must be trustworthy, look for opportunities to create synergy, think win-win, and take risks in order to learn.

## Introducing VIP Strategic Leadership into Your Workplace

In an ideal world, introducing the VIP model into your working life would begin when you start your own company and design it as you like, or when you arrive in a new organization to assume a new position. If you're starting your own company, you can devise your organization's mission with your partners and colleagues and determine the strategic positioning you want to adopt and the value proposition you want to offer. You can introduce the Balanced Scorecard™ approach into the organization's culture from day one and ensure that an entrepreneurial environment, highly networked culture, and sound human values are adopted. The activity sets, required core competencies, and strategic system can be mapped out on paper or computer before a single brick is laid. Employees can be hired having understood and accepted the mission and culture, and between them possess all required core competencies and have VIP Leadership capability. You can build a strong HR emphasis and ensure that everyone's personal development is planned and checked. Irrespective of your behaviour in the past, you can concentrate on building trust with all of your employees and stakeholders from the day you start planning the company. Of course, for most, this ideal situation is unrealistic and you are more likely feeling "stuck" and frustrated in your present position when you come across this book. If that is the situation, what should you do?

You really have three choices: (1) change nothing and continue as you are at present, (2) begin to implement VIP Personal Leadership in your current organization and position, and (3) look for a new position either within your current organization or elsewhere, where colleagues are more open to learning and change and where you can start with a clean slate. Any of these choices are fine, depending on your circumstances. If you are three years from retirement and a healthy pension (if you don't rock the boat), then the first option sounds like the perfectly appropriate response. But if you are looking at one of the other two options, the process outlined below might just allow you to start introducing VIP without any great fanfare, but with great effect.

## The VIP Start-up Process

Arriving at your office on a Monday morning and announcing a big program of change—that your team will forthwith be adopting a new "VIP Model" of business operation—is likely to raise more laughs than a serious re-evaluation of your organization's mode of functioning. VIP Leadership is a set of skills that you can start learning, practicing, and using today but whose use does not require any big announcements. Let your change in behaviour lead the way. Seeing a real personal change in you is the only thing that people will really believe in and by the time they begin to take interest in the catalyst that has improved results, it will be the evidence that persuades them rather than any grandiose announcements.

So how can you start using the VIP model if the organization where you are working is already operational?

### 1. Start "Walking the Talk" *(You: The Foundation)*
Irrespective of your past behaviour, today is the first day that you can start being trustworthy and begin building trusting relationships with colleagues. If these are already in place, great. If when doing the trust exercise (see Chapter 9, page 170) you feel that there are very few colleagues whom you trust or who would trust you (more that 50 percent), then its time to do a little homework and to start changing your behaviour. If they don't trust you, why should they be led by you? It's impossible to be a good People Manager without a solid base of trust.

### 2. Analyze Macroenvironmental Trends *(The Visionary)*
David Hurst talks about organizations needing a crisis before they change their ways. One way of increasing people's awareness of the need to change is to organize a session to analyze the macroeconomic, technological, political, and other trends that impact the organization today and in the future. This can easily be added to any planned meeting agenda and within sixty to ninety minutes of brainstorming, you can generate a long list of trends and potential impacts that is certain to crush compla-

cency and signal just how ill-prepared your organization is to face the changes taking place in the environment. If you're the head of a manufacturing or sales department, generating a list of ways that each of the trends (particularly technological and demographic) could impact the way you and your competitors run your businesses can be very effective. The process doesn't need to generate a crisis atmosphere, but it can make people more cooperative in accepting change.

### 3. Introduce the Balanced Scorecard™ *(The Implementor)*

If appropriate (and if you have the power to do so), it is sometimes useful to announce the introduction of the Balanced Scorecard™ on an organizational scale. Often, however—and irrespective of your position— you can start encouraging target setting, measuring and rewarding increasing levels of customer satisfaction, improving processes, and improving the competencies of your employees without enormous fanfare. Looking at these factors is logical when you explain that doing so will help you to perform better in the future and be prepared for any of the macroenvironmental changes you've identified as a team.

*VIP Leadership is a set of skills that you can start learning, practising, and using today.*

The beauty of the Balanced Scorecard™ approach is that it's tied to the organization's strategic positioning. As a result, it can force you to look at your core competency portfolio or generate a corporate challenge, and it can be linked vertically throughout the organization to either corporate objectives or to individual performance, depending on your particular post in the organization. It's the lever that allows you to facilitate the introduction of some major changes. I use the word "facilitate" rather than "make" because everyone can follow the logic of improving customer satisfaction and your colleagues should collaborate with you on implementing any required changes.

### 4. Introduce DR.GRAC *(The People Manager)*

The introduction of DR.GRAC agreements drives down the measured parameters of the Balanced Scorecard™ to an individual level and ensures that everyone understands the results being sought, that everyone is accountable for their efforts, that feedback is obtained and, most importantly perhaps in terms of motivating any change of behaviour, that they are rewarded appropriately—that is, for achieving the multifaceted desired results of the Balanced Scorecard™ performance indicators. As mentioned before, you may not be able to change the way that your people are financially rewarded, but there are many nonfinancial benefits you can use to stimulate the desired behaviour.

These four steps can take you along way towards adopting the VIP model yourself and implementing major changes within a team in any existing organization. All of them can be taken at your level of the organization, irrespective of what that happens to be, without the support or even the knowledge of your superiors.

Processes such as preparing an organizational or team mission statement can then be done over a longer period once people have become used to your changed behaviour and have started to learn a little about the VIP paradigm themselves. The results from having everyone focused and rewarded for their efforts in improving customer services, businesses processes, and organizational learning as well as achieving financial targets will certainly generate some notice—and then you can start encouraging people to start carrying out all the VIP activities at their particular level or job function.

# Becoming a VIP Strategic Leader

Implementing the model of VIP Leadership in an organization starts with you, as an individual. You need to adopt the VIP paradigm and behaviours yourself. Then, by example and by explaining your personal challenges to colleagues, they will see that you are trying to improve the way you work and deal with them. Communication is key here: they should be a part of your project and should not be asking themselves, "What's wrong with Mark?" They may be cynical at first—it depends on your past record in dealing with them—but once they see that you are sincere and making an effort, most people will show a supportive attitude.

But how do you go about adopting the VIP paradigm yourself?

The first step mentioned in the process outlining the introduction of the VIP model into your organization is "walking the talk." Nothing undermines initiative or peoples' attempts to build trusting relationships more than others who don't practice what they preach. This behaviour is regarded as dishonest and hypocritical, and warrants the mistrust and cynicism that it generates. Making mistakes is allowed—that's a vital part of learning—but you need to include your colleagues in your learning process, acknowledge mistakes, and learn to apologize. After all, in a people-based organization you are a human being—not your position.

Each of us must decide and take responsibility for what we are ready to do in order to achieve our personal visions and to what extent we are willing to develop ourselves. The first step in moving forward is to address questions as basic as these: Who do you want to be? What you want your legacy to be? What are you willing to do to achieve that?

In Chapter 2 I presented my definition of leadership: The ability to move yourself and others towards who you want to be. Obviously, then, to be a leader as defined by this definition, you need to know who it is you want to be! What's more, in discussing VIP-based organizations, it's already been established that you should only hire individuals who share the organization's mission. Therefore, you must know yourself, your own vision and legacy, and understand your own 4Ls.

## Defining Personal Success: Your Mission

Each person in the world is unique. Consequently, each person also has a unique personal mission, contribution, and path to tread in life. However, as discussed in Chapter 3, it is very easy to become distracted from a personal pathway. From childhood, people are influenced—perhaps by their parents or by favourite teachers—to pursue careers that are secure and well-paid, careers that perhaps the parents or teachers themselves pursued or would have liked to have pursued, or careers that the parents or teachers think are best suited to their child's talents. As the child grows and matures, society, spouses, peers, and mentors can all influence career choices. As a result, individuals often end up "following the flock": doing what is expected or socially acceptable, or taking the option that may be easier or more financially rewarding. Yet if you develop a certain self-awareness in your life, you are destined to always live with a feeling of "what might have been" if you do not follow your own path. (Read the book *Jonathan Livingston Seagull* by Richard Bach for more on this topic.) What's more, your fourth L, your Legacy, will never be quite satisfied. So-called "midlife crises" are often the result of an awakening after many years of pursuing other peoples' or society's definition of success.

One of the first steps you must take, then, is to actually define what you regard as success and what you want to do or to be in your life. This is not an overnight process; creating your own personal and unique definition of success requires deep reflection and an ability to think clearly for yourself.

To start the process, you can first examine how society, family, friends, peers, and anyone else whose opinion you value measure success today. You can also look at which individuals you consider to be successes and why. These could be historical figures, friends, colleagues at work, or famous people you know only through the media. Having prepared your list, you then to need reflect on the why. Why does your particular society measures success in a particular way? Do you agree with it? If so, why? If not, why? Why do you consider a certain politician, athlete, or friend successful? What makes someone a success and what makes someone a failure in your eyes? Are you judging them by your own standards or by society's? What does that tell you about what you want out of your own life?

Other short exercises that can help you define your terms of success include the following:

- ⮑ Find a poster-sized sheet of paper and an assortment of magazines. Without analyzing your decisions, clip out images that represent what you want out of life. Glue the images onto the paper to make a collage. How do you interpret the collage when you step back and look at it?
- ⮑ Make a list of the five most important things in your life. Do you allocate your time and energy to these things or have you lost your way or focus?
- ⮑ Examine your 4Ls: Living, Loving, Learning, and Legacy. What basic and financial requirements do you, your family, or your dependants need? What sort of social environment do you want to work in? What do you want to be learning? What legacy would you like to leave behind? How can you start pursuing these four Ls?
- ⮑ Think about what type of work you would choose to do if you were independently wealthy. How does that differ from what you do now?
- ⮑ Prepare a list of your strengths and weaknesses. Ask four other people (a family member, a good friend, and two work colleagues) to also prepare an "honest" list of these strengths and weaknesses for you. How different are the lists? How similar are they? What do those differences or similarities tell you?
- ⮑ Imagine that it is your fiftieth birthday. A dear friend has to make a ten-minute speech about you and your life. Write the speech that you would like that person to make. Then ask yourself these questions: Is that what would be said today? If not, what are you going to do to make this speech a true representation of your life? Alternately, write the obituary that you would like to appear in the newspapers upon your death. Is that what people would write about you now?

By doing these short but quite challenging exercises, you should be able to come up with an improved version of your definition of success and be in a better position to elaborate a mission statement that can help you decide where you should be working and what you should be doing in your career.

### Building Trusting Relationships (or Terminating Them)

If you haven't already, do the trust exercises described in Chapter 9 (see page 170). If your colleagues, friends, and family don't consider you trustworthy, then you will never be in a position to lead them. If you can't trust the people around you, you have only two choices: (1) deal directly with the people concerned and see if they're willing to build the sort of relationship you now desire or (2) terminate the relationship.

### Leadership Characteristics: Do You Possess Them?

As highlighted in Chapter 2, Warren Bennis outlines four things people need from their leaders. If you haven't already, look at Table 2.1 (see page 31). The four points are presented with some questions that should help you decide whether you do have what it takes to be a leader.

I believe that anyone who has progressed to this final part of the book and has completed the exercises along the way can probably be reasonably confident that they are on the right track in each of these four leadership areas. Double-check by asking the trusted friends and colleagues you picked to list your strengths and weaknesses to also rate you on these four points.

# Building Organizations of VIPs

The VIP Strategic Leadership model gives all individuals a simple yet powerful tool for implementing personal change and for building long-term success in organizations operating in the knowledge economy. Today's core fundamental reality is that organizations can only develop if (a) their employees are developing personally and professionally and (b) they can establish a culture of trust and collaboration in order to generate synergy between individuals and/or business units. Remember the equation we've considered throughout the book:

$$\text{Organizational Growth and Development} = \sum (\text{Individual Growth and Development})^n$$

Adopting the VIP model of strategic leadership facilitates the accelerated growth of both these functions.

The most important elements of the VIP model are (1) that the adoption of the model represents a very real and practical win-win arrangement for both individuals and their organizations, (2) that it allows more people access to some tried and tested theoretical management tools created by acknowledged experts and management gurus, and (3) that the model can be adopted by any individual, irrespective of their position.

### Why Is It Win-Win?

The model recognizes the new reality of the business world: that people are the foundation, the "citizens" of every organization and that an organization can only grow if its people grow too. It is not an adaptation of the existing "financial" model, but it does not ignore the financial aspects of building a business. It is a new way of seeing the world that recognizes the owners of the real assets—the capital intelligence—are the employees. However, it does not argue that we should now only take care of the employees; it says—and shareholders will be relieved to hear this—that we must take care of *all* stakeholders. And that, in turn, has been shown to improve shareholders' returns anyway!

It is clear that as we build organizations based on "intelligence," we need to make the most of that intelligence. We need to develop it and we need to use it to its maximum: intelligent people like to learn and be challenged. By giving them VIP roles, irrespective of their level within the organization, they can each scan for new developments that might improve the organization's performance while building up their own expertise at the same time. This allows all employees to contribute value creation and to play their full role. They can build their own networks, they can take risks and learn, they can work in an atmosphere of trust and

> *Everyone will play a full role in the organization's delivery of its value proposition and in filling its strategic position.*

collaboration and, being hired by an organization whose mission they share, they know they are always moving towards creating their own legacy. By working in an environment structured to encourage "entrepreneurship," employees know that their performance will be enhanced—not limited—by the organizational structures in place. They are liberated, free to be creative, innovative, and to satisfy their clients with better products and services. And if they "fail," they can accept that it was their own failure (i.e., it wasn't on account of the organization or lack of support) and that they have something to learn from it. Then they can try again and succeed.

The model gives all adoptees a very simple framework to use and access to some of the most advanced yet simple tools to improve their job performance and their levels of satisfaction at work. Even if no one else in the organization ever hears of the VIP model, the person who adopts it will find their quality of work life improving, their stress levels declining, and they will be taking steps that bring them closer to achieving their personal 4Ls.

By giving employees what they need, you will be able to build a rigorous organization that will be able to flourish in the rapidly changing networked-based macroenvironment in which we now live. You will be able to build an organization that is entrepreneurial and liberated, where everyone shares a common mission. It will be an organization that develops, generates, and exploits capital intelligence. The employees will share a sense of belonging and community and each unit and every individual will constantly drive forward to achieve balanced goals and to satisfy all stakeholder needs. It will be a place where individuals feel able to learn, collaborate with colleagues, be creative, and create synergy—everyone will play a full role in the organization's delivery of its value proposition and in filling its strategic position. It will be an organization built on networking, values, guidelines, and individual and team stretch. It will be built up from a base of trust and individual professional and personal development. You will be building an organization based on leadership at all levels, and more precisely, on VIP Strategic Leadership.

### Access to "New" Management Tools

The business tools referred to in this book represent my interpretation of the latest and most innovative material from some of the most distinguished business theoreticians, consultants, and leaders of the day. Some of the models used are relatively new, others have been around for decades, but most have already been applied in numerous leading organizations—sometimes throughout the company and sometimes by individuals demonstrating initiative, vision, and leadership. One of the book's main objectives is to make this material available to the many individuals who have never been exposed to it before. Along the way, the models have been compiled, synthesized, massaged, developed, and then finally broken down again into the sizeable chunks represented by the Visionary, Implementor, and People Manager roles—roles that each of us play to some extent in our working lives.

## Adopting the VIP Model Today

What are the risks in adopting the VIP paradigm? The main one is being ridiculed as people start noticing that you are no longer following the crowd in order to achieve their approval and your success. You have chosen your own route and are risking failure in their eyes as you move forward. This is a powerful pressure and should not be underestimated. However, if you have done your personal work well and you have become aware of what you want in life, this is a small price to pay for the happiness, satisfaction, and self-esteem that will grow as a result of your pursuing your own dream.

If, having determined your personal definition of success, you find that it already matches with what you have been trying to achieve, great—the only challenge that remains is to take the four steps outlined earlier in this chapter:

1. Build trust by walking the talk.
2. Organize a session to analyze the macroenvironmental trends that can impact your organization or team.
3. Start implementing a Balanced Scorecard™ approach.
4. Start using DR.GRAC agreements.

Finally, if you need a final argument to be convinced, check the following list and see if you disagree with any of the following premises:

1. In this era of knowledge-based business, the main assets and real owners of organizations are their intelligent employees.
2. Organizations are more likely to achieve long-term success when they devise unique value propositions rather than offer "me too" products and services to their clients.
3. Organizations are more likely to achieve long-term success when they devise unique and sustainable value creation activities and processes to achieve their strategic positions.
4. Giving employees simple rules to follow empowers them to be creative and to make decisions that are consistent with the organization's strategy.
5. Organizations represent a relatively lower risk when each person is continually horizon scanning for future developments in their field of expertise.
6. Organizations competing in a knowledge-based market should always keep developing and improving their knowledge (i.e., core competencies).

7.  Organizations should balance the risks they are taking by shaping and adapting, and perhaps by not playing in some markets.
8.  There is reduced financial risk and employees feel more pride in working for an organization that cares about all its stakeholders.
9.  People are more motivated and less likely to leave an organization that they have helped develop or when they share its mission and values.
10. Employees are more conscientious and produce more work of better quality when they feel that their employer and executives "care" and believe that the organization's success is built upon their employees' professional and personal development.
11. Employees are more relaxed and effective when they work in a trusting and collaborative environment and produce more creative and innovative work therein.
12. It's unfair and self-defeating to give employees projects without explaining exactly what you expect from them, what resources they will have, and what guidelines they must follow in order to achieve the desired results.
13. Employees are more likely to behave in the way favoured by their rewards.
14. Organizations are better prepared to make profit in the future if they are continually seeking to improve customer satisfaction, business processes, and organizational learning.
15. Organizations and individuals both "win" when each person develops and assumes their roles of Visionary, Implementor, and People Manager.

I hope this book brings as much enjoyment and learning to you, the reader, as it has to me while I've been writing it. As demonstrated with the Discover, Invent, Produce, Observe cycle, however, reading this book will have been a waste of your time and no real learning can actually take place until you apply the material and learn from the results. Ready? This is the first step towards becoming a VIP in your own eyes.

Have a great trip; I'd be interested to have news of your progress. Have fun on your exclusive adventure in change, learning, and personal growth, offered to all people who aspire to be VIPs!

## Key Points in Chapter 11

↻ You now have all the knowledge and tools to grow yourself, your people, and your organization.

## Questions to Consider

↻ What will you do today to make it happen?

**Works Cited**

1. Abell, D.F. *Defining the Business: The Starting Point of Strategic Planning.* Englewood Cliffs: Prentice-Hall, 1980.

2. Allaire, Yvan and Mihaela Firsirotu. *L'Enterprise Strategique.* Montreal: Gaetan Morin Editeur, 1993.

3. Argyris, Chris. "Good Communication That Blocks Learning." *Harvard Business Review* (July/Aug. 1994): 77–85.

4. Bartlett, Christoper A. and Sumantra Ghoshal. "Changing the Role of Top Management: Beyond Strategy to Purpose." *Harvard Business Review* (Nov./Dec. 1994): 79–88.

5. Bartlett, Christoper A. and Sumantra Ghoshal. "Changing the Role of Top Management: Beyond Systems to People." *Harvard Business Review* (May/June 1995): 133–42.

6. Bartlett, Christoper A. and Sumantra Ghoshal. "Rebuilding Behavioural Context: A Blueprint for Corporate Renewal." *Sloan Management Review* 37.2 (Winter 1996): 23–36.

7. Bartlett, Christoper A. and Sumantra Ghoshal. "Rebuilding Behavioural Context: Turn Process Reengineering into People Rejuvenation." *Sloan Management Review* 37.1 (Fall 1996): 11–23.

8. Bartlett, Christoper A. and Sumantra Ghoshal. "Release the Entrepreneurial: Hostages from Your Corporate Hierarchy." *Strategy & Leadership* (July/Aug. 1996): 131–37.

9. Conger, Jay A. "The Necessary Art of Persuasion." *Harvard Business Review* (May/June 1998): 84–95.

10. Cooper, Robert K. *Emotional Intelligence and 21st Century Leadership: Excelling Under Pressure While Everyone Else is Just Competing or Falling Behind.* Robert K. Cooper, 1999.

11. Courtney, Hugh, Jane Kirkland, and Patrick Viguerie. "Strategy Under Uncertainty." *Harvard Business Review* (Nov./Dec. 1997): 67–79.

12. Covey, Stephen R. *The 7 Habits of Highly Effective People: Powerful Lessons in Personal Change.* New York: Simon & Schuster, 1989.

13. Davis, Stan. *Future Perfect.* Reading: Addison-Wesley, 1996.

14. Eisenhardt, Kathleen M. and Donald N. Sull. "Strategy as Simple Rules." *Harvard Business Review* (Jan. 2001): 107–16.

15. Fry, Joseph N. and J. Peter Killing. *Strategic Analysis and Action.* Scarborough: Prentice-Hall Canada Inc., 1986.

16. Goleman, Daniel. "What Makes a Leader?" *Harvard Business Review* (Nov./Dec. 1998): 93–102.

17. Hamel, Gary and C.K. Prahalad. *Competing for the Future: Breakthrough Strategies for Seeking Control of Your Industry and Creating the Markets of Tomorrow.* Boston: Harvard Business School Press, 1994.

18. Hamel, Gary . "An Interview with Gary Hamel." In *Thought Leaders: Insights on the Future of Business*, edited by Joel Kurtzman, 134–49. San Francisco: Booz-Allen & Hamilton Inc., 1998.

19. Handy, Charles. *The Age of Unreason.* Boston: Harvard Business School Press, 1989.

20. Handy, Charles. "The New Language of Business." *Director* 52.7 (Feb. 1999): 50–54.

21. Handy, Charles. "Where Are You on the Sigmoid Curve?" *Directors & Boards* 19.1 (Fall 1994): 22–25.

22. Hersey, Paul and Kenneth H. Blanchard. "Life-cycle Theory of Leadership." *Training & Development* (Jan. 1996): 42–50.

23. Hurst, David K. "Cautionary Tales from the Kalahari: How Hunters Become Herders (And May Have Trouble Changing Back Again)." *Academy of Management Executive* 5.3 (Aug. 1991): 74–86.

24. Hurst, David K. "Crisis & Renewal: Ethical Anarchy in Mature Organizations." *Business Quarterly* 60.2 (Winter 1995): 32–41.

25. Kaplan, Robert S. "Devising a Balanced Scorecard Matched to Business Strategy." *Planning Review* 22.5 (Sept./Oct.): 15–19.

26. Mintzberg, Henry and Alexandra McGugh. "Strategy Formation in an Adhocracy." *Administrative Science Quarterly* 30.2 (June 1985).

27. Mintzberg, Henry and James Brian Quinn. *The Strategy Process: Concepts, Contexts, Cases*, 3rd ed. Upper Saddle River: Prentice-Hall Inc., 1996.

# Works Cited

28. Moore, Geoffrey A. *Crossing the Chasm: Marketing and Selling High-Tech Products to Mainstream Customers.* New York: HarperBusiness, 1991.

29. Porter, Michael E. "What Is Strategy?" *Harvard Business Review* (Nov./Dec. 1996): 61–78.

30. Quinn, James Brian and Frederick G. Hilmer. "Strategic Outsourcing." *Sloan Management Review* 35.4 (Summer 1994): 43–55.

31. Senge, Peter. "Making a Better World." *Executive Excellence* 12.8 (Aug. 1995): 18–19.

32. Senge, Peter. "Systems Thinking." *Executive Excellence* 13.1 (Jan. 1996): 15–16.

33. Senge Peter. *The Fifth Discipline: The Art & Practice of the Learning Organization.* New York: Doubleday, 1994.

34. Treacy, Michael and Fred Wiersema. "How Market Leaders Keep Their Edge." *Fortune* 131.2 (6 Feb. 1995): 88–98.

Many peoples' work has contributed to my own learning over the years. In particular I would like to acknowledge the following masters in their areas. I encourage you to seek out and read as much of their work as possible:

- Yvan Allaire
- Christopher A. Bartlett
- Warren Bennis
- Stephen R. Covey
- Gary Hamel
- Charles Handy
- David K. Hurst
- Henry Mintzberg
- Geoffrey A. Moore
- Michael E. Porter
- Peter M. Senge

In addition to the titles that appear on the Works Cited pages, the following books and articles were major contributors in the development of my VIP Personal Leadership model:

Bartlett, Christopher A. and Sumantra Ghoshal. "Changing the Role of Top Management: Beyond Structure to Processes." *Harvard Business Review* (Jan./Feb. 1995): 87–96.

Covey, Stephen R. *Principle-Centered Leadership: Strategies for Personal & Professional Effectiveness.* New York: Simon & Schuster, 1992.

Hamel, Gary. "Attend to the 3Ds." *Executive Excellence* 12.2 (Feb. 1995): 8–9.

Hamel, Gary. "Corporate Challenge." *Executive Excellence* 12.3 (Mar. 1995): 7–8.

Hamel, Gary. "Strategy as Revolution." *Harvard Business Review* (July/Aug. 1996): 69–82.

Handy, Charles. *Beyond Certainty: The Changing World of Organizations.* Boston: Harvard Business School Press, 1998.

Handy, Charles. *The Age of Paradox.* Boston: Harvard Business School Press, 1995.

Handy, Charles. *The Empty Raincoat: Making Sense of the Future.* Toronto: Random House Canada, 1995.

Handy, Charles. *The Hungry Spirit: Beyond Capitalism.* New York: Broadway Books, 1999.

Kaplan, Robert S. "Having Trouble with Your Strategy? Then Map It." *Harvard Business Review* (Sept./Oct. 2000): 167–76.

Kerr, Steven. "On the folly of Rewarding A, while hoping for B; More on the folly." *Academy of Management Executives* 9.1 (Feb. 1995): 7–16.

Long, Carl and Mary Vickers-Koch. "Using Core Capabilities to Create Competitive Advantage." *Organizational Dynamics* 24.1 (1995): 6–22.

Moore, Geoffrey A. *Inside the Tornado: Marketing Strategies from Silicon Valley's Cutting Edge.* New York: HarperCollins, 1999.

Moore, Geoffrey A. *Living on the Fault Line: Managing for Shareholder Value in the Age of the Internet.* New York: HarperBusiness, 2002.

Pfeffer, J. "Competitive Advantage Through People." *California Management Review* 36.2 (Winter 1994): 9–28.

Ray, Michael and Alan Rinsler, eds. *The New Paradigm in Business: Emerging Strategies for Leadership & Organizational Change.* New York: Jeremy P. Tarcher, 1993.

Index

# Index

# Index

# Index